Psychiatry and Religion

PSYCHIATRY
AND
RELIGION

Samuel Z. Klausner

THE FREE PRESS OF GLENCOE

COLLIER-MACMILLAN LIMITED, LONDON

For information, address:

The Free Press of Glencoe
A Division of The Macmillan Company
The Crowell-Collier Publishing Company
60 Fifth Avenue, New York, N.Y. 10011

DESIGNED BY ANDOR BRAUN

Library of Congress Catalog Card Number: 64–16961

Collier-Macmillan Canada Ltd., Toronto, Ontario

To my father—my instructor

To my mother—my teacher

PROV. 1:8

. . . the most remarkable effect of the division of labor is not that it increases the output of functions divided, but that it renders them solidary.

Emile Durkheim

ACKNOWLEDGMENTS

THE SKELETON OF THIS BOOK evolved out of my encounter with the writings of religion and psychiatry. Its flesh and marrow evolved in meetings with colleagues and friends. They are represented here by the few to whom I am able to offer public gratitude. This project was initially conceived and supported by members of the American Foundation of Religion and Psychiatry. Dr. Smiley Blanton, Psychiatric Director of the Religio-Psychiatric Clinic, has been a constant spirit behind the endeavor. Dr. Iago Galdston of the New York Academy of Medicine was responsible for turning the Foundation's attention in an academic direction. Dr. John M. Cotton, Director of Psychiatry at St. Luke's Hospital, succeeded him as chairman of the Foundation's Research Committee. His associates on the Research Committee include Professor Bernard Barber of Barnard College, Professor Thomas J. Bigham of General Theological Seminary, Professor Abraham N. Franzblau of Jewish Institute of Religion-Hebrew Union College, Professor Earl Loomis, Jr., of Union Theological Seminary, and Professor Elmer L. Severinghaus of the Columbia University School of Public Health. This committee bore the tedium of reading and commenting upon early research reports.

Whatever success was enjoyed in the early stages of research within the Religio-Psychiatric Clinic owes much to the support of the Clinic staff, Dr. Howard S. LeSourd, as business manager of the Foundation, helped with financial and organizational matters. The discussion groups which provided early data were organized with the assistance of Renée Fodor, the Clinic psychologist; Elizabeth Lyons, the Clinic psychiatric social worker; and the Rev. Elizabeth Ehling, then a Clinic trainee and later a pastoral counselor. Ideas for the original hypotheses were developed in discussions with the late Dr. Eugene Braun and with Dr. Maria Fleischel, psychiatric counselors at the Clinic; Dr. Fred Tate,

Assistant Psychiatric Director; and Dr. Preston McLean and Dr. Herbert Holt, psychiatric participants in the pastoral clinical training program. I am also indebted for these ideas to the Rev. Frederick C. Kuether, Director of Training at the Clinic; the Rev. Frank West, the Rev. Hugh Hostetler, the Rev. Ridgley Lytle, and the Rev. Clinton Kew, pastoral counselors at the Clinic; and the Rev. Herman Barbery, pastoral minister of the Marble Collegiate Church. The Rev. Arthur Tingue, Administrator of Clinical Services, and the Rev. Charles DiSalvo, Assistant to the Director of Training, actively encouraged me in my efforts to complete the manuscript.

My colleagues at the Bureau of Applied Social Research of Columbia University helped me maintain a sociological perspective on the topic. Professor Charles Y. Glock, former Director of the Bureau, contributed to the research design. During the course of the work he was succeeded as Director by Dr. David Sills, Dr. Bernard Berelson, and Professor Allen Barton, all of whom took an active interest in the project and commented helpfully on the developing report. Professor Edmund deS. Brunner, Member of the Bureau's Board of Governors, was gracious with his time in providing detailed remarks on a late draft of the manuscript. Jann Eckert Azumi and Vivian Biasotti Vallier provided administrative, secretarial, editorial, and intellectual assistance through long months of sustained effort. Clara Shapiro was a constant guardian of the project's financial solvency. Professor Robert K. Merton gave me more time and counsel than I deserved in an effort to raise the level of the work. This final version does not pretend to have met his standards.

Comments by Professor Amitai Etzioni of the Department of Sociology of Columbia University helped me avoid some pitfalls. Professor Talcott Parsons of the Department of Social Relations of Harvard University inspired solutions to some problems arising in the course of the work.

The work owes a subtle debt to Bracha Klausner. Rina and Jonathan Klausner will come to understand their contribution with the passage of time. Gabriella Grant devoted many hours to manuscript drafts. Francine Shacter aided in the arduous task of manuscript revision. Antonette Simplicio lent her deft skill to the preparation of printer's copy. Publication at this time owes much to the kindness of Dr. Robert T. Bower, Director of the Bureau of Social Science Research, who granted me a leave of absence from his employ. Professor Charles

Kadushin, at first my assistant and later my colleague, was an intellectual friend as the report evolved sentence by sentence. Would that I could realize the instruction of these colleagues and friends.

"Wisdom crieth aloud in the street . . ."

Prov. 1:20

Samuel Z. Klausner

Bethesda, Maryland
December, 1962

CONTENTS

LIST OF TABLES

Tables followed by A or B will be found
in the Notes following each chapter.

Psychiatry and Religion

PART ONE

Religio-Psychiatry: A Social Institution

Chapter I

Introduction

A PROTESTANT MINISTER in New York leaves his pulpit to become a full-time psychological counselor. A church dignitary accuses him of perverting his ministry. In Barcelona, a Catholic psychiatrist helps patients find a new relationship with God. His colleagues attack him for scientific irresponsibility. The minister and the psychiatrist discover one another and make a common cause. Thus, a psychological ministry and religious psychiatry create an unorthodox alliance to battle personal misery. The religio-psychiatric movement is born through several thousand similar encounters. This book reports on pressures and counterpressures surrounding that movement.

MAJOR AND MINOR THEMES OF THIS BOOK

The religio-psychiatric movement is a social movement rooted in social conditions. These social conditions, which lead ministers and psychiatrists to abandon traditional ways of behaving and thinking, will be studied through the literature of the movement. Psychological ministers and religious psychiatrists depart from tradition in three principal role[1] relations: the relations between ministers and the church and between psychiatrists and psychiatry, the relations between these individuals as counselors and their clients, and the relations between pastoral counselors and religiously oriented psychiatrists. The religio-psychiatric movement will be studied through the sociological perspective of these changing relations. We will not develop new social theory as much as we will apply theoretical insights to the understanding of this movement.[2]

What the reader finds in this book may be conditioned by his perspective. A sociologist might interpret this as a study in the sociology of knowledge, since ministerial and psychiatric attitudes are linked to the positions they occupy in the social structure. The study might be seen as an application of specific social theories. Reference group theory, for example, is used to bridge the distance between social position and ideas. This book might be considered by some as a contribution to the sociology of religion or the sociology of science. A historian of ideas might see the work as a case study of the cultural relations of religion and science and of the social mechanisms through which they influence each other. The concluding chapter will summarize the findings from this point of view.

A minister or psychiatrist not involved in the movement might read this study as an analysis of the influence of the religio-psychiatric movement within his institution. Pastoral counselors and religiously oriented psychiatrists, the subjects of this study, already sensitive to psychodynamic factors in their relations to their institutions, their clients, and one another, might find interest in the social factors conditioning these relations. The range of possible ways to organize these relations becomes apparent when the experiences of a number of counselors are brought between the covers of a single book. The methodologically oriented reader is likely to discover some of the problems involved in adapting interview and survey research methods to the analysis of library materials, and the difficulties involved in selecting adequate indicators for highly abstract concepts.

Certain outcomes should not be expected from this book. The effectiveness of the counseling relationships described will not be judged, nor will we evaluate the theological status of the ministers' attitudes and the psychological theoretical status of the psychiatrists' attitudes. Ways of dividing the counseling jurisdictions and qualifications which might be demanded of candidates for the counseling role will be described, but the study will not judge the right provinces for ministerial and psychiatric endeavors, nor recommend qualifications for the counselor. The evidence to be presented in this study is not adequate to support one or another judgment. The author will endeavor not to allow his personal attitudes on these issues to intrude upon the analysis. Any position on these issues which seems implied by the presentation is to be considered inadvertent.

The following pages include a brief note on past relations of religion and psychiatry, and descriptions of the method of the study, of the literature and its authors, and of the argument of the book.

PAST RELATIONS OF RELIGION AND PSYCHIATRY

Early classical society had no social institution devoted exclusively to healing or exclusively to science. Both were interwoven in what we would today term a religious context. Gradually science evolved an independent status alongside religion and, in time, medicine emerged as an independent branch of applied science. Psychiatry has been designated as a specialty within medicine for little more than a century. Religion, for its part, underwent a parallel differentiation. For centuries pastoral, sacerdotal, and educational activities were intertwined. Gradually, different churches or, within a church, different orders or roles occupied themselves more with one of these activities than with the others. The pastorate has but recently emerged as a specialized ministerial role. Renewed interest in pastoral activities in religious circles was contemporaneous with psychiatry's self-assertion as an autonomous medical specialty. Mid-nineteenth-century religion and medicine were turning to mental healing in what appeared to be separate developments. The "warfare of science and theology" obscured their common roots. Yet each constituted the world in which the other lived. Theologians were surrounded by a spreading scientific hegemony. Some accepted the new scientific revelation of the physical universe and awaited archeological authentication of Holy history and philological insights in Holy Writ. Many scientists had grown up in a church atmosphere and some were ministers' sons. Even those who had abandoned religion were faced with patients speaking in religious tongues. At the dawn of the twentieth century, religion and psychiatry were related like the tree tops of a jungle rain forest. Branches of the tallest trees might intertwine above separate trunks, but there was scant awareness of the roots knotted around one another.[3]

Religio-psychiatry, a discernible movement of ideas for the past three-quarters of a century, has assumed organizational form only recently.[4] The Emmanuel Movement at the turn of the century was an early clinical organization in which Episcopal priests and psychiatrists cooperated. Development of the hospital chaplaincy brought ministers and psychiatrists together in clinical settings. During the 1930's the Council for Clinical Training provided a meeting ground for pastoral counselors engaged in this work. St. Elizabeth's Hospital in Washington, Boston Psychopathic Hospital, and the Religio-Psychiatric Clinic in New York became training centers for ministers. Recently the Academy of Religion and Mental Health has been organizing community groups of Jewish, Protestant, and Catholic psychiatrists and clergymen.

The religio-psychiatric movement has its own professional journals. During the first decade of the century a journal entitled *Psychotherapy* provided a common platform for ministers and psychiatrists. This was followed by *Religion und Seelenleden* in Germany, and the *Journal of Psychotherapy as a Religious Process,* and recently the *Journal of Religion and Health* in the United States. Journals directed more specifically to ministers, such as *Pastoral Psychology* and *Lumen Vitae*, also carry material in this field. These and other journals have been accompanied by books, some of which will be mentioned below, filling many library shelves. It is through these books and articles that the movement will be studied.

HOW THE RELIGIO-PSYCHIATRIC MOVEMENT WAS STUDIED THROUGH ITS LITERATURE

Studying a movement through its literature is like inferring an iceberg from its visible cap. For each pastor or psychiatrist who publishes an untold number serve quietly in churches and offices.

But here is the limit of the iceberg analogy. The cap and body of the iceberg are of the same material and the inference from one to the other principally quantitative. Prolific ministers and psychiatrists, however, are not typical of their colleagues. Nevertheless, the inventory of written ideas catalogs the unwritten. It is in the relative distributions of these ideas that the two populations might differ. We cannot know the way these distributions differ until some parallel study establishes parameters for the nonwriters similar to those described in this book for the writers. Though we shall speak of the field of religion and psychiatry on the assumption that it reflects its literature, the reader should be cautious about generalizing beyond the literature. Further, limitations of our sample require that this study be looked upon principally as exploratory. Generalization from the sample of items to be studied to the universe of literature and authors is hazardous.

How was this literature assembled and studied? Bibliographic work was limited to writings bridging the fields of religion and of psychiatry in their concern with mental or spiritual health. Books and articles subsuming religion under a psychiatric or psychological rubric, by and large, were not included. This decision eliminated items such as Sigmund Freud's *Totem and Taboo* and Edwin Starbuck's *Psychology of Religion*. Discussions of emotional disturbances written solely from the point of view of religion were excluded. This decision eliminated items such as Mary Baker Eddy's *Science and Health with a Key to the Scriptures*. On these grounds works on spiritual guidance, pastoral letters, and faith healing were deemed outside the scope of the study. By and large, the study was restricted to "scholarly" writings, defined not by their technical level but by their intent to analyze or to instruct. This decision eliminated most of the popular inspirational literature. Ultimately, a bibliography of 1,364 books, articles, pamphlets, and dissertations was assembled. Seventeen of the items were penned anonymously. This study is based on the remaining 1,347. These are listed and annotated in Volume II[5] of the present study. The increasing difficulty in locating additional items at the close of the bibliographic phase of our work suggests that this number approaches the universe of items in all languages published in the field through 1957. Of these works, 739 were read and abstracted by the investigator, assisted by a group of graduate students and seminarians.

The writings were the work of 780 authors. Each author's vitae, as available, were entered on a McBee card along with the abstract of the item he had written. Of 1,132 items for which we were able to identify the author's profession, 67 per cent were penned by ministers, 21 per cent by psychiatrists, 8 per cent by psychologists, and 4 per cent by philosophers, journalists, and members of other professions.

The unit of analysis for this study is the book, article, or dissertation. All of these will be referred as "items." The report will speak of the characteristics of ministers and psychiatrists. These should be understood as elliptical expressions referring to items authored by ministers and psychiatrists possessing the given characteristics. The Appendix will show that the populations of authors and of items have similar parameters. This suggests that our findings probably would not have differed significantly had individuals rather than items been the units of analysis.

Original coding categories were established on the basis of a case study of relations among ministers, psychiatrists, and patients at the Religio-Psychiatric Clinic in New York City. These categories were revised after coding a sample of 100 abstracts of the literature. The final code classified some of the author's personal characteristics. This information was obtained, by and large, from directories of professional associations and from a questionnaire returned by the authors. Date and place of publication and the general subject matter of the writing were available from the title page and table of contents. For items that were abstracted it was possible to classify norms advocated by authors for regulating relationships between ministers and psychiatrists and norms governing their relations to patients, their theories of mental deviance, their formulations of the pressures driving them either to reinterpret or to reassert traditional roles, types of changes they would introduce into these roles, goals they recommended for counseling, their reference groups, the psychiatric orientations of their writings, a religious belief index, and a psychiatric belief index. All of the items were coded by the researcher. While this optimizes the consistency of the coding (comparable to a "coefficient of stability" as a reliability measure) it raises a problem concerning "construct validity," the appropriateness of classifying a particular indicator as a sign of a particular concept. Some studies allow for this by comparing the judgments of several coders (often referred to as "intercoder reliability"). As a substitute for this, as each topic is introduced, several examples will be given of indicators used for classifying an item in the given category.[6]

The method of data-gathering was modeled on the interview method, with the code book as the interview schedule and the item abstract as the respondent. Because the object of study was literary, the method in some respects resembles content analysis. There are certain differences, however. Content analysis tends to focus on a small number of themes and to employ a quantitative procedure for deciding upon the classification of a given item. An interview generally involves a great battery of questions. Relatively more flexible interpretive criteria are used for classifying the respondent.

In this study, questions were "asked" of the abstract. The statements or themes in the abstract used as indicators are the "responses." A live interviewee may search his mind for an answer. Here, if the author did not deal with the question, no answer was obtainable. On the other hand, if he did have a position on the question, he could not refuse to reply. Since the items covered a variety of subjects, few provided "responses" to all questions. For example, a theoretical discussion of the concepts of sin and sickness would not be likely to provide information on qualifications for admission to the counseling role. Consequently, a rather large "no answer" category appears in our tabulations. Some of these "no answers" may be due to the abstractor's failure to transmit the relevant information in the item. This is similar to the "don't know" responses in an interview, especially where the respondent may not recall the information, or the case in which an interviewer fails to ask the question. Most of these "no answers," however, are more like the "question not relevant" category of an interview. In view of this, the "no answer" categories will not be considered in the data analysis. Calculations will be based on the "response" categories alone. As a result the numbers in some tables become relatively small or may vary from table to table as different questions with different proportions of "answers" are considered. The coded data were entered on both McBee and IBM cards. The McBee code permitted examining each classification qualitatively in the context of the abstract. The IBM code allowed the multivariate analysis upon which most of this report is based.[7]

MANIFEST CONTENT OF RELIGIO-PSYCHIATRIC LITERATURE

Manifestly the literature of the religio-psychiatric movement concerns the relation between religious and psychological ideas about emotional disturbances. As a sociological study, this book uses analytic categories to examine the relation between the ideas espoused and the social positions of the ministers and psychiatrists. Analytic topics do not always follow the organization of substantive problems. Consequently we pause at this point to give the reader a sense of what the literature is explicitly about. We shall do this by presenting some characteristic titles under six broad themes: religious and psychological theories of deviant behavior, religious and psychological theories of counseling, role and institutional relations, training of pastoral counselors, history of relations between religion and mental health, and bibliographic and reference works. Subtopics are included under the first four headings. Table 1 summarizes the number of publications classified by their major themes.

Religious and Psychological Theories of Deviant Behavior

Almost a third of the 1,347 writings analyze and compare religious and psychiatric theories of neurosis. About half of these deal with philosophical issues: human nature, morality, truth, and responsibility. Pryor Grant, for example, examines "The Moral and Religious life of the Individual in the Light of the New Psychology" (509).[8] Rudolf Allers' *The Successful Error* (11) executes a meticulous Thomistic critique of Freudianism. Benjamin Sanders seeks to validate Christian religion through psychoanalytic theory in his *Christianity after Freud* (1110). James H. Van der Veldt and Robert P. Odenwald judge psychiatry in the light of moral law in *Psychiatry and Catholicism* (1252).

A slightly greater number of these items analyze specific concepts in psychological and religious theories of deviant behavior. Charles Macfie Campbell in his *Delusion and Belief* (242) defends the role of beliefs as "adaptive mechanisms" by which man takes his stand in the cosmos. Anton T. Boisen describes psychosis as a spiritual crisis to be resolved by *The Exploration of the Inner World* (133). Louis Beirnaert is concerned with neuropsychiatry's exegesis of *The Question of Miracles* (82).

Table 1—Number of Publications in Religion and Psychiatry Classified by Major Themes

		Number
I. Religious and Psychological Theories of Deviant Behavior	452	
1. Broad Philosophical Considerations		212
2. Specific Concepts		240
II. Religious and Psychological Theories of Counseling	558	
1. Value Considerations		372
2. Problems of Technique		186
III. Role and Institutional Relations	217	
1. Psychology and the Pastoral Counselor		103
2. Religion and the Psychiatrist		19
3. Relations Between Ministers and Psychiatrists		42
4. Counseling in Religious Institutions		28
5. Religion in Psychiatric Institutions		25
IV. Training of Pastoral Counselors	50	
1. Principles of Training		34
2. Training Materials		16
V. History of the Relations Between Religion and Mental Health	37	
VI. Bibliographical and Reference Works	33	
Total	1347	

Religious and Psychological Theories of Counseling

Almost half of the books and articles deal with theories of counseling. Chrysostumus Schulte discusses moral responsibility in the "Pastoral Treatment of Psychopaths" (1138). For Rollo May, overcoming egocentricity is one of *The Springs of Creative Living* (837). Hans Schaer analyzes counseling as *The Experience of Salvation and its Psychological Aspects* (1118). Maurice S. Friedman recommends a dialogic encounter between counselor and counselee in his "Healing Through Meeting: Martin Buber and Psychotherapy" (447). Some write of psychotherapeutic technique. Lewis Joseph Sherrill relates *Guilt and Redemption* (1155) through a dynamic relationship with a therapist who gives *agape* love. Seward Hiltner says a balance between emotional involvement and mechanical treatment exemplifies "Empathy in Counseling" (565).

Role and Institutional Relations

Over two hundred items deal with role relations between ministers and psychiatrists or the institutional relations of religion and psychiatry or psychology. H. Flanders Dunbar instructs clergy-men in the connection between "Mental Hygiene and Religious Teaching" (369). Anton T. Boisen presents scientific insights useful to "The Minister as Counselor" (142). Victor White compares "The Analyst and the Confessor" (1295). Clinton J. Kew is con-cerned with the problems of "Group Psychotherapy in a Church Setting" (697). George A. Gross defines "The Function of a Chaplain in Psychotherapy" (520) as expediting the psycho-analytic process.

Training of Pastoral Counselors

Training is an issue among ministers entering psychological work. Rollin J. Fairbanks establishes "Standards for Full-Time Clinical Training in the Light of the New England Experience" (400). Richard White Boyd explains "The Use of Group Psycho-therapy in the Professional Training of Ministers" (173). Kilian William McDonnel's description of "Psychiatrists in an Abbey" (853) tells of the psychiatric workshop for clergymen at the Benedictine Abbey of St. John's in Collegeville, Minnesota.

History of Relations Between Religion and Mental Health

Historians of religion and psychiatry may count Andrew Dickson White among their predecessors. His *A History of the Warfare of Science with Theology in Christendom* (1290) remains a classic. Years later, Gregory Zilboorg and George W. Henry out-line *A History of Medical Psychology* (1343) from primitive times. John Thomas McNeill traces *The History of the Cure of Souls* (869) from the guides of Israel to the classical philosophers and the church fathers to the more recent Protestant tradition. Need-less to say, some nonhistorical works carry retrospective introduc-tions to special themes.

Bibliographical and Reference Works

Bibliographies on religion and mental health are becoming available. Seward Hiltner has prepared a "Bibliography and Read-ing Guide in Pastoral Psychology" (574). Robert C. Leslie has compiled one on "Religion and Healing" (766). Karl A. Men-ninger's *A Guide to Psychiatric Books and some Reading Lists* (875) includes titles in the religio-psychiatric field.

SHIFTING INTERESTS AND GROWTH OF THE FIELD

The number and distribution of items in Table 1 are functions of our definition of the field and of the categories in which these items are grouped. One cannot infer the relative concern with these topics on the part of other ministers and psychiatrists from this distribution. Certain tendencies or emphases, however, are suggested. The religio-psychiatric literature is more involved with theoretical than with applied problems. Even works on counseling place value considerations ahead of techniques. Perhaps those actively engaged in counseling, and consequently interested in application, are less likely to write. The cultural confrontation of religion and psychiatry gives this literature its central theme. Works on role relations and training show more concern with the implications of psychology for the pastor than of religion for the psychiatrist. Even when ministerial and psychiatric items are examined separately, relatively more works picture religion looking to psychiatry for guidance than conversely. This tendency will appear repeatedly in our study. The fact that training guides are published and that the field has its historians and bibliographers suggests that this literature indeed reflects a developing movement.

Literary emphases have changed in the course of the religio-psychiatric movement. A theme significant during an early period may be unimportant in later years. Table 2 summarizes the proportion of items written on each of the above themes in each decade.

Over half of the items published before 1918 are concerned with religious and scientific conceptions of man and theories of his deviant behavior. Interest shifted to practical issues of counseling after the war, and the next decade was characterized by growing concern about relationships between ministers and psychiatrists. During and following the Second World War interest in philosophical discussions decreased, interest in counseling and in role relationships continued, and concern with training ministers for the counseling role increased slightly.

This shift in concern hints at an evolution of psychologically oriented counselor and religiously oriented psychiatrist roles. Theoretical discussion prior to World War I tested the possibilities of religio-psychiatric relations. An experience with a specialized counseling ministry was provided by the wartime military chaplaincy. Postwar growth of a hospital chaplaincy brought ministers into

**Table 2—Proportion of Writings on Each Subject Published
in Each Decade (in Per Cent)**

Decade	Theories of Deviant Behavior	Theories of Counseling	Role Relationships	Training	History and Bibliography	Total Published	
Before 1918	59	25	4	—	12	100	(48)
1918–1927	40	42	9	2	7	100	(65)
1928–1937	40	40	15	2	3	100	(138)
1938–1947	31	41	16	8	4	100	(217)
1948–1957	31	43	17	4	5	100	(851)
Total							(1319)a

a. This and all of the following tables are based on cross-tabulations. They will not total 1,347 because information on classifications will be lacking for some items. Here the difference between 1,319 and 1,347 is due to the fact that information on date of publication was not available for 28 items. Most of these are organizational pamphlets.

counseling situations alongside medical personnel and exposed psychiatrists to ministers as collegial professionals. This confrontation may account for interest in theories of counseling and, particularly, for interest in role relationships during the postwar decades. The lack of specific material on training early in the movement suggests that the pastoral counselor role, the one with which this training literature is concerned, must have rested upon general ministerial training. The recent increase in training literature may reflect the institutionalization of the psychological pastoral role and, consequently, crystallization of the procedures for socialization.[9]

The extreme right-hand column in Table 2 presents a picture of the growth of the movement as reflected in publication figures.[10] Twice as many publications appeared during the second postwar decade as during the first; the third decade almost doubled the second. Between 1948 and 1957 almost four times as many items were published as between 1938 and 1947. Over the last four decades the publication rate increased thirteen-fold.[11]

Proportional increases of relatively small numbers may give an illusion of growth. Yet one cannot help but be impressed by the insistent upward trend and the recent quadrupling. The graph shows an exponential curve of growth. This may be seen from the fact that the logarithmic curve of the publication figures is nearly a straight line. The shape of the graph indicates that by 1957 the field had not yet reached its peak.[12] Continued rapid growth may be predicted for the next few decades. The next section outlines the plan for study of the movement reflected in this literature.

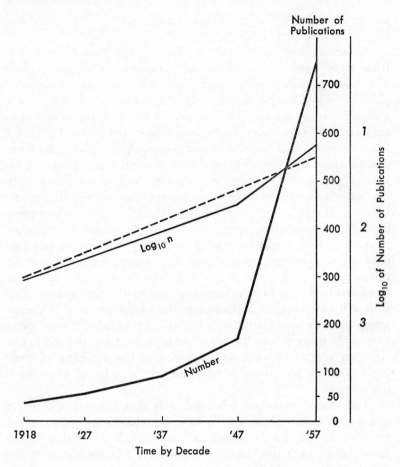

PLAN OF THE BOOK

The first part of this report will describe and analyze the relations between minister-authors of this literature and the church and between psychiatrist-authors and psychiatry. Most of these ministers and psychiatrists choose nontraditional approaches to healing or counseling. They level criticisms against their institutions which express some of their reasons for breaking with tradition. The institutions, through the voices of the more traditional ministers and psychiatrists, respond with countercriticisms. Study of the sectors of society from which the movement recruits these ministers and psychiatrists will suggest social conditions which promote and inhibit literary participation.

By accounting for some factors leading ministers and psychiatrists away from their institutional traditions, we do not explain why these ministers adopt psychiatric norms or why these psychiatrists adopt religious approaches to counseling. The reference group chosen by an individual influences him to conform or not to conform to his institution and also influences the types of goals set for counseling. A shift in reference group might explain why some psychiatrists introduce religious elements and some ministers introduce psychiatric elements into their work, and perhaps explain the latter's favorable disposition toward seeking psychiatric assistance. The fact that some ministers establish their own psychological-type counseling services requires additional explanation. This phenomenon will be related to their perception of the psychoanalytic movement as simultaneously a negative and a positive reference group. A question remains. Why do they shift to a nonmembership group as a reference group in the first place? This shift will be related to implicit approval of the potential reference group by their own institutions, opportunity to interact with members of the other group, the impact of occupying a high rank in one situation and a low rank in another, and the widening of their horizon to new behavioral possibilities through a broad educational background.

The second principal relationship is that between counselors and their clients. "Ideal type" counseling relations of ministers and psychiatrists will be developed as base lines. We will then follow their change from the "ideal type" of their own institution in the direction of one which is more characteristic of members of the other institution. Changes in relation to the client will be shown to be concomitant with alienation from their institutions. Three types of nonconformists will be described. One is the ritualist who continues the traditional counseling practices of his institution but puts them into the service of goals set by the other institution. The second is the innovator who imports procedures from the other institution but applies them to attain goals set by his own institution. Third is the rebel who adopts the other institution's definition of both the means and the goals of counseling. In the order presented, each of these types is increasingly nonconformist.

Ministers and psychiatrists adopt these new attitudes and behaviors in an effort to escape certain problems they face in counseling. These very changes, however, disrupt the relation of the individual to his institution and expose him to new pressures. These new pressures derive from "punitive" measures taken by their institutions and from the painful conscience which pursues their break with tradition. To attenuate these new strains, they justify their behavior to themselves and to others. These behavioral rationales may rely on a reinterpretation of the rules or on a claim that, in breaking with tradition, the individual is following the example of honored members of the group. An individual is encouraged to use one or another type of rationale by the extent of his nonconformity and by the social group to which he is oriented.

The relation between pastoral counselors and religiously oriented psychiatrists is the third principal focus of study. This relation is contingent upon what each considers the appropriate counseling jurisdictions of each profession. Authors will be classified according to whether they believe counseling is solely a psychological or solely a religious affair or involves a combination of both. In addition, they will be classified according to whether they believe either a minister or a psychiatrist alone is sufficient for counseling or whether counseling requires two specialists, one religious and one psychiatric, cooperating with one another. We will analyze some influences leading individuals to support one or another type of jurisdictional position. However the jurisdictional question is settled, personnel must be chosen to fill the roles. Ministers and psychiatrists debate the qualifications they seek in a potential counselor. Some define counselling as an ascribed role, for which the incumbent qualifies by virtue of inherent personality characteristics or a state of Grace. Others define it as an achieved role for which he qualifies by virtue of skills or training. The qualifications advocated will be related to the conception of the counseling task, to the culture of the institution with which individuals identify when counseling, and to the nature of the public for whom they write.[13] A concluding chapter will speculate about the function of the religio-psychiatric encounter for the broader institutions of religion and science.

Chapters IX and X present a case study of the Religio-Psychiatric Clinic in New York City. In the research chronology this preceded the study of the literature, but here it is placed after the latter study to serve as a concrete illustration of the relationships described through the literature.

Throughout, certain terminological conventions will be followed. The general terms "minister" and "clergyman" will refer to official leaders of religious institutions regardless of the specific titles by which they may be addressed in their groups. The term "psychiatrist" will be used when the intent is to refer to a medical practitioner who is concerned with the treatment of emotional problems. To refer to the body of knowledge upon which this practice draws, the term "psychology" will be used. The term "counseling" will refer to the relation of psychiatrists and ministers to their clients. The client may be called a parishioner or a patient. The goal of counseling will be referred to either as "healing" or as "therapy."

NOTE ON TECHNICAL TERMS

A few technical terms, such as "role" and institution," have intruded into our opening remarks. Some of these terms are shared by psychology and sociology and will not trouble the reader. Others have special sociological meanings. A few terms central to the study will be defined here.

Repeated reference will be made to norms of religion and psychiatry. The term "norm" indicates a set of rules which either enjoin or prohibit behavior. They are called "institutionalized norms" when shared by individuals belonging to the same group so that each expects the others to behave according to these rules.[14] A norm, for example, might state that a person in a given position is expected to explain arithmetic to a group. A second norm might direct him not to develop deep emotional ties with the members of that group. A third norm could require that he apply the same standards in evaluating each of the group members. A cluster of such expectations defines the status of classroom teacher. We shall study clusters of norms defining the statuses of minister and psychiatrist. The "teacher" or the "minister" or the "psychiatrist" defined by these norms is not an individual but is, on the one hand, that aspect of the individual expressed through his participation in a social position and, on the other hand, a definition of the social position itself. An individual occupies several social statuses.

At least two statuses must be related for the status norms to be enacted. For example, the norm requiring the teacher to explain arithmetic is realized in behavior when the teacher is paired with a student. The student, in turn, is expected to listen and learn arithmetic. This relation between statuses defines a role. We speak of the psychiatrist-patient role, the minister-parishioner role, and the psychiatrist-minister role. In the first two instances the related statuses are within the same institution. The last role links statuses in two institutions. What, then, is an institution?

The normative cluster defining the status "classroom teacher" is linked to another status defined by the norms that its occupant decides upon the curriculum and hires teachers. This is the status of "school administrator." A third status may be defined by the expectations that its occupant keep school records and periodically report to the administration. These expectations define the "school clerk." Just as norms cluster to define a status, so statuses themselves cluster to form an institution. An institution links statuses around the pursuit of a central social activity such as education, worship, or healing. The cluster of teacher, administrator, and clerk contributes to the definition of the education institution. A religious institution could include such statuses as bishop, priest, and parishioner. The statuses of psychiatrist, patient, and nurse are related in the psychiatric institution.[15]

On what basis are norms selected? Why may an employer in one society hire workers according to a rule of competence and in another favor members of his family? The standards according to which one norm is selected as appropriate and another rejected are termed values or value standards. Value standards do not only guide the choice of norms, the appropriate means for executing an act, but also are a basis for selecting goals for action. We will be concerned with the values of ministers and psychiatrists in the psychotherapeutic role.

Certain individuals claim membership in a social group but do not support certain of its norms. This may be expressed attitudinally as disagreement. Behaviorally they may be rebels, reformers, criminals, insane, or the clarions of progress. Departure from the prescribed norms is termed variation. The person whose behavior is inconsistent with the norms of his group is called a variant. The embezzler varies from the norms regulating an employee's relationship to his employer. The teacher who beats a pupil varies from the norms our society sets for the teacher-pupil role. A man refusing to fight is a variant in a warrior society. A man who does fight is a variant in a pacifistic society. To say that a person is a variant is not to judge the ethics of his act. Saints and sinners are both variants from their surroundings.[16]

NOTES

1. See the Note on Technical Terms appended to this introduction for definitions of some sociological terms occurring in this study.

2. Almost every cross-tabulation in this book will be explained in terms of an accepted social science proposition. Some sociologists among the readers may want to know in what way this study advances theory beyond the already accepted. The modest theoretical contributions take the form either of some slightly new perspective on an old issue or of a small extension of accepted propositions to a new substantive area. For example, in Chap. III the problem of choosing a reference group will be examined for the case where an individual selects a nonmembership group as a reference group. In the process, reference group theory will be linked with propositions about status consistency. Chap. V will try to relate two popular theories of variant behavior—Merton's theory of institutional variation and Parson's theory of variation generated in role interaction. The discussion in Chap. VI on ministers' and psychiatrists' self-justification will connect psychological concepts of mechanisms of defense and sociological ideas about the content of the defense employed. The analysis of the division of labor in Chap. VII deals not only with the emergence of new, more differentiated specialist roles but extends the discussion to account for development of a new generalist role. The same discussion also deals with the priority of task or problem area differentiation over role differentiation. The conception of an appropriate division of labor is then related to the criteria used for allocating personnel among roles. Finally, throughout the book there will be evidence that in the process of polarization which accompanies certain types of social change, the two opposed polar types—here, rebels and militant conformists—tend to be alike in many respects. These theoretical points are merely suggestive. They are based on regularities observed in a very special sample with no guarantee that they would be found in a study of another population.

3. For a more detailed history, see items 869 and 1343 in the Bibliography of Cited Religio-Psychiatric Works.

4. The term "movement" is used in two senses. Expressionism may be called a movement in painting or Romanticism a movement in literature. In this sense, "movement" signifies a convergence in the work of a number of individuals. The "members" of such a movement are usually aware of one another, study one another's paintings, read one another's books, single out common intellectual or artistic ancestors, and manifest opposition to a common enemy endeavor. They need never meet in a face-to-face group, identify with each other, or espouse a common objective. Sometimes their designation as "members" of the same movement awaits their historian. The sociologist prefers to reserve the term for "social movements" such as the Falange in Spain or Henry George's Progress and Poverty of turn-of-the-century United States. These groups are organized in the pursuit of a common goal.

For examples of studies of social movements see Herbert Blumer, "Collective Behavior," *New Outline of the Principles of Sociology*, ed. Alfred McClung Lee, pp. 167–224; Hadley Cantril, *The Psychology of Social Movements*; and Leon Festinger, Henry W. Riecken, and Stanley Schacter, *When Prophecy Fails*.

5. Vol. II refers to "Annotated Bibliography and Directory of Workers in the Field of Religion and Psychiatry" (Bureau of Applied Social Research, Columbia University, 1960). (Mimeographed.)

6. A much larger number of examples of indicators is filed for inspection with the Bureau of Social Science Research in Washington, D.C.

7. Basic references on the methods of data-gathering and data analysis include Robert K. Merton, Marjorie Fiske, and Patricia L. Kendall, *The Focused Interview*. On content analysis, see, for example, Bernard Berelson, *Content Analysis in Communications Research*; and Harold D. Lasswell et al., *Language of Politics, Studies in Quantitative Semantics*. This study exemplifies survey research using library materials. For a general reference on survey methods see Herbert Hyman, *Survey Design and Analysis*. The topic of multivariate analysis is covered in Paul F. Lazarsfeld and Morris Rosenberg (eds.), *The Language of Social Research*.

The Appendix provides more detailed information about the methodology of the study.

8. The numbers in parentheses refer to the locations of the items in the Bibliography of Cited Religio-Psychiatric Works at the end of this study. In Vol. II the reader will find the complete bibliography of the 1,347 items and often a short summary of the content of the item as well as biographical information about the author.

9. We are assuming that training for a specialized role follows rather than precedes the institutionalization of that role. This is consistent with the common belief that education prepares individuals to enter established roles more often than it acts as an agent of social change by anticipating the

emergence of new roles. Once individuals are trained for a new role, there is pressure to maintain the direction of change. Training creates a vested interest in that role, legitimizes the role in the eyes of competitors and detractors, makes for more efficient execution of the role, and gives the trainers control over recruitment of new personnel.

Following these conjectures, one would anticipate a future increase in the proportion of the literature dealing with training and role relationships. The demands of training, in turn, will lead to further writings on counseling. Proportionately less work, though not absolutely less, may be done on philosophical problems as the role itself becomes accepted and individuals turn to the concrete issues arising from it.

10. Rate of publication is a conservative indicator of interest and activity in a field. Religio-psychiatric ideas infused the general literature of religion and psychiatry before a specialized literature emerged to signify a differentiation of the cognitive culture. There is also a sociological reason for supposing that publication would lag behind general interest. A specialized literature presupposes an audience prepared to read it. This is particularly true where publication is responsive to consumer demand, as most of this is, rather than subsidized by interest groups.

11. These figures can be appreciated in comparison with statistics on general publication in the United States. This will not lead us too far astray because although the figures in Table 2 refer to publications in all languages, 72 per cent are published in the United States and Canada. Since the religio-psychiatric literature is directed to professionals, its production should be compared with that of other professional literatures. These comparisons are made in Table 2A. The figures for medicine and hygiene, science, religion, and all books published were taken from the yearly statistical summaries of *Publishers Weekly*. They refer only to books published in the United States. The psychology column is summarzied from *Psychological Abstracts* and includes books and articles in all languages (as do the religion and psychiatry figures which are shown separately); this publication did not appear during the first decade considered.

Table 2A—Number of Books and Articles Published in Religion and Psychiatry and Some Cognate Fields in Each Decade Since 1918

| | BOOKS AND ARTICLES | | BOOKS ALONE | | | | |
| | Religion and | | Religion and | Medicine and | | | All Books Published |
Decade	Psychiatry	Psychology	Psychiatry	Hygiene	Science	Religion	in U.S.
1918–1927	65	—	41	3,961	3,947	6,629	77,484
1928–1937	138	22,951	57	3,726	4,264	7,269	95,142
1938–1947	217	27,734	84	3,756	4,343	6,421	92,432
1948–1957	851	42,204	202	4,797	7,203	8,099	116,726

Between 1918 and 1957 the total number of books published in the United States increased by slightly more than half. Population rose by two-thirds during this time, so this would not indicate increased reading. Certain groups of the population may, however, read more today while others read less. Evidence on this and related questions may be found in Bernard Rosenberg and D. M. White, *Mass Culture*, Sec. 3 on "Mass Literature"; and in D. Waples, Bernard Berelson, and F. Bradshaw, *What Reading Does to People*. The number of books published in medicine and hygiene rose by about 63 per cent and those in science by about 89 per cent during this same period. This corresponds with the general population rise but lags behind the increase in medical, health, and scientific personnel. The number of religious books rose by only about 22 per cent, while the books and articles in psychology nearly doubled through the last three decades. The proportionate expansion in religion and psychiatry exceeds by far that of these other professional fields. This type of finding would be anticipated for the literature of nuclear physics or aerodynamics, where new fields have emerged.

12. Not only is the number of publications increasing, but the rate of publication is still rising. The point of inflection of the curve has not yet been reached. On similar curves for technological growth, see William F. Ogburn, *Social Change with Respect to Culture and Original Nature*.

13. By this time the reader must have the sense that he will be facing a number of typologies and taxonomies in the coming manuscript. In every such case, analysis begins with the classification. It does not end with it. The types or classes of phenomena become the variables examined in the analysis. Their usefulness is demonstrated by their discriminatory power when cross-tabulated with other variables.

14. For a discussion of "normative orientation" of action in terms of "expectations" of behavior, see Talcott Parsons, *The Social System*. See also Muzafer Sherif, *The Psychology of Social Norms*.

15. No institution is self-sufficient. The educational institution has, for example, economic requirements relating it to economic institutions. Sociologists often reserve the term "society" for a self-sufficient cluster of institutions. Anthropologists tend to refer to this as "culture" and reserve the term "society" for the case of a population enacting institutional roles.

16. The terms "variant" and "variation" are used here in the sense in which "deviant" and "deviance" appear in the sociological literature. See for example, Talcott Parsons' chapter on "Deviant Behavior and the Mechanisms of Social Control," *loc. cit.*; Robert K. Merton's chapters on "Social Structure and Anomie" and "Continuities in the Theory of Social Structure and Anomie," *Social Theory and Social Structure*; and Albert Cohen, *Delinquent Boys*.

Chapter II

Cultural Encounter and Institutional Change

WHY DO SOME MINISTERS abandon a traditional ministry to specialize in psychological pastoral counseling? Why do some psychiatrists introduce religious elements into therapy?[1] Two types of explanation will be offered for the genesis of variant behavior. Both of these assume that individuals are not prone to change unless their accustomed ways produce some "problem." One type of explanation posits social stability based upon conformity of individuals to behavioral expectations. When a role occupant becomes subject to incompatible demands[2] he is said to experience a role or value conflict. Variant behavior emerges as the individual attempts to deal with the conflict.[3]

A second type of theory employs an image of individuals striving by socially legitimate means to attain socially established goals. It may happen that either the means are not adequate to the goal or that the individual does not have access to adequate means.[4] Variant behavior emerges as an adaptation to the malintegration of institutional means and cultural goals.[5] We shall not select one or the other of these approaches but shall call upon each in turn when it seems applicable.

In this and the next two chapters we will seek some of the conditions which lead these ministers and psychiatrists to elect unorthodox paths. We shall begin by listening to their own complaints about their institutions. Some of these will suggest role conflict and others will suggest the individual's frustrations at his inability to attain certain goals. Complaints alone would not establish these individuals as variants. The counterattacks they engender, however, show that some sectors of their institutions consider them so. The formulations of these attacks and counterattacks may not necessarily reflect the underlying conditions producing estrangement. Analysis will show, however, that these remarks do indeed reflect the situation that they may be taken at face value. Individuals whose complaints suggest role conflict are indeed those more likely to be exposed to conflicting demands. Those who express frustration in regard to their aims do indeed have less access to the needed means. In attempting to specify the nature of the conflicts in which these individuals are caught, we will examine role conflicts related to class, educational, denominational, and age factors. In particular, it will be suggested as a hypothesis that the variants are caught in value conflicts peculiar to industrial society. These conflicts produce a "push" away from their institutions. The chapter concludes with an examination of some ways in which religious institutions exert authority to prevent ministers from varying and to encourage psychiatrists belonging to those institutions to engage in behavior which is variant with respect to traditional psychiatry. The next chapter will examine the "pull" of religion upon psychiatrists and of psychiatry upon ministers.

CRITICISMS AND COUNTERCRITICISMS

Let us examine some ministers' criticisms of religion and psychiatrists' criticisms of psychiatry and, in each case, the countercriticisms aimed at the dissidents. It would be enticing to weigh the correctness of each criticism and countercriticism but we shall resist this temptation. To succumb to it would divert us from the main object of this chapter—to discover why, at all, these ministers and psychiatrists become interested enough to write books and articles on the subject of religion and psychiatry.

Ministers Criticize Religion

Ministers' complaints may be subsumed under four headings: (1) inconsistencies between religious and scientific values, (2) discrepancies between actual and ideal religious values, (3) the ineffectiveness of religion in helping parishioners with their emotional difficulties, and (4) the ministers' personal ineffectiveness in the face of parishioners' emotional difficulties. The first two criticisms reflect conflicting conceptions of the ministerial role. The latter two criticisms suggest that institutional means are not adequate to cultural goals or a personal lack of access to adequate means. Complaints based on an inconsistency of religious and scientific values are found in the earliest literature of the movement. At the turn of the century, George Albert Coe, a liberal minister, called for a reconstruction of the whole scheme of Christian living in view of the theory of evolution (282)[6] Some years later, Clifford Barbour, a Presbyterian minister with a doctorate in psychology, demanded that Christianity recognize truth even at the expense of its most cherished ecclesiastical dogma (55). Walter Horton, a Congregationalist professor of theology, suggested that theology cannot be allowed a doctrine of man which conflicts with the findings of psychology and anthropology (589).

The discrepancy between actual and ideal religious values is most frequently expressed as a complaint that religious institutions have, in some sense, departed from true religious values. Rollo May, a minister engaged in psychological counseling, would free persons from the false compulsion to morality of fundamentalist religion (837). Seward Hiltner, a professor of pastoral psychology, found fault with literal and legalistical interpretations of doctrine (572).

Some ministers blame lack of success in helping parishioners on the structure of the church. Wayne Oates, a Southern Baptist, complained that executive and administrative responsibilities make the minister more of a corporation executive than a shepherd of the flock (974). Joseph Fletcher, an Episcopal priest trained in sociology and anthropology, believed the ministry would be more effective if it remembered that prophetic and pastoral roles must complement one another (413). Looking at the healing cults, John Sutherland Bonnell charged that their very existence is a judgment on the Christian church for failing to follow the Master's injunction to exercise a ministry of healing (156).

Self-blame in terms of insufficient training in psychology is the most common of the complaints. Frederick Kuether, Jr., an Evangelical and Reformed minister and a founder of the Council for Clinical Training, would implement religious ideas through clinical training (742). Reuel C. Howe, an Episcopal priest with a doctorate in pastoral theology, argues that seminarians without training in counseling may evade their problems or deal with them by compulsive religious observance (596).

Table 3 summarizes the proportions of items written by ministers advancing each type of criticism. Each item is classified by its major line of complaint.

Table 3—Proportion of Items Written by Ministers Advancing Each Type of Complaint Against the Church and the Ministry

Feeling of Personal Ineffectiveness	41%
Discrepancy Between Actual and Ideal Religious Values	33
Ineffectiveness of Church and Ministry in Helping Parishioner	15
Inconsistency Between Religious and Scientific Values	11
Total	100%
	(226)

A feeling of incompetence in the face of their problems is the single most important reason given by ministers for seeking change. Along with those disturbed by the church's ineffectiveness in helping parishioners they are complaining about a malintegration of means and goals. Slightly less than half of the complaints concern value discrepancies between religion and science or within religion itself. These ministers may be reflecting conflicting role demands. From the nature of the countercriticism of these ministers we sense that these are not inconsequential musings, but that these ministers are truly regarded as variant by some elements in the church.

The Church's Countercriticism

The complaints are not manifest in a revolution in religion or psychiatry. This is due, in part, to group constraint of the complainers.[7] The extreme nonconformist may be expelled from his status. The minister may be defrocked or the psychiatrist have his license revoked. Generally sanctions take the less severe form of attitudinal "punishments." Nonconformist variants are subjected to criticism and opprobrium.

The following are examples of statements by ministers who are, in this respect, militant conformists.[8] They function as a social control on the nonconformists. The vast majority of ministers and psychiatrists are neither non- nor militant conformist variants but are indifferent to the religio-psychiatric movement. These are the conformists. They are not variants. Militant conformists do not belong to this silent mass but are moved to write critical books and articles. Their conformity is vividly assertive. They become part of the religio-psychiatric movement by being locked in struggle with the nonconformists. Militant conformists and nonconformist variants emerge in response to similar social forces.[9] In addition, however, militant conformists adapt to a strain created in the institution by the existence of nonconformists.

Militant conformists attempt three approaches to the nonconformist variants. "Ideal typically," these approaches might be sequential, though in the present case we lack evidence to that effect. One approach is to cajole the dissidents. Critique takes the form of "come let us reason together." The militant conformists express tolerance or perhaps broad agreement with some of the new ideas but hint at their limitations. A second approach is to attack the dissidents. The critique is sharp and bitter. Venom is directed at the deceptively attractive ideas which beguile the dissidents. A third approach is to entice the dissidents. What they seek can be discovered within their own group. To encourage their return to the traditional fold, a reward may be dangled before them.[10] By and large, though not always, agents of social control criticize members of their own group. Even when they attack the source of the new ideas in another group, they generally do so for its impact on their colleagues.

Early dissidents were not taken seriously. They were cajoled by having their attention called to possible consequences of their position. A psychologist rather than a minister was an early critic of the nonconformists. H. Munsterberg, writing about the Emmanuel Movement in 1900, argued that since pleasure is not the main goal of religion, involving the church in other than miraculous treatment of illness may destroy the whole significance of the ideal of religion. The church will have to give its explanation in psychological rather than religious or philosophical terms (931). Cyril Edward Hudson, in examining the relation between *Recent Psychology and the Christian Religion*, admits some resemblances between confession and psychoanalysis but thinks they are grossly exaggerated (601).

Catholic literature, unlike Protestant, reflects little dissidence among priests. Nevertheless, a sizeable proportion cautions both clergy and laymen against any contemplated variation. Noel Mailloux says the theologian is never contemptuous of the faltering efforts of human reason and welcomes the efforts of science to build up a body of conclusions to serve as documentation for sacred doctrine (813).

Cajolery is accompanied and followed by attacks. Thomas H. Hughes judges Freudianism a menace to Christianity which should be vigorously combatted (609). Fletcher, in America, decries the error of ethical neutrality in therapy (415). Robert J. Watson, in a dissertation at Union Theological Seminary, argues that if behavior were determined by unconscious forces, there would be no attribution of individual responsibility and the foundations of moral law would crumble (830). In the midst of generally appreciative obituaries of Freud, William McGarry, an American Catholic priest, criticizes Freudianism for helping those who would outlaw modesty and concludes with the expectation that God will judge this man Freud (856). A. McDonough cautions lay people that psychoanalysis was originated by a sex-mad atheist (854).

When Pope Pius XII spoke before the Fifth International Convention of Psychotherapy and Psychology in Rome in 1953, Catholic psychotherapeutists were caught between growing general acceptance of psychoanalysis, on the one hand, and anti-Freudian priests on the other. As guidance, Pius XII discriminated between those aspects of psychoanalysis which are acceptable and those which remain legitimate targets for attack. All psychical drives are rooted in the soul but since they are *in* the soul they cannot be said to *be* the man. Therefore, the autonomy of the free will may not be displaced by a heteronomy of instinctual drives. To consider man as controlled by the subconscious beyond the control of the conscious would place him on a par with the animals (1034).

Besides cajoling and atacking the dissidents, the forces of church control remind them that, after all, what they seek is found within the traditional church. Only God's Holy Spirit brings the gift of *aqape* (598). The Cross of Atonement is necessary. The self may be unified only through God (863). William Hulme, an American Lutheran with a Ph.D. in the psychology of religion, recognizing the pastor's feeling that he has failed as a counselor, explains that some falsely identify theology with dogmatism (611). Hans Prinzhorn, an Anglican priest writing in England during the thirties, finds psychotherapy weak because the therapist, unlike the confessor, is unable to grant absolution (1054). This point is rarely made by Protestants but looms large in the Catholic critique of psychotherapy.

The voices of tradition show the dissident that the relationship he desires with his parishioner is available in the church. Oscar Robert Pfister, a Swiss Lutheran who carried on a friendly correspondence with Freud, explains that cure is more effective in religion because the religious community derives its power not from an idea but from a supreme reality which elicits love and inspires deeds of moral greatness (1023). Dissidents bemoan church constraints. The church retorts that these ministers must blame themselves for the situation. William A. Quayle says preaching takes more courage than being a gladiator (1059). William A. Cameron says that the confessional centered in the love of Christ is more efficacious than psychotherapy (239). John C. Ford, a doctorate from Gregorian University and a professor of theology involved in the alcohol studies at Yale, writes that a theologian need not rewrite his treatise *De Actibus Humanis*, since the idea of unconscious influences has long been recognized. The operation of Divine Grace is an example (421). Agostino Gemelli, in the mid-fifties, finds that psychoanalysis is recognizing the importance of moral values in moving from the positivism of Freud to the mythology of Jung, the spiritualism of Binswanger, and logotherapy of Frankl (469).

Psychiatrists Criticize Psychiatry

The ministers' complaints that the church is ineffective are paralleled by psychiatrists' complaints about the ineffectiveness of traditional psychiatry. Psychiatrists are also troubled by inconsistencies between religious and scientific values. Ministers' complaints about a discrepancy between actual and ideal religious values are cognate to psychiatrists' calls to reformulate psychiatric theory. Instead of reviving a primaeval purity, the ideal is to be created.

The disenchantment of psychiatrists with their ability to help is expressed in a critique of the role of effort or physical treatment in therapy. Fritz Kunkel resents his dependence upon the patients' will to be helped. He envies the minister commissioned by God (744). F. J. Braceland, a Catholic psychiatrist, is concerned about the adverse effects upon personality and spiritual development of electroshock and psychosurgery (174). Others attribute failure to conceptual error. Gregory Zilboorg, who has been Russian Orthodox, Catholic, and Episcopalian, argues that Freud and his followers fell into the error of "psychomechanistic parallelism" in identifying religion and compulsive neurosis because both are functionally similar in psychological mechanisms (1347).

Some psychiatrists are concerned with discrepancies between scientific and religious ideas. In Germany, Wilhelm Bitter asks for a theory of human existence that embraces the entirety of material and spiritual existence so that scientific nature and revelation can aid and abet one another (115). Sol Ginsburg notes that religion and psychiatry originally were inseparable in their concern for the cure of souls and interest in the nature of evil. He blames the rise of materialism for the clash and for widespread atheism (482). Karl Stern, a psychoanalyst converted to Catholicism from Judaism after his release from a concentration camp, writes that the notion of transference being "used" is instinctively unpleasant to anyone with a Christian morality (1193).

Others would reformulate psychiatric theory in terms of a new ideal. Aleck D. Dodd, with a doctorate in psychology and a background in missionary and pastoral work, would reformulate theory in terms of humanism (349). Camilla M. Anderson, identifying with both Lutheranism and Unitarianism, evolves an eclectic theory "beyond Freud" (25).

Various complaints are not equally frequent in our sample of psychiatrists. Table 4 shows the items written by psychiatrists according to the main line of their complaints.

Table 4—Proportions of Items Written by Psychiatrists in which Each Type of Complaint Against Psychiatry is Advanced

Ineffectiveness of Psychiatric Approach	49%
Inconsistency Between Religion and Psychiatry	36
Reformulation of Psychological Theory	15
Total	100%
	(103)

Half of all psychiatric complaints impugn the effectiveness of psychiatry in achieving its goals. Given the basic orientation of psychiatry to "doing," it is not surprising to discover strain in this area.

Complaints about personal competence do not appear among psychiatrists as they did among ministers. Ministers in that group seek training in psychology. Psychiatrists who would introduce religious elements into therapy do not suggest that training in religion might be involved but tend to consider these elements as states or attitudes to be embraced. Those concerned with inconsistencies between religious and psychiatric values, and those who recommend the reformulation of psychiatric theory to include religious elements, may well be subject to competing institutional demands. The countercriticism of the militant conformists will be presented as evidence that these nonconformists are looked upon as institutional variants.

Psychiatry's Countercriticism

Psychiatric countercriticisms, like the ministerial ones, may be classed "ideal typically" as those which cajole, attack, or entice the dissidents. Psychiatric "cajolers" admit some visible relationship between psychiatric and religious elements. "Buts" and "limitations" follow closely behind. Theodor Reik, a Ph.D. in psychology and an early student-acquaintance of Freud, agrees that a study of the origin and development of religious and moral concepts is of greatest significance for therapy (1068). Lawrence Kubie, Abraham Franzblau, and Sandor Rado see a possibility not of the psychiatrist introducing religion into therapy but of allowing limited participation of the ministry in therapy (741, 441, 1062). E. B. Strauss says that the determinist teachings of psychology apply to the psyche but not to the soul (1205).

Psychiatrists attacked religion before the days of psychoanalysis. Josiah Moses' 1906 book, reflecting an older tradition, argues that disordered religious emotions lead to grotesque and pathological deeds. Mysticism is a theistic narcosis thriving best in the neurotic soul (920). Ernest Jones warns analysts involved with religion that religions represent crude solutions of the Oedipus complex. Arguments for free will derive from an internal psychic need for a sense of security. Even the feeling of being free to choose is unconsciously motivated (653). F. B. Elkisch, trained in Jung's analytic psychology and with a medical degree from Berlin, attributes many nervous disorders to the moralistic emphasis of religion (385).

Psychiatrists entice their dissident colleagues by arguing that what they seek is to be found only in psychiatry. Cavendish Moxon reminds them that psychoanalysis enables man to substitute realizable ideals for the illusory, leading toward human betterment on earth (922). David Forsyth argues that a peaceful and sane world will come only when people cease to dissipate their energies upon imaginary pursuits and accept the discipline of science (425). Kurt Robert Eissler, recognizing that the minister can reduce mental pain at the deathbed, expects that the demand for the psychiatrist during the terminal pathway will increase (383).

TESTING THE VALIDITY OF THE COMPLAINTS

We are not concerned with the substantive validity of the statements, that is, whether the contentions are true or false. We are concerned, however, with whether the inferences we are making on the basis of their manifest content truly reflect the situations of their authors. Are the ministers and psychiatrists who complain about an inconsistency between religious and scientific ideas or between actual and ideal religious or scientific ideas themselves really torn between two types of role demands?[11] Are those who complain about lack of pastoral training or about the ineffectiveness of the church in helping parishioners or of psychiatry in helping clients themselves denied adequate means for attaining their goals?

It is not at all obvious that we may directly infer social structural problems from individuals' formulations of the difficulty. The manifest formulations may mislead because the individual is ignorant of the roots of his discomfort or because the "real" problem is disguised by mechanisms of defense. Through reaction formation or denial the situation might be reported inversely. The painfulness of the difficulty might encourage its disguise through rationalization by specifying an alternative source of discomfort. These distortions might influence interpretation of a role conflict or goal frustration of an individual personality. How much more might a discrepancy exist between manifest complaints and difficulties inherent in the structure of certain social positions.[12]

The Net of Competing Role Demands

An individual not strongly identified with his own institution is more open to role demands of another institution. This assumes that there cannot be a vacuum of role expectations.[13] A minister or psychiatrist in this position and suffering a conflict of institutional loyalty would be more likely to be concerned with value or normative inconsistencies. Individuals more clearly identified with their own institutions, especially with the goals of these institutions, and yet prevented from attaining these goals, might be more likely to complain of ineffectiveness.[14]

Let us test this hypothesis first for the minister. Identification with the church would be reflected in adherence to religious belief. The minister low on religious belief would be open to accept other beliefs and also subject to a discrepancy between what the institution expects his attitude to be and what it actually is. To determine the degree of adherence to religious belief, the books and articles were classified on a seven-step religious belief index. Each item was classified on a holistic basis according to the statement which seemed most closely to reflect the author's position. The guiding statements, with the percentage of ministerial and psychiatric items classified in each category, are shown in Table 5.

Table 5—Proportion of Ministers and Psychiatrists Classified in Each Category of Religious Belief Index

Category of Religious Belief	Ministers	Psychiatrists (in Per Cent)
1. I believe in a Divine and personal God who is my redeemer, and I am accountable to him.	7	4
2. I believe in a merciful and loving God who listens to prayers.	35	16
3. I believe in a supreme but impersonal being or force.	32	19
4. I believe in a general moral force or God as expressed in men's relations or God as a symbolic archetype.	19	44
5. There is no personal creator. The world is governed by natural laws.	7	11
6. I neither believe nor disbelieve in religion.	—	4
7. Religion is not a positive force.	—	2
Total	100 (478)	100 (140)

Based on this distribution, categories 1 and 2 were called high, 3 was called medium, and 4 to 7 were called low on religious belief. We find that 31 per cent (35) of ministers high on religious belief complain about value inconsistencies [a number in parentheses following a per cent refers to the number of cases within the category which are involved in the calculations on this point; here, 31 per cent of 35 of the ministers high on religious belief complain about value inconsistencies], but 39 per cent (62) of those low on religious belief do so. The ministers who are low on religious belief are more likely to suffer role conflict and, apparently, are slightly more likely to express complaints in role-conflict terms.

The assumption that complaining in role-conflict terms is a result of being pulled by another belief system and, in effect, being caught between the two, may be tested. Parallel to the religious belief index, a psychiatric belief index was developed. This index measures adherence to "science" not as a set of cognitive norms but as an ultimate value system; that is, it measures the tendency to take science as a "religion." A scientist is not only committed to follow the scientific method but may be expected to support values relating to the worthwhileness of the endeavor. Each writing was classified holistically in one of seven categories. The guiding statements with the percentage of ministerial and psychiatric items classified in each category are shown in Table 6.

Table 6—Proportion of Ministers and Psychiatrists Classified in Each Category of Psychiatric Belief Index

Category of Psychiatric Belief	Ministers (in Per Cent)	Psychiatrists (in Per Cent)
1. Science is the final judge of the good in life.	11	1
2. The good is achieved through science. Even religion is a function of science and may be judged by science.	50	18
3. Science provides a good general approach but it is not final. It may help clarify religious problems.	29	47
4. Science is good in its own limited area, but certain areas, such as the religious life, are not open to science.	8	30
5. Personality is not open to scientific investigation, so science has little to tell us about therapy.	1	4
6. Science has done more harm than good in the area of psychology.	1	—
7. Science is harmful and should be opposed.	—	—
Total	100 (478)	100 (140)

A minister high on this psychiatric belief index would be caught in conflict between what he believes and what his institution traditionally expects of him.[15] Defining categories 1 and 2 as high, 3 as medium, and 4 to 7 as low, we find that 64 per cent (37) of the ministers high on psychiatric belief interpret their problem in terms of value inconsistency but that only 34 per cent (130) of those medium and low on psychiatric belief do so. The minister high on psychiatric belief, identifying with a group of which he is not a member, tends to see his problem as a conflict of ideas. The psychiatric belief index is a much better predictor of the formulation of ministerial complaints than is the religious belief index. This may be a function of the content of the scales. In our culture the contrast between the attitudes at the two ends of the psychiatric index is probably more meaningful for distinguishing social groups than that marked by the extremes of the religious index. There is less contrast between a person believing in a merciful God and one believing in a general moral force than between one who believes good is achieved through science and one who believes personality is not open to scientific investigation.

This argument would be further buttressed were the same phenomenon, but in reverse, observed among psychiatrists. Psychiatrists low on the psychiatric belief index, while they might be committed to the cognitive norms of science, might have a problem identifying with psychiatrists as a social group. Of psychiatrists high or medium on psychiatric belief, 32 per cent (31) are concerned with the inconsistency of norms but 76 per cent (33) of those low on psychiatric belief couch their complaints in these terms. These latter are less clearly identified with their institution and more open to the influence of another institution.

Pursuing the argument, psychiatrists high on religious belief should experience conflict. Testing this corollary, we find that of psychiatrists high or medium on religious belief 66 per cent (35) complain of inconsistencies of norms as compared with 42 per cent (31) of those low on religious belief. Psychiatrists high on religious belief, like those low on psychiatric belief, formulate their problem in terms of inconsistent role- and value-demands rather than in terms of their effectiveness.

Keeping in mind the limitation noted in footnote 14, the above findings may be stated in the reverse. Ministers identifying with religious values and psychiatrists identifying with psychiatric values are clear about the goals for which they strive. If they become disgruntled it is more likely to be over the adequacy of the means at their disposal for attaining their goals, and they are more likely to express the problem in these terms. A direct relationship seems to exist between the manifest content of the complaints and the nature of the individual's relation to his institution.[16]

Youth's Sense of Ineffectiveness

The question may be approached from the other side—which individuals might be concerned about effectiveness? In one sense, this concern is the obverse of the loyalty problem. Concern with attaining a goal presupposes identification with it. Beyond this, however, our individual complaining about his ineffectiveness is accepting the possibility of change or attainment through active intervention. Younger persons might tend more than older ones to believe that they should be able to offset their situation through action. If so, they would more likely express disappointment in terms of a failure of means. In addition, younger professionals are less well established and have less experience. They are "underprivileged" in their access to adequate means. The aged, on the other hand, would be more aware of inherent limitations, conflicts, and contradictions among the procedures and so less likely to be disappointed at their efficacy. They would also be more experienced and so less likely to be ineffective, and to have a more realistic perception regarding goal attainability.[17] Ministers of age 45 and below at time of publication will be classed as younger. Psychiatric authors, who are generally older than clergymen authors, will be called young if they are 55 or below at time of publication.[18] We find that 68 per cent (66) of the young ministers and psychiatrists and 41 per cent (22) of the older ones express their complaints in terms of ineffectiveness rather than in terms of inconsistency of ideas.[19]

In sum, there is sufficient connection between the problem to which the complainers are exposed by virtue of the group relations or position in the age structure and the formulation of their complaints to justify considering these manifest formulations seriously. We have found tendencies which accord with both theories of the genesis of variant behavior: some individuals are caught in a problem of choice between incompatible demands and some seem acutely sensitive to the failure of their efforts. It now becomes our task to discover how ministers and psychiatrists become exposed to these incompatibilities. Our data, however, do not always allow us to discern which incompatibility is at work; they so often appear intertwined in a concrete situation.

SOCIAL CONDITIONS FOR CULTURAL ENCOUNTER

Interest in the religio-psychiatric movement is far from universal among ministers and psychiatrists. The relatively few attracted to the movement are concentrated in certain societies and in certain sectors of those societies. They appear only in a handful of countries and among members of a small number of religious denominations. In age and education they are not a representative cross section of ministers and psychiatrists.

The charatcer of the societies, or sectors of society, in which the movement emerges may enable us to infer some social and cultural factors contributing to its emergence.[20] Presuming (see footnote 9) that the same broad conditions lead to both nonconformist and militant conformist types of participation, both will be treated together here. In the next chapter we will specify their differentia.

Industrial Culture As a Setting for Role Conflict

A classification of items according to the country in which they were published locates their principal audiences and, by and large, their authors as well. Table 7 shows the geographic location of publishers of books and articles on the relation of religion and psychiatry.[21]

Seventy-nine per cent of the writings have been published in English-speaking societies, while 9 per cent have appeared in German and 6 per cent in French-speaking areas.[22] The literary membership of this movement is American and Western European. Asian and African countries do not appear, since psychiatry is little developed in those lands.[23] Eastern Europe and the Soviet Union contribute little to the literature. Since religious institutions in these nations are discouraged from entering the psychotherapeutic field, a liaison between the institutions is unlikely. Prewar Hungarian and earlier Russian analysts tended to publish through German and Swiss houses and would be included in those categories.[24]

Countries contributing to this literature, in contrast to the nonparticipating rest of the world, are the urbanized and industrial societies. Japan, however, is highly industrialized but contributes no

Table 7—Publications in Religion and Psychiatry According to Location of Publishers

	Percentage
United States, Canada	72
Germany, Switzerland (German), Austria, Low Countries	9
Great Britain, Ireland	7
France, Switzerland (French)	6
Italy, Spain, Greece	3
Scandinavia	1
Other and Unknown	2
Total	100
	(1347)

writings to the movement.[25] This may be due to the small number of psychiatrists there. Psychiatry is, however, developed in Poland, Spain, and Italy.[26] Yet the movement hardly stirs in these countries. Considering the relative size of their populations, the Scandinavian countries contribute proprotionately more than do Poland, Italy, Spain, or France. The movement seems most vigorous in countries that are both industrial and Protestant. Catholics, in fact, seem to publish most when they are among Protestants.

This apparent association between Protestantism, industrialization, and the development of the religio-psychiatric movement suggests a hypothesis. In the following pages this hypothesis will be presented as a way of accounting for ministerial participation. Subsequently, it will be found useful in explaining psychiatric participation. We do not have the data for an adequate test of the hypothesis but, at the conclusion, will be able to present some data consistent with what would be expected were the hypothesis true.

In social and economic organization, industrialization is associated with rationalism and empiricism. Relative to religious healing, a psychologically oriented pastorate also is rational and empirical in its approach.[27] Max Weber has related this rational mentality, characteristic of industrial society, to the Protestant ethic.[28] What is it, however, about the rationalism and empiricism of industrial society that might be relevant to our problem? Some authors have noted that a trend toward "depersonalization" in human relations accompanies the growth of industrial society.[29] Looked at factually rather than ethically this suggests a reduced importance of personal considerations in establishing and fashioning social relations and increased mediation of these relations by impersonal norms. This has been termed a universalistic orientation. Further, industrial society typically allocates positions on the basis of achievements. This has been termed a performance orientation. These two orientations are linked when universalistic standards are applied to judge the adequacy of performance. The culture of industrial society tends to be characterized by universalistic-performance norms. Its principal roles, such as the occupational, tend to instiutionalize these norms.

Religious culture tends toward a converse cultural pattern. Within the Christian tradition, the devotional orientation is to the Person of Christ. The worldly religious community is based on an inherent relationship of the believer to the church. Sin is a failure to accept this belongingness. As opposed to the universalistic orientation to impersonal rules, this concern with a relationship for its own sake is what has been termed a particularistic orientation.[30] Relative to science, which is basically a set of methodological rules for operating and classifying, all religion is particularistic.[31]

Religion shows relatively more concern with inherent qualities than with performances. Membership in the church, for example, depends on a spiritual state rather than upon earned credentials. Individual performances may signify a state already enjoyed. That the religious orientation to inherent qualities has not been unmixed is apparent from the Grace-works controversy.[32] Most of Protestantism, Calvinism in particular, stresses justification through faith. Salvation cannot be earned, but through the death of Christ, it is *irresistibilis* in the elect. Roman Catholicism also holds that justification is by faith but admits thoughts and deeds as relevant to the quality of that faith. On the whole, relative to the dominant universalistic-performance culture of industrial society, religion retains a particularistic-quality culture.[33]

How does the contrast between these cultures relate to the involvement of ministers in psychological pastoral counseling? The relation may be examined on the cultural level. If these two value systems are segregated or each considered applicable in its own time and place, an individual would have no problem in living by both of them. If, however, both are accepted as legitimate guides for the same situation, a dilemma may arise. Psychiatry, arising in industrial societies, applies universalistic-performance norms to healing.[34] The religio-psychiatric literature may be viewed, in part, as a response to the confrontation of these norms, especially in the counseling area, with the particularistic-quality norms of religion.

How, though, do two sets of norms become relevant to the counseling area? The mechanisms by which this comes about may be analyzed on the social relational level. Within an industrial system the demand of efficiency and the concomitant problems of urbanization advance the division of labor to a degree not experienced in other societies.[35] The professions in these societies also evolve toward specialization. The medical psychiatrist and the subspecialty of the psychiatrist concerned with neuroses appear in this type of a situation.[36] Psychiatrists, while abjuring interest in values, attempt to change behavior and attitudes and, thus, have a real impact on the patient's values.[37] In the Judeo-Christian tradition the church sees itself as a guardian of behavioral norms. It can hardly ignore the challenge of another institution in this area. Ministers who do not accept psychiatric values may still become interested in psychiatric procedures. Thus, the universalistic-performance values of industrial society become relevant to an area of ministerial concern.[38]

The spirit of rationality penetrates the clerical outlook via other routes. In industrial cultures there is an overriding emphasis on effectiveness and accomplishment.[39] The Protestant minister in these countries, more than his Catholic colleague, participates actively in the economy as a consumer. His class position is also more closely linked to the achieved status of his family of origin. If the orientation of his other social positions spills over into his religious position, he may be disturbed about empty pews on Sunday morning, about his inability to "cure" parishioners who come to him with emotional problems, and about his own relatively low economic status. It may seem to some of these ministers that psychological sophistication will provide "group dynamics" techniques to attract people to worship and supply counseling techniques to aid parishioners. Psychological concepts in sermons might also attract higher-status parishioners or open the way to appointment to a church of higher socioeconomic status. The values of industrial society thus affect the pastorate from within.

Under these conditions, the church, through its leaders, may become wary of the encroachment of psychiatry in the area of the "cure of souls" and of the internal seduction of its ministers to secular values.[40] Other types of nonchurch specialists with an empirical approach to guiding "souls," such as mesmerists, palmists, and spiritualists, have been opposed by the church. However, they engage in individual practice, are unorganized and less likely to take a stand unfriendly to religion. As such, they are less of a threat to the church than are the psychiatrists backed with the prestige of the organized medical profession. Thus, the emergence of ministerial militant conformists opposing the psychiatrists and the ministers influenced by them is socially coincident with the attraction of ministers to psychiatric thinking.[41] One way to test this hypothesis would be to compare the proportion of religio-psychiatric writings to all writings by ministers and psychiatrists in situations where these two culture patterns conflict with the proportions of religio-psychiatric writings in situations where these patterns do not conflict. Another way of testing the hypothesis would be to compare the social locations of individuals who contribute to this literature with the social locations of ministers and psychiatrists who write as much but do not write in this field. We do not have data on the total writings of ministers and psychiatrists, and consequently, we cannot decisively test the hypothesis. We can, however, examine the ratio of publication in this field of Protestant and Catholic ministers and psychiatrists to the population of these religions in the various countries. Table 8 gives these figures in terms of publications per million inhabitants in that country of each faith.[42] Let us first examine this table in terms of ministerial participation. Keeping in mind the tentativeness of the table, it appears that in each country the Protestant ministers, whom we have assumed to be

Table 8—Numbers of Items Published Per Million of Protestant and Catholic Population in Several Countries by Protestant and Catholic Clergymen and Psychiatrists Respectively (526 Ministerial and 217 Psychiatric Items)

Religion and Profession	United States	Great Britain, Ireland	France, French Swiss	Germany, German Swiss	Southern Europe
Protestant					
Ministers	5.40	4.0	7.0	.53	—
Psychiatrists	.76	—	1.4	.85	—
Catholic					
Priests	2.16	3.8	.92	.22	.34
Psychiatrists	2.32	2.0	—	.22	.12

more exposed to the universalistic-performance norms, have a higher production rate than do the Catholic priests (excepting in Southern Europe where there are few Protestant clergymen). Catholic clerical production is highest in the English-speaking countries where they live among Protestants.[43] If this is due to their exposure to Protestants, the German exception may be due to the greater geographic segregation of Protestant and Catholic populations in that country than in England or the United States. The expected relationship between degree of industrialization and production of ministerial material in this field seems to hold up. The high productivity of French Protestants may be related to their concentration in highly industrialized areas. We shall return to examine psychiatric participation later. Meanwhile, since the various Protestant denominations are differentially exposed to the universalistic-performance pattern, this fact may be used for a further check on the hypothesis.

Denominational Affiliation and
Exposure to Industrial Culture

Perhaps too much of an edifice has been built on scant information about the geographic distribution of the literature. Let us examine the distribution of participants in American society. If our conjecture has value, the ratio of ministerial publication to population in American society should vary with the extent of institutionalization of the universalistic-performance pattern in each sector of the society.

Studies of social class suggest that higher socioeconomic groups institutionalize the universalistic-performance pattern to a greater degree than lower socioeconomic groups.[44] Membership in Protestant denominations corresponds more or less with socioeconomic status. Episcopalians tend to be of highest class status, and then in descending order are the Presbyterians and the Congregationalists, the Methodists and the Lutherans, the Baptists, and the Disciples of Christ. The more sect-like Pentecostal groups such as the Assembly of God tend to be relatively low on the social ladder.[45]

Congregationalists, Presbyterians, Episcopalians, Lutherans, and Methodists are responsible for 88 per cent (361) of the items by Protestant ministers. This is what we would expect on the assumption that class position, and its correlate, the universalistic-performance pattern, is related to participation. Since class is correlated with education and, presumably, with writing, ministers of

these denominations probably contribute a disproportionate share of
all religious literature. We lack data to test the influence of class
on religio-psychiatric writing independently of the general propensity to write. The bias, however, is not likely to be so profound
as the above figure would indicate. We will, however, be able below
to allow for the influence of education. Our argument is not that
religio-psychiatric writing by ministers is directly influenced by the
universalistic-performance pattern but that it gains additional im-
petus as a response to the clash of this pattern with the particularistic-quality pattern of religion.

The correlation may be specified for each denomination by rang-
ing them in order of the class position of their members and
comparing their publication to population ratios (see Table 9).[46]

**Table 9—Ratio of Items Written by Ministers of Various
Protestant Denominations in the United States per Million
Adherents of Those Denominations (Population Figures
From World Almanac, 1961) (349 Ministerial Items)**

Episcopalians	25.9
Congregationalists, Presbyterians	15.9
Lutherans, Methodists	4.0
Baptists	3.1

The extent to which publication ratio follows socioeconomic
status of the denomination is quite striking. Impressionistic information about the authors suggests that even within these groups, the
writings are produced by ministers of the higher socioeconomic
factions. Ministers of the wealthy rather than poor Baptist groups
contribute to this literature.

How does the minister in these higher social class denominations
become exposed to the universalistic-performance pattern? In the
first place, his class origin is likely to coincide with that of his denomination. Secondly, he is likely to have grown up with people
occupying bureaucratic positions, professionals, and policy-makers.
Specifically relevant to the religio-psychiatric influence, higher-status
parishes are more likely to include psychologists and psychiatrists
among their members as well as individuals who have studied psychology in college. The minister would be influenced by their expectations. Further, more of his parishioners are likely to visit psychiatrists.

This finding might be, in part, a result of education, since the amount of formal education is positively correlated with social class. Formal academic education, literally "discipline," implies socialization in rational thoughtways. The above findings, however, hold independently of education.[47] Nevertheless, the fact that 77 per cent of these ministerial authors hold a doctoral degree suggests that education must be a significant factor in generating participation.[48] Academic socialization may be necessary even if it is not a sufficient condition for ministers to write on religion and psychiatry. When we examine the proportion of items by doctoral ministers of each denomination, we find an interesting distribution. This is shown in Table 10.

Table 10—Proportion of Ministerial Items Written by Doctoral Clergymen in Several Denominations

Denomination	Percentage	Number
Episcopalians	43	56
Congregationalists, Presbyterians	59	81
Lutherans, Methodists	81	100
Baptists	80	51
Catholics	95	118

The proportion of items by doctoral ministers, among all minister authors in each denomination, tends to be inversely related to the social-class position of the denomination. Since a minister of a higher-status church is more likely to hold a doctorate, we may infer that the proportion of doctoral authors in each denomination is inversely related to the proportion of clergymen in each denomination who hold that degree. The more the universalistic-achievement pattern is present in the milieu of these denominations, the less important is educational socialization for creating interest in the movement. It takes less exposure to education in a higher-class denomination to bring a minister into the movement. The factors of education and social class seem to stand in an either/or type of supplementary relation.

Age Group and Cultural Attitude

The argument to this point has been that individuals tend to participate in the movement as a consequence of being caught in a conflict between the demands of two value systems. Our examples have concerned ministers, whose status is embedded in a particularistic-quality culture but who are exposed through their broader social status to the universalistic-performance culture. Another way of analyzing the problem is in terms of a broad human status which a person occupies by virtue of his position in the age structure. Ministers and psychiatrists differ in the age at which they participate in the movement. Ministers tend to write in the field at a median age of about 40. Assuming that clergymen begin their professional careers at 25, their participation follows about 15 years of professional effort. Assuming the psychiatrists begin their careers at age 30, we find that Catholic psychiatrists tend to publish after some 20 years of professional life, at a median age of 50, while Protestant psychiatrists do not participate until they have seen some 30 years of service, or have attained a median age of about 60.[49]

These differences in age at publication may be understood in relation to the broad human orientations of individuals at various ages. Early home and family life is predominantly governed by particularistic-quality relationships. In adulthood, the universalistic performance occupational status becomes more salient. In old age, and with approaching death, interest increases in maintaining solidary human relations based on the particularistic-quality ethos. The return to religion during these later years is an expression of the trend.[50] Younger ministers, involved in an institution dedicated to the particularistic-quality pattern, may experience it as in conflict with their age-group life orientations. This type of role conflict accounts for their early interest in the movement. For psychiatrists, the broad age-group and professional outlooks are consistent during their earlier years, so they are less prone to enter the movement. In later years, however, the psychiatrist's renewed interest in particularistic-quality relations conflicts with his professional orientation. This may account for the interest of relatively older psychiatrists in the movement. Conceivably the more devout Catholic psychiatrist, more exposed to religious culture, may reach this point earlier than his Protestant colleague. This conjecture will be pursued below.

Church Polity as an Influence on Parish Ministers

Relatively high status and high education, as factors increasing exposure to universalistic-performance culture, also supplement one another as conditions encouraging ministerial participation in the movement. What factors, however, may curb participation? The militant conformist examples earlier in this chapter reveal that there are forces within the church that oppose adoption of psychological concepts by pastors. What enables the church to make these attitudes effective? Some insight is provided by a classification of ministers according to the institutional setting in which they work. Eighteen per cent of the items written by ministers were written by men in the parish, 21 per cent by those in clinical settings, 22 per cent by teachers of pastoral subjects in seminaries, and 39 per cent by teachers of other subjects (553). This is a rather odd distribution. Parish clergy are the foundation of each denomination. They far outnumber chaplains and seminary professors. Yet the proportion of items written by them is generally low.[51] Conceivably the parish clergymen are most exposed to pressures to conformity so that their participation is curbed more than that of other ministers. Relatively low in the church hierarchy, they may be more subject to church disciplinary forces. They are also more directly involved with laymen who tend to have traditional expectations for ministerial behavior. The clinical minister meets only a narrow range of pastoral expectations in his less religious or nonreligious setting. The seminary professor enjoys the license of rank for experimenting with new ideas.

Variations in the proportion of items written by parish rather than other ministers in each denomination would be a rough indicator of the effectiveness of these pressures curbing participation. Churches differ, however, in their ability to exercise authority over the parish clergy. Under an episcopal form of church polity parish ministers are answerable to bishops who can censure them and influence their appointments. In congregationally organized churches the parish minister has greater freedom to elect an independent course of action. For purposes of this discussion, churches having legitimate clerical authority and office above the parish level will be classed as episcopal and those not having such a hierarchical structure of clerical authority will be classed as congregational. Following this definition, Episcopalians, Roman Catholics, Methodists, and Lutherans may be considered as relatively episcopal in church polity and Jews,[52] Presbyterians, Congregationalists, and Baptists as relatively congregational.[53] If authority is a variable, parish ministers in congregationally organized churches would, relative to other classes of ministers in the same denomination, be more likely to participate than would parish ministers in episcopally organized churches. The socioeconomic factor already discussed may obscure the influence of church polity. Clerical salaries will be used as an indicator in controlling for socioeconomic status.[54] The cultural and social milieu, the extent of exposure to the universalistic-performance ethos, which accompanies salary, rather than the salary level itself, is the significant referent here.

Rabbis have the highest salaries among clergymen. Among Protestants, Episcopal priests are slightly better paid than Congregationalists and Presbyterians who, in turn, have higher salaries than Lutheran, Methodist, and Baptist clergy. Much of the Catholic priest's salary is indirect. His economic level as measured by style of life would seem to be lower than that of rabbis and Calvinist ministers but higher than that of the Lutherans and Methodists. It is hypothesized that relative to other clergy, the parish contribution would be greater where their economic level is highest and the church congregationally organized and relatively smaller where salaries are low and the church episcopally organized. This is examined in Table 11. The vertical ordering in the table is relative within each organizational form. Baptists receive lower salaries than Methodists but among the congregationally organized churches they are lower than Presbyterians.

Table 11—Proportion of Participating Clergy in Each Denomination Who are Parish Ministers, According to their Relative Salary Levels and the Structure of their Institutions (Total Number of Ministers 598)

Average Ministerial Salary	TYPE OF CHURCH ORGANIZATION (in Per Cent)			
	Congregational		Episcopal	
High Salary	Jews	53	Episcopalians	26
Medium Salary	Presbyterians, Congregationalists	14	Catholics	7
Low Salary	Baptists	10	Methodists, Lutherans	2

Among rabbis, who enjoy relatively high income and are congregationally organized, 53 per cent of the items are penned by men in the pulpit. That is to say, the remaining 47 per cent of items by rabbis were written by chaplains or those in clinical settings or by members of theological school faculties. Episcopalian parish priests have relatively high salaries, a factor encouraging participation, but are in hierarchically structured situations, a factor discouraging participation. They experience cross pressures.[55] Congregationalists, Presbyterians, and Baptists are lower salaried but have relatively independent parishes. Forces work in opposite directions. Catholics, Methodists, and Lutherans would be expected to have low parish participation from both points of view and do indeed. Comparing the vertical with the horizontal differences, socioeconomic level is more important than church polity in determining participation of parish clergy in this movement.

The influence of socioeconomic level on ministerial participation has already been discussed, and no more will be said about it. Church polity acts as a social structural screen which permits or restrains participation by ministers otherwise desirous of entering the field. Screening may be effective in three ways besides that of direct social control. First, hierarchical churches tend toward rational bureaucracy and so are apt to choose leaders for organizational ability.[56] This might encourage a drift from the parish into administration of ministers with universalistic-performance orientations. The serious book and article writers might then be those who have risen in the hierarchy rather than parish clergy. Hierarchical churches, as rational bureaucracies, are more likely to segregate the role of developer of ideas from that of pastor of the flock. In congregational churches, on the other hand, organizational responsibility is heavier at the community level. Talent is less likely to be "promoted" out of the parish, and so larger proportions of their authors are found there. Second, a congregational parish is relatively autonomous and so shoulders more responsibility for decisions. Debate on new ideas, with participation of the clergy, is more likely to occur on the parish level. In structured churches the parish minister is less involved, since debate on new forms would tend to occur more readily in the theological seminaries or in higher clerical councils. Finally, the congregational minister, as more of a personal charismatic, is more likely to introduce new forms. The episcopally organized minister enjoying charisma of office is part of a traditional structure and less likely to introduce change.[57] All of these factors conspire to increase the probability of parish participation in congregationally organized churches and to decrease it in episcopally organized churches. They are all outgrowths of the greater ability of episcopal churches than of congregational churches to exercise authority in support of tradition.

How Religion May Influence the Psychiatrists

This is a convenient place to pick up the thread of the story about psychiatric participation. To the extent that church authority is a factor it should operate in opposite directions for ministers and psychiatrists. If a church is able to exert authority over its psychiatric communicants, as well as its clergy, it will increase the probability that they will adhere to religious tradition. While this means greater religious conformity for the ministers, it means greater nonconformity to psychiatric norms for the psychiatrists. With this in mind, let us return to Table 8 and examine psychiatric participation in the various countries.

The ratio of clergymen to psychiatrists in the general population is very high—it is about 30:1 in the United States and probably higher in other countries. Table 8, however, shows that the ministerial and psychiatric publication to population ratios are of nearly the same order. This suggests that psychiatrists are more likely to enter the field than are ministers. This is to be expected, since the pastoral office is but one aspect of a minister's calling and not of major concern to all ministers while therapy is the principal function of psychiatrists. Most interesting is the heavy participation of Catholic as compared with Protestant psychiatrists in the English-speaking countries. Catholicism in these countries is influenced by the relatively more conservative Irish Catholics. The effect of religion becomes more apparent when we trace psychiatric participation through the years. Table 12 shows the proportion of writings

Table 12—Proportion of Protestant and Catholic Writings in Each Decade Which are Authored by Psychiatrists

Decade	PROTESTANTS		CATHOLICS	
	Percentage	Number	Percentage	Number
Before 1918	15[a]	13	9	11
1918–1927	10	19	29	14
1928–1937	19	58	39	18
1938–1947	12	104	45	51
1948–1957	18	368	26	201

a. The remaining 85 per cent of the Protestant items written before 1918 were authored by and large by ministers.

by psychiatrists to all items among Protestants and Catholics by decade.

The ratio of psychiatric to other (mainly ministerial) contributors among Protestants has remained rather stable through the years. The proportion of psychiatrists among Catholic contributors has climbed sharply. Also, while the movement as a whole is growing more rapidly among Protestants due to sharply increasing ministerial participation, among Catholics psychiatric participation is increasing at a greater rate than that of priests. The relative drop in the proportion of psychiatric (and thus, increase in priestly) participation in the last decade among Catholics is of especial interest.

From the basic theme of this chapter it follows that factors underlying psychiatric interest complement those accounting for ministerial involvement. Psychiatry in general emerges in urbanized industrial societies as a universalistic-performance approach to healing. Where members of a psychiatrist's community hold that his therapeutic role should be guided by particularistic-quality norms or where he accepts these norms as legitimate for his role, he may be caught in a value conflict similar to that of the minister. Participating in the movement could be one form of resolution of this conflict.

When might religion and its particularistic-quality ethos become salient for the psychiatrist? This could occur either by the psychiatrist accepting the legitimacy of religious authority over his role or by the religious institution possessing the power to exert coercive authority. Psychiatric participation would then vary according to the religiousness of psychiatrists and the strength of religious authority. On the first count, 39 per cent of Catholic psychiatrists (56) but only 11 per cent (55) of Protestant psychiatrists were classed as high on the religious belief index. The Catholic psychiatrist is more likely to be devout than the Protestant psychiatrist. Since the measure is based on writings about mental health, a Catholic psychiatrist seems more likely than a Protestant psychiatrist to accept his religious status as relevant to his professional status.

On the second count, the Roman Catholic Church is more likely than the Protestant church to choose to exert authority in the area of the "cure of souls." The change in the ratio of priests and psychiatrists in the last decade is revealing in this respect. During the thirties and forties Catholics actively debated the role of psychoanalysis. In 1951 and again in 1953 the Pope declared the method, though not the philosophy, of psychoanalysis acceptable. The immediate consequence was "permission" for clerical participation and the lessening of church pressure on psychiatrists.

Church influence on psychiatrists is exerted in still another fashion. Catholic psychiatrists are more dependent for their clientele upon the favor of the church than are Protestant psychiatrists. Catholic laymen, for their part, are more likely to consider the church position in selecting a physician than are Protestants. A Catholic point of view also is supported through a separate psychiatric association. Since physicians are dependent upon referrals from other physicians, the Catholic professional association becomes another way in which religious group influence is brought to bear.[58] Finally, as an episcopally organized church, it is better able to communicate its influence beyond the parish. This brings us back to our discussion of the ability of an episcopal church to control its communicants.

The effect of episcopal organization in increasing psychiatric participation may be examined among Protestants. This influence was demonstrated among ministers by comparing parish with other ministerial participation in the several denominations on the assumption that episcopal organization, while reducing ministerial participation, increases psychiatric participation. Protestant psychiatric participation is, relative to ministerial, heaviest among Episcopalians, where 17 per cent (108) of the items are written by psychiatrists. We find that psychiatric participation is relatively higher among the episcopally organized, 10 per cent (128) of the Lutherans and Methodists, than among the congregationally organized, 4 per cent (116) of the Congregationalists and Presbyterians, despite the fact that the latter are of higher socioeconomic status. In the specific case of Episcopalians, the higher social status of the Episcopal priest enables him to interact socially with the psychiatrist and influence him directly.[59] This finding is the converse of what we discovered among ministers where an episcopal polity discouraged interest. These findings dovetail. Both are examples of the greater ability of churches with an episcopal polity to maintain conformity to traditional church norms.

SUMMARY

Several bits of evidence have been presented to account for participation in the religio-psychiatric movement. An examination of complaints suggested that both role conflict and frustration at perceived inability to measure up are significant factors. The critical source of competing role demands is in the encounter of the univeralistic-performance culture of industrial society and the particularistic-quality culture of religion in the situation of healing. The movement emerges in highly industrialized and urbanized societies. Ministerial participants come from sectors of these industrial societies where they are most exposed to the universalistic-performance pattern. They tend to be from denominations of the "Protestant ethic," especially those of higher socioeconomic status, and from among the more highly educated clergymen. In these societies, the medical specialty of psychiatry provides a service paralleling the traditional religious "cure of souls." This overlap exposes the minister to an alternative set of norms for the pastorate. The proportionate contribution of parish clergy is highest where the parish minister is a member of a congregationally rather than an episcopally organized church. On the other hand, psychiatrists affiliated with episcopally organized churches are relatively more likely to participate. An episcopal church polity is more able to exert authority which inhibits ministerial interest in psychiatry but which encourages psychiatric interest in religion. Finally, the movement attracts younger ministers, who are more exposed to the universalistic-performance culture, and older psychiatrists, who tend to be attracted to particularistic-quality relations.

These conditions do not explain why these specific ministers or these specific psychiatrists choose to respond to this cultural encounter by participating in the field of religion and psychiatry. Ministers who write serious theological works, or appeal for neo-orthodoxy in Protestantism, or support the social gospel, are also likely to be from urban centers, from the higher socioeconomic and more highly educated strata. Many psychiatrists may suffer role conflict, be devout, or accept church authority and face their problems of old age and yet not participate in the religio-psychiatric movement. These sociocultural factors are necessary but not sufficient explanations for their choice of the religio-psychiatric movement. Our discussion of their complaints hinted at a necessary factor: the nature of their group identifications or loyalties. This hint will be pursued in the next chapter in terms of the concept of reference group.

NOTES

1. The question in this form might lead us to seek motives through analysis of personality. Observing, however, that those who vary from traditional forms seem concentrated in certain parts of the society suggests a sociological analysis of the question. What conditions exist which increase the probability that individuals located in certain parts of the social structure will depart from tradition? Psychological issues will be raised from time to time, but the study will focus principally on sociological conditions producing the religio-psychiatric movement. Both social and psychological factors are involved in any concrete situation. Sociological factors would have to be linked to personality factors to account for an individual variant. On the differentiation of these levels of analysis, see Talcott Parsons and Edward A. Shils, "Values, Motives, and The Theory of Action," *Towards a General Theory of Action*, ed. Talcott Parsons and Edward A. Shils, pp. 54ff.

2. For example, during a strike at the mills of Gastonia, some ministers were caught between the demands of the workers that they oppose intolerable working conditions and the demands of the mill owners, who were important contributors to the church, that they maintain work discipline. Liston Pope, *Millhands and Preachers*.

3. An account of role conflict as a source of deviant behavior is given in Parsons, *op. cit.*, pp. 280–283.

4. For example, lower-class children are imbued with the success goals of American society, but partly because of their social placement and the experiences which they have in these positions, it is difficult for them to attain these goals. Under such conditions, they may adopt illegitimate means, i.e., become delinquents. Cohen, *op. cit.*

5. This is the theory of Merton, "Social Structure and Anomie," *Social Theory and Social Structure*, pp. 131–194. The two theories of the genesis of deviance differ in their accounts of "what" happens and "where" it happens. According to Parsons, the strain arises when one individual does not behave as his role-partner expects. According to Merton, strain arises from failure to attain a goal. Parsons locates the difficulty in the interactive system and Merton finds it on the institutional level. These two points of view have a

psychological analog in the contrast between Lewin, who is concerned with "success and failure" and "goals" and "barriers" and only secondarily with selection among goals of different valences, and Tolman, who begins with the problems of "deprivation" but then focuses on "choice" behavior. See Kurt Lewin, *A Dynamic Theory of Personality;* and Edward C. Tolman, "A Psychological Model," in Parsons and Shils, *op. cit.,* pp. 279–361. The Parsons approach tends to be applied more easily to the decisions or choices of leaders, to fit the situation of the "privileged" who must select among several alternatives. The Merton approach tends to be applied more easily to "underprivileged" individuals.

6. These statements are given essentially in their authors' words but are edited or paraphrased sufficiently so that they flow in our narrative.

The illustrative statements in this and the following chapters are examples of indicators for categories to be treated statistically and at the same time to provide insight into the content of the religio-psychiatric literature. Some allusions to the religion and occupation of the authors will be made along with the citations in this chapter to give the reader some sense of the type of participants in the movement.

7. No group depends entirely upon external constraints. Members of the group "police" themselves through indentification with its standards. They anticipate external sanctions and attitudinally punish themselves for violation of group norms.

8. The statements which follow are used as indicators for classifying items as having been authored by militant conformists. The sentence contains the phrase "in this respect" because the same concrete individual who criticizes the nonconformists in one writing may be found to be a nonconformist himself in another writing.

9. A movement does not consist only of the protagonists of some idea but of their antagonists as well. Thus, the Russian revolution involved Bolsheviks, Mensheviks, and the Czarist forces. All of these had in common a political interest which differentiated them from the apolitical masses. The Reformation and Counterreformation were two aspects of a movement of religious change in early modern Europe. This commonality lends a backdrop for study of the specific differentia of the antagonists and protagonists. This departs form the general usage of the term movement but allows us to treat the entire religio-psychiatric discussion as a single movement.

10. This discussion is organized according to the paradigm for social control developed by Talcott Parsons. See Parsons, *op. cit.,* pp. 227–320.

11. It is an oversimplification to say that these ministers are subject to only two sets of demands. We will, however, limit ourselves to the two-way pull for purposes of the analysis.

12. This problem of the "validity of reasons" is discussed in Paul F.

Lazarsfeld, "Evaluating the Effectiveness of Advertising by Direct Interviews, in Lazarsfeld and Rosenberg, *op. cit.*, pp. 411–419.

13. This follows the notion that, excluding autisms, behavior not conforming to the norms of one group conforms to the norms of another. A delinquent violates the norms of the broad society but conforms to the norms of the delinquent subculture. See the account of this in Cohen, *op. cit.* The condition that rejection of the norms of one institution, either religion or psychiatry, implies substitution of the norms of the other institution is built into this study by the fact that analysis is limited to these two groups. Those who simply reject one without accepting the other would "withdraw" from the field and would not be included in the sample. There is a possibility of "anomie," a situation where the normative requirements are not so much rejected or accepted but lack clarity or are not well integrated.

14. Strictly speaking, the following analysis will not substantiate the link of complaints of effectiveness to malintegration of means and goals. This is a consequence of our using a dichotomy where those who did not offer one type of complaint offer the other. The analysis allows only one degree of freedom. It would substantiate both categories only if they were the reverse of one another or were two ends of an ordered series.

15. The religious and psychiatric belief indices are negatively correlated. For ministers $Q = -.49$ and for psychiatrists $Q = -.40$. In both cases the coefficients are significantly different from zero at the .001 level by a χ^2 test. For examples of classifications on these indices see the Appendix.

16. Extent of identification is not, of course, a static quantity. A Catholic will have a lower threshold of conflict than will a Protestant. A small variation on the part of a Catholic priest may produce as much strain as a greater departure by a Protestant minister.

17. From the point of view of the individual, a goal is not objectively fixed but is set partly by his "aspiration level." The experience of failure would be contingent upon realizing an aspiration. See Kurt Lewin *et al.*, "Level of Aspiration," *Personality and the Behavior Disorders*, ed. J. McV. Hunt, pp. 333–378.

18. Sixty-six per cent of the ministers (330) were 45 or younger at the time of publication, while only 18 per cent (59) of the psychiatrists were that young. However, 52 per cent of the psychiatrists were age 55 or below at publication. Age at publication was determined by subtracting the year the B.A. was received from the year of publication and adding 22.

19. A social movement may also be considered young or old. This association between youth and concern with the effectiveness of means may be characteristic of the movement as well as of its individual members. Early adherents are likely to be committed to simple goals and to belief in achieving them by getting out and doing something. Later, more tempered, and shouldering more responsibility, members of the movement are more accept-

ing of the limits of action. Their aspirations are more realistic and so less likely to fail. We find that 59 per cent (83) of items printed by 1947 and 53 per cent (151) of the more recent items stress complaints about ineffectiveness. This difference is small. However, looking at the growth curve of the movement in the previous chapter, we see that the decline has not yet begun. The supposition is that as the movement goes into its zenith there will be an increase in complaints about ideological goals with less attention to the procedures. This recalls the question raised in footnote 5 that the malintegration of means and ends is a characteristic problem of the "underprivileged" and role conflict a problem of the "privileged." Following this we might conjecture that after the movement passes its zenith and goes into decline, there will be an increase in concern with the adequacy of the means. It is interesting in this respect that Merton illustrates the malintegration of means and goals with Gilbert Murray's description of decline in ancient Greece.

20. As will be indicated below, this is a "second best" type of procedure. The contexts in which the movement does and does not appear differ in so many respects that it is difficult to fix the relevant dimension. We will be trying to "squeeze" analytical information from what are essentially descriptive statistics by importing *ad hoc* yardsticks. It would be better to compare the characteristics of individuals who do and who do not participate in the movement. In later chapters we shall try to approximate this by comparing individuals within the movement who differ in the extent to which they have departed from tradition.

21. Place of publication rather than residence of author is used as an indicator of distribution of interest in the movement. This information is available from the item itself. Undoubtedly, the distribution of interest in the movement is not as clear-cut as the table would suggest, since an author may publish in a country in which he does not reside and an item may be read in other than its country of origin.

22. Though an effort was made to be thorough in covering foreign language material, there may be a bias in the direction of the English items since the search was conducted in American libraries (see the Appendix).

23. Why psychiatry has not emerged in some cultures where medicine is accepted is a significant question but beyond the scope of this discussion.

24. The distribution suggests that the dominant psychiatric and theological ideas of the movement would be those enjoying currency in English-speaking countries. Consequently, the spirit of the movement might be expected to be activist rather than contemplative, individualistic rather than collectivistic, ascetic rather than ecstatic, and naïvely meliorist and optimistic rather than imbued with the "tragic sense of life."

25. Some "faith healing" movements have emerged in postwar Japan but these do not involve psychiatry. After the closing date for inclusion in this

study, work on psychotherapy and Eastern religion appeared in Japanese psychological journals.

26. Since the close of this study, interest has been increasing slightly in Italy and Spain. It is significant that in Spain the development is occurring primarily in industrialized Catalonia.

27. Rational organization is one in which means are selected in terms of their efficiency for attainment of the end. Max Weber, *The Theory of Social and Economic Organization*, pp. 117f.

28. Max Weber, *The Protestant Ethic and the Spirit of Capitalism*. The "rational" is an "ideal typical" construction. Weber finds certain elements of it in India, China, and ancient Israel, but it remains for Protestantism to evolve a more thorough going rationalization of life. A number of recent studies have supported the contention that Protestants are more achievement oriented than Catholics. See, for example, Fred L. Strodtbeck, "Family Interaction, Values and Achievement," *Talent and Society*, ed. D. C. McClelland, pp. 135–198. More recently Joseph Veroff, Sheila Feld, and Gerald Gurin, "Achievement Motivation and Religious Background," *American Sociological Review*, XXVII (April, 1962), pp. 205–217, found higher achievement motivation among Catholics than among Protestants especially among those in their 30's and 40's. Catholics at this age seem to expend their energy in the family while Protestants focus on economic achievement.

29. See, for example, Erich Fromm, *Escape from Freedom*; and David Riesman, *The Lonely Crowd*.

30. This usage of the terms "universalistic" and "particularistic" to distinguish an orientation toward rules from an orientation toward a personal relation in its own terms is not to be confused with a widespread usage of those terms as synonymous with nonparochial and parochial. In this latter sense, of course, Pauline Christianity would be "universalistic."

31. Some religions, however, are more particularistic than others. Viewed in terms of intragroup relations, Judaism is more universalistic or less particularistic than Christianity. The Jewish relational bond between man and God, man and man, and of both with the people of Israel is established by contract or covenant. The covenant involves observance of Torah, a set of rules through which the relationship is realized. Transgression is the sin which disturbs the relationship.

32. See the discussion on the debate between Augustine and Pelagius in Adolf Harnack, *Outlines of the History of Dogma*, pp. 363ff. Judaism is, in a sense, "pelagian" in relating salvation to "good deeds" or observance of the law. Membership in the group, however, is only in an extreme situation contingent upon these performances.

33. The distinction between the universalistic-performance and the particularistic-quality cultures follows that of Parsons, *op. cit.*, pp. 180ff. This parallels the earlier *gemeinschaft-gesellschaft* distinction of Toennies. Par-

sons' terminology will be used here because of our interest in the norms operative in each type of relationship. One should not think of *gemeinschaft* and *gesellschaft* relations as existing in concretely separate societies. They are two polar types of relationship which exist side by side in the same group. This is what Durkheim showed in the relation of organic and mechanical forms of solidarity. See Emile Durkheim, *The Division of Labor in Society*. Each form tends to be institutionalized in different parts of the society. Ordinarily, religious and family relationships tend to be *gemeinschaft*, but relations among siblings in a family and the economic activities of monasteries partake of universalistic-achievement elements. An example of a *gemeinschaft ecclesiola* in a more *gesellschaft ecclesia* is given in the study of Peter L. Berger, "Sectarianism and Religious Society," *American Journal of Sociology*, pp. 41–44.

34. See Talcott Parsons, "Illness and the Role of the Physician," *American Journal of Orthopsychiatry*, pp. 452–460 and *op. cit.*, pp. 428–479. For alternative forms of the healing profession see W. H. R. Rivers, *Medicine, Magic and Religion*. Chap. IV is devoted to the way these norms are realized in the healing relationship.

35. Weber, *The Theory of Social and Economic Organization*, p. 219ff., discusses division of labor as a response to the demands of production and Durkheim, *op. cit.*, relates it to the moral and material density of society.

36. See Gregory Zilboorg and George W. Henry, *A History of Medical Psychology*, for evidence on the development of psychiatry as a specialty.

37. Henry Lennard and Arnold Bernstein, *The Anatomy of Psychotherapy*, shows how patient values change in the direction of those of the therapist.

38. Another illustration of the way developments in one profession, psychology, influence developments in a second profession, sociology, as a result of an area of overlapping concern, social psychology, is described in William J. Goode, "Encroachment, Charlatanism, and the Emerging Profession: Psychology, Sociology and Medicine," *American Sociological Review*, pp. 902–914.

39. David C. McClelland, *The Achieving Society*.

40. Two recent studies of secularization in the church are Harold W. Pfautz, "Christian Science: A Case Study of the Social Psychological Aspect of Secularization," *Social Forces*, pp. 246–251; and David Graybeal, "Churches in a Changing Culture," *Review of Religious Research*, pp. 121–128.

41. This development of a psychologically oriented pastorate may also be related to the emergence of the mental health movement. This movement is also part of the "secularization" of the approach to individual deviant behavior alluded to above. The geographic distribution of the mental health movement parallels that of the religio-psychiatric movement. Of 132 member

associations of the World Federation of Mental Health, 38 are in the United States and Canada, 15 in the United Kingdom, 5 in France, and 5 in Germany. The remaining 59 associations are scattered among 39 other countries. World Federation of Mental Health, *First World Mental Health Year: A Record*, p. 96.

42. This table conveys only a rough impression of the situation. Since the ratios are not given per unit of time they are not rates. Publications have appeared over a period of some 60 years. Most of the population figures on which this table is based are from the last decade. During the last several decades the religious composition of the populations, the size of the populations as a whole, and the boundaries of the territories to which they refer have been changing. The sources used included: *The World Almanac*, 1960; *World Christian Handbook*, 1952; Catholic Welfare Conference statistics which are gathered periodically by student mission crusade (these data for June 30, 1961); Constant H. Jacquet, Jr., *Missionary Research Library Occasional Bulletin*, 1954; the 1961–62 *Stateman's Yearbook*; German Republic's 1960 census of religions.

43. This may be due to a greater tendency for Protestants and those in a Protestant environment to write or to different ratios of clergy to laymen in various countries, rather than to a greater interest in this field.

44. See for example, August B. Hollingshead, *Elmtown's Youth*; Herbert H. Hyman, "The Value Systems of Different Classes: A Social Psychological Analysis of Stratification," *Class, Status and Power*, eds. Reinhard Bendix and Seymour Lipset; and Bernard C. Rosen, "The Achievement Syndrome: A Psychocultural Dimension of Social Stratification," *American Sociological Review*, XVI (1951), pp. 766–774. Recent research has shown that this pattern internalized as the "achievement motive" is related to occupational mobility especially in the middle classes. See Harvey J. Crockett, Jr., "The Achievement Motive and Differential Occupational Mobility in the United States," *American Sociological Review*, pp. 191–204.

45. This stratification of American Protestantism has been noted, for example, by Robert S. Lynd, *Middletown*; W. Lloyd Warner and Paul S. Lunt, *The Social Life of a Modern Community*; Richard H. Niebuhr, *The Social Sources of Denominationalism*; and Donald J. Bogue, *The Population of the United States*, pp. 700–708. The above ordering is modal. The membership of each denomination overlaps in class status with that of other denominations. The class position of a denominations' churches also varies from community to community. A careful study in which the ascribed factors conducive to economic achievement were controlled to measure the contribution of the religious factors restates the same order among Protestant denominations. See Albert J. Mayer and Harry Sharp, "Religious Preferences and Worldly Success," *American Sociological Review*, pp. 218–227.

Edmund de S. Brunner believes that the question of the class position of denominations is not a closed one. In his own studies he found no uniformity in the denominational affiliation of the elite church from community to community. Lutherans appeared to be at the top in many places in Wisconsin, Minnesota, and the Dakotas, while Congregationalists outrank Episcopalians in many places in New England (Personal Communication, June 25, 1961).

46. The same limitations apply to interpretation of this table as were noted for Table 8. This table is based only on those Protestant ministers whose specific denomination is known. Though Lutherans and Methodists overlap a good deal in socioeconomic status, the fact that the former is a liturgical and the latter a nonliturgical group might be important enough to merit their separate consideration. Doing so, the Lutheran ratio is 3.3 and the Methodist is 4.4. Apparently the socioeconomic difference outweighs these other considerations in this case.

47. Among ministers holding a doctorate, the publication to population ratios of the denominations in the order given in Table 9 are 8.3, 7.6, 4.3, and 2.1. Among those with less education the ratios are 11.0, 5.2, 1.1, and 0.5. In the high education groups denominational differences become less important and in the low-education group they become more important. The suggestion is that the class position of the denomination is not as important a factor in determining the outlook of a highly educated as of a less highly educated minister. The selective factors among those holding a doctorate probably make of them a rather homogeneous group whatever their denominational affiliation. For explanations of this type of relationship see Paul F. Lazarsfeld, "Interpretation of Statistical Relations as a Research Operation," in Lazarsfeld and Rosenberg, *op. cit.*, pp. 115–125.

48. A sample of serious ministerial writings in any field would include a higher proportion of authors holding a doctorate than would be found in the ministry in general. The actual proportion of doctorates would vary with the subject matter. Fewer doctorates would be found among authors of inspirational books whereas nearly all systematic theologians would hold the degree.

49. These figures refer to the age at which participants published any work. Since some publish more than one work, the age of initial interest would be slightly below these medians. In 1957, the median age of all ministers who had written anything at any time and were living was about 50. The corresponding median age for psychiatrists was about 60. This did not differ among the various ministerial and psychiatric institutional settings. The medians are rounded to the tenth year because the data were coded in ten-year intervals with interval mid-points at the middle of a life decade.

50. This value shift has been noted by C. G. Jung, *Modern Man in Search of a Soul.*

51. We do not have exact figures on the total number of ministers in each institutional setting. We may estimate that with over 300,000 clergy in parishes in the United States, those in hospitals, clinics, and academic positions probably number under 10,000. The above discrepancy cannot be due solely to the fact that academicians write while the parish clergy are expected to preach. No "writing norm" accounts for the fact that clinical ministers write proportionately more than parish clergy. It might be argued that the clinical ministers may overproduce somewhat in the field because they are a special interest group in religion and psychiatry. One wonders whether the production could be so disproportionate.

52. Rabbis have not been included in the previous discussion because the reasons for their participation differ from those of other clergymen and will be discussed at the end of Chap. III.

53. For a discussion of church constitutions, see Joachim Wach, *Sociology of Religion*, pp. 143ff. Presbyterians are classed as congregational since their Presbyteries and Synods are not strictly clerical hierarchies.

54. Salary levels in each denomination are reported in F. Ernest Johnson and J. Emery Ackerman, *The Church as Employer, Money Raiser and Investor.* It would be better if we had information on the incomes of the individual authors and compared this with data on the income of nonauthors. Not having this information, however, we use average income in the group as a "global indicator."

55. On the notion of "cross pressures," see Bernard Berelson, Paul F. Lazarsfeld, and William McPhee, *Voting.*

56. On the relation between bureaucracy and rationality, see Weber, *Theory of Social and Economic Organization*, pp. 329–340.

57. Weber, *ibid.*, pp. 358f., defines charisma as a "quality of an individual personality by virtue of which he is set apart from ordinary men and treated as endowed . . . with exceptional powers or qualities." In hierarchical churches this quality becomes "routinized." For Weber charisma is a source of innovation. *Ibid.*, p. 361. See also Wach's discussion, *op. cit.*, pp. 337ff. Some evidence that personal charisma is associated with nonliturgical rather than liturgical denominations is presented in W. Seward Salisbury, "Faith, Ritualism, Charismatic Leadership, and Religious Behavior," *Social Forces*, pp. 241–245.

58. The referral system is discussed by Oswald Hall, "The Informal Organization of the Medical Profession," *Canadian Journal of Economic and Political Science*, pp. 30–44, see especially p. 43.

59. On the means by which this kind of influence is transmitted, see Elihu Katz and Paul F. Lazarsfeld, *Personal Influence.*

Chapter III

Shifting Reference Groups and Institutional Variation

THE PREVIOUS CHAPTER closed with a question. Why do these nonconformist ministers in attempting to escape contradictions in their traditional role move toward psychiatry rather than some other field? Likewise, why do these nonconformist psychiatrists move toward religion? We observe that these nonconformist ministers, while remaining within the church, tend to judge themselves and their pastoral work by psychiatric standards. Psychiatrists who follow the same standards, unlike these ministers, are abiding by the norms of the group to which they belong, their "membership group." From a psychological point of view, some of these ministers may be said to identify with psychiatrists. Sociologically speaking, they are taking psychiatry, a nonmembership group, as their "reference group."[1] The situation is similar for nonconformist psychiatrists who take religion as their reference group. When a person's reference group is not identical with his membership group, he may be seeking to transfer membership to his reference group.[2] Despite their shift in reference group, however, the ministers in this study are not likely to become psychiatrists, nor are the psychiatrists apt to assume the cloth. Both remain as nonconformist variants within their membership groups.[3]

Several recent studies of variant behavior have employed the concept of reference group as an intervening or independent variable. These studies use the concept of identification with a nonmembership group to explain variation from membership group norms.[4] Following these studies, it will be shown that selection of a nonmembership group as a reference group leads to changed attitudes toward counseling. The adoption of a group's judgmental standards will be shown to underlie advocacy of the behavioral norms of that group. A new reference group explicitly serves as a guide for restricted types of behavior. Nevertheless, its adoption is associated with a broad ideological shift touching the very core of institutional allegiance. It will also be contended that psychoanalysis serves simultaneously as a positive and negative reference group for some ministers. This ambivalence underlies the establishment of a ministerial counseling service as an alternative to counseling by analysts.

Demonstrating the significance of reference groups for variation pushes the unknown but a small step back. Reference group must be examined as a dependent as well as an independent variable. What is it that induces ministers and psychiatrists to select a nonmembership group as a reference group? The chapter concludes with a consideration of this question.

Indicators for Reference Group

In many of the items reviewed the minister or psychiatrist, besides advocating some counseling goal or procedure, expains his selection. This explanation is given in terms of a standard which, by and large among these authors, derives either from a traditional religious or from a traditional psychiatric position. The tradition from which the standard is selected is the basis upon which this study classifies a book or an article according to its author's reference group. For example, a minister who says prayers should be selected because of their tension-reducing value is taking a psychiatric standard, emotional tension reduction, as a basis for judging the worthwhileness of prayers. His membership group is the church, but his reference group is psychiatry. A minister who argues that confession is good for its salvatory qualities, regardless of its influence on mental health, is taking religion as his reference group. A psychiatrist who evaluates prayers according to their contribution to mental health has a psychiatric reference group. The psychiatrist who would discern the religious convictions of a fellow practitioner before referring a patient to him has a religious reference group. An author who judges counseling about equally in terms of a psychiatric and a religious reference group may be said to have a double reference group.

"Emotional catharsis" and "mental health" are attributed to psychiatry and "salvatory qualities" and "religious conviction" to religion on the basis of a distinction between the two as cultural systems to which these symbols belong. This assumption is supported by the fact that the militant conformist ministers and psychiatrists in our sample do indeed tend to select the symbols which we are calling traditional for their respective groups. These classifications are not based upon what the author says he does or believes, but upon the group whose symbols he uses to legitimize his action or belief. Descriptions of their behavior and attitudes will be used later to determine variant types.

This method permitted classification of the authors of 699 books and articles according to their reference groups. Of these, 44 per cent were classified as having a double reference group, 28 per cent a psychiatric reference group, and 25 per cent a religious reference group. The remaining 3 per cent look to other groups for their standards. They are not considered in the ensuing analysis.

Validation of the Indicators

A minister may have a psychiatric reference group when engaged in counseling and a religious reference group when teaching Sunday School.[5] That is, he might look to psychiatry for guidance in the mental health area without abandoning religious criteria on the nature of God or the purpose of prayer. On the other hand, reference group studies tend to assume a reference group "halo effect." A minister might take a psychiatric reference group in several areas. His shift of reference group in the mental health area could be but symptomatic of a general alienation from religion. Similarly, a psychiatrist electing a religious reference group with respect to counseling might or might not look to religion to guide other areas of his life. Members of a group may accept its authority as legitimate in one area and not in another.[6] Medical authority is legitimate in the area of physical therapeutics, but not for deciding a technicality of baseball. A baseball player's endorsement of a food item assumes an extension of the scope of his legitimate expertise. It will be shown that ministers and psychiatrists who look to the opposite group for mental health standards tend to extend that group's legitimacy to other areas. Shifting a reference group corresponds with alienation from the individual's commitment to the core of his group's ideology. The religious belief index in this study attempts to capture commitment to the core beliefs of western religion, and the psychiatric belief index attempts to capture commitment to beliefs on the efficacy of psychiatry. If the indicators for reference groups reflect a general shift of allegiance from the membership and to the reference group, they should be highly correlated with the belief indices. This finding would also be a test of validity for the indicators of reference group. Table 13 compares ministers and psychiatrists who are high, medium, or low on the religious belief index according to whether they have a psychiatric, double, or religious reference group.

Table 13—Religious Belief of Ministers and Psychiatrists According to Reference Groups[a]

Reference Group	RELIGIOUS BELIEF (in Per Cent)		
	High	Medium	Low
Ministers			
Psychiatric	3	29	54
Religious	63	17	5
	(183)	(161)	(120)
Psychiatrists			
Psychiatric	8	18	58
Religious	35	10	5
	(26)	(29)	(80)

a. The double reference group is not shown but accounts for the difference between the sum of the percentages given and 100 per cent. The number in parentheses at the base of each column indicates the number of cases upon which that column is based.

High religious belief is associated with the selection of a religious reference group and low religious belief with a psychiatric reference group for both ministers and psychiatrists. An intermediate position on religious belief is associated with double reference group. This is to say that the selection of a religious reference group in the mental health area is correlated with adherence to fundamental religious conceptions.

This relation between reference group and general ideological commitment also may be measured by our psychiatric belief index. As noted in the previous chapter, this index does not reflect the norms of science, but rather the tendency to look to psychiatry for fundamental values. Table 14 shows the relation between reference groups and psychiatric beliefs. Selection of a psychiatric reference group for therapeutic guidance is associated with acceptance of psychiatry as a broad source of values for both ministers and psychiatrists.

Table 14—Psychiatric Belief of Ministers and Psychiatrists According to Reference Groups[a]

Reference Group	PSYCHIATRIC BELIEF (in Per Cent)		
	High	Medium	Low
Ministers			
Psychiatric	73	30	5
Religious	2	10	69
	(51)	(234)	(175)
Psychiatrists			
Psychiatric	96	43	5
Religious	—	2	32
	(25)	(63)	(43)

a. The double reference group is not shown but accounts for the difference between the sum of the percentages given and 100 per cent. The number in parentheses at the base of each column indicates the number of cases upon which that column is based. For ministers, category 1 is classed as high, 2 as medium, and 3 to 7 as low. For psychiatrists, 1 and 2 are classed as high, 3 as medium, and 4 to 7 as low.

Despite the fact that selection of a reference group in one area does not necessarily imply its selection for other areas, our findings suggest that ministers who select a psychiatric reference group tend to be alienated from traditional religious ideology and probably disenchanted with religious institutions as well. Psychiatrists selecting a religious reference group tend not to look to psychiatry as a fundamental source of values and are probably disenchanted with psychiatric institutions. Once loyalty to the membership group weakens in one area, disaffection may tend to generalize.[7] Substantively, this finding will help us understand why changing a reference group has such a significant influence upon behavior and attitudes. Methodologically, the above correlations provide "construct validation." They are also evidence of "internal consistency" or reliability of the indicators of reference group and the belief indices.

THE INFLUENCE OF A NEW REFERENCE GROUP

Reference Group Influence Upon the Direction of Institutional Variation

The social conditions, such as the exposure to competing role demands examined in the previous chapter, account for general interest in the movement. Why, however, under these conditions does one minister or psychiatrist become a nonconformist, complaining against his institution, and another become a militant conformist, asserting his institutional allegiance and attacking the dissidents?[8] The direction in which they vary seems to depend, in part, upon which reference group they select. Table 15 shows the relation between reference group and the direction of variation.

Table 15—Percentage of Ministers and Psychiatrists with Each Type of Reference Group Who are Nonconformists Rather than Militant Conformists (in Per Cent)

| | REFERENCE GROUP | | | |
	Psychiatric	Double	Religious	Total
Ministers	96	94	44	79
	(115)	(208)	(151)	(474)
Psychiatrists	68	95	100	83
	(56)	(68)	(15)	(139)

Seventy-nine per cent of the ministers and 83 per cent of the psychiatrists for whom we have reference group data are nonconformists. Ninety-six per cent of the ministers with a psychiatric reference group, 94 per cent of those with a double reference group, and 44 per cent of those with a religious reference group are nonconformists. (The remaining 4 per cent, 6 per cent, and 56 per cent respectively are militant conformists.) Similarly, almost all of the psychiatrists with a religious or double reference group, but only about two-thirds of those with a psychiatric reference group, are nonconformists.[9] Those taking a nonmembership group as a reference group are more likely to be institutionally nonconformist, to follow the counseling norms of the other group, and to criticize their own group. The mechanisms by which this comes about are understandable. A group would tend to institutionalize those goals and procedures (the indicators of conformity and nonconformity) which are favored by the group's standards (the indicators for reference groups). An individual whose behavior accords with the legitimate means and goals of his membership group, but who judges his behavior by the standards of a nonmembership group, may come to question the validity of his behavior. A minister who judges his hymns according to their cathartic value may find them wanting. A psychiatrist who seeks spiritual outcomes for his work may judge it as failing. One solution is to accept the prescriptions of the nonmembership group so that the behavior advocated becomes consistent with what is believed good. By advocating, or even following, behaviors of another group an individual does not necessarily shift institutional membership, but may remain as a nonconformist variant in his own group.

This explanation treats shift in reference group as the influencing factor, assuming that a sense of alienation from the group's standards precedes a behavioral and attitudinal change. The reverse may be true. An individual may change his counseling because he has been studying psychology, and yet remain primarily oriented to the church as his reference group. These techniques might then appear questionable when judged by religious standards and he might, as a consequence, seek a new set of standards, a new reference group, as a rationale for what he is already doing. Whichever way the influence flows, the association between taking the nonmembership group as a reference group and being a nonconformist variant is quite clear. Most likely a shift in reference group precedes nonconformity, since almost all of those who take a nonmembership group as a reference group are nonconformists, but almost half of the ministers and a third of the psychiatrists who take their membership as a reference group are also nonconformists. One can be a nonconformist without changing reference group, but one who does change his reference group is almost certain to be a nonconformist.

Having become a nonconformist and attained greater consistency between the criteria of evaluation and the behavior he advocates, the individual is subject to new pressures. The nonconformist variant is criticized by his colleagues, especially by the militant conformists among them. A crucial distinction exists between these two situations of strain. An individual following the norms of his own group, while having a nonmembership group as a reference group, may suffer a sense of inconsistency or experience "guilt." On the other hand, were he to become a nonconformist, he might still be troubled with some "guilt" for having abandoned his own, previously internalized, group norms. In addition to this "guilt," however, the criticism levelled by his colleagues might cause the nonconformist to suffer "shame." Perhaps there is a psychological insight here. The minister or psychiatrist who shifts his reference group is caught between the "guilt" of remaining a conformist, despite accepting the standards of another group, and the "shame" of living as a nonconformist suffering attacks by his colleagues.[10] Perhaps those who fear "guilt" the more become nonconforming variants and bear the "shame." Those who fear "shame" the more may become militant conformists, working out their "guilt" in aggressive assertiveness.

Reference Group Influence upon Therapeutic Goals

Reference groups have been related to the variations from institutional norms and goals. The indicators for this variation, as will be indicated in Chapter V, are the religious or psychological formulations of the terms referring to counseling. The question might arise as to whether a psychiatrist using the language of "spirit" becomes any less "psychiatric" or a minister referring to "neurosis" any less "religious." The argument for the influence of the reference group gains cogency by showing that a more fundamental aspect of what it means to be "psychiatric" or "religious" is affected. To demonstrate this we follow a commonly held contrast between religious and scientific concerns. Science constructs its world in functional or instrumental terms. The idea of one phenomenon operating upon another is central. Religion, on the other hand, approaches the world in evaluative terms. It is concerned with purpose and meaningful relations.[11] This distinction may be applied to ministers' and psychiatrists' conceptions of the outcome of therapy. Each book or article was categorized globally, not according to the cultural system to which the linguistic symbols belong but according to this distinction in the character of the therapeutic goals it supports. Items were divided into those advocating therapy as a way to provide meaning or purpose, assumedly reflecting a religious orientation, and those advocating therapy to help the patient adapt to his surroundings or to operate more smoothly, assumedly reflecting a psychiatric orientation. The first are termed goals of "meaning," the second "instrumental" goals.

Some authors described their therapeutic goals in almost these words, saying, on the one hand, that therapy helps the patient discover meaning in life or, on the other hand, that therapy enables him to function better in his surroundings. Beyond this items were categorized as advocating "meaning" goals if they said that therapy clarifies confused interpretations of the world, helps man accept Christ, or enables him to recognize the difference between piety and scrupulosity. Expressions to the effect that therapy enables the individual to cope with stress, manage his human relations better, or carry out his occupation were classified as instrumental goals.[12] Items giving about equal stress to both types were categorized as advocating meaning and instrumental goals.

The usefulness of the distinction is apparent from the differing frequencies of the categories among items written by ministers and by psychiatrists. Setting the mixed type aside for the moment, we find that 56 per cent (325) of the ministers but only 34 per cent (94) of the psychiatrists advocate meaning in preference to instrumental goals. (Considering militant conformists alone the percentages are 83 per cent [64] and 9 per cent [23] respectively.) Thus, even in our atypical sample of ministers who have moved toward psychiatry and of psychiatrists who have moved toward religion, we find the expected contrast in the formulation of therapeutic goals. If we assume that the distinction is correct in principle, then this finding is evidence for the validity of the indicators.

With this confidence in the indicators, we may examine the relation between reference groups and goals of therapy, as shown in Table 16.

Table 16 demonstrates a clear association between a religious reference group and meaning goals, and between a psychiatric reference group and instrumental goals for both ministers and psychiatrists. The combination of meaning and instrumental goals is characteristic of those with a double reference group. A person with a double reference group, suspended between religion and psychiatry, selects therapeutic goals from both groups.[13] In fact, the character of the goals of therapy is more closely related to reference than to membership groups. Ministers with a psychiatric reference group are almost as likely to advocate instrumental goals as are

Table 16—Ministerial and Psychiatric Reference Groups
According to Whether Meaning or Instrumental Goals
are Advocated as an Outcome of Therapy

| | THERAPEUTIC GOALS (in Per Cent) | | | |
Reference Groups	Meaning Goals	Meaning and Instrumental Goals	Instrumental Goals	Total
Ministers				
Psychiatric	22	18	60	100 (114)
Double	34	41	25	100 (192)
Religious	59	28	13	100 (138)
Psychiatrists				
Psychiatric	13	21	66	100 (53)
Double	24	52	24	100 (68)
Religious	54	33	13	100 (15)

psychiatrists with a psychiatric reference group. Psychiatrists with a religious reference group, like ministers, advocate meaning goals.

It is important to check whether the relation between reference groups and therapeutic goals shown in Table 16 is not a function of the correlation of both of them with a third factor, institutional variation. Testing the relation of reference groups and therapeutic goals with variant type held constant, the same relationship holds.[14]

The association of reference groups and therapeutic goals may be explained in the same way as the relation of reference groups and variant types has been explained. When an individual accepts the standards of a nonmembership group for judging his counseling, takes it as a reference group, he may soon adopt the goals recommended by that group.[15] The therapeutic goals of his membership group tend to be abandoned under the impact of negative evaluation by the new reference group standards. Thus, a shift in reference group is related not only to a change in the linguistic formulation, our indicator for variant types but also to a common "definitional" contrast between the institutions in terms of instrumental versus meaning orientations.

Thus, we may surmise that given the strains of role conflict or of the malintegration of institutional norms and cultural goals as described in the previous chapter, ministers who retain a religious reference group tend to enter the religio-psychiatric movement as militant conformists. Other ministers, subject to these same strains and with a similar interest in counseling, take a psychiatric reference group. They tend to become the nonconformist variants. These latter become not only institutionally alienated, but also change their therapeutic goals in the direction of those usually associated with psychiatry. Conversely, psychiatrists subject to these strains who nevertheless retain a psychiatric reference group, tend to enter the movement as militant conformists. Those who, in this situation, take a religious reference group become the nonconformist variants. They also become not only institutionally alienated, but change their therapeutic goals in the direction of those usually associated with religion. The attraction to one or another reference group has powerful import for the direction in which the variant behavior is expressed.

Throughout this section ministerial and psychiatric variation have been treated as parallel. There is a significant difference, however, in the consequences of their variation. Psychiatrists introduce religious elements into therapy. They do not found churches. Some ministers not only introduce psychological elements into their traditional role but establish counseling centers and offer psychological services. The next section attempts to account for this aspect of the religio-psychiatric movement.

Reference Group Ambivalence and the Development of Pastoral Counseling

Taking psychiatry as a reference group might explain why ministers and their parishioners seek these services or why ministers are drawn to psychological thinking. This does not fully account for these ministers attempting to provide their own psychological services. Some say they do so because there are too few psychiatrists. Yet pastoral counseling services are most likely to be established, as suggested in Chapter II, in urban centers, precisely where there is the greatest density of psychiatric services.

While these pastoral services are being established, religious leaders charge that psychiatry is hedonistic, materialistic, deterministic, mechanistic, and, perhaps, antireligious. These ideological charges might be levelled by representatives of any Western religion. In fact, however, they are most often expressed by Catholics, less often by Protestants, and rarely by Jews. Catholics and Protestants have been more active than Jews in developing ministerial counseling services.

Why are the attitudes of Jews toward psychiatry and pastoral counseling different from those of Christians? Perhaps this difference is a reflection of Jewish and Christian attitudes to science. The warfare of science and theology, a doctrinal dispute, has not occurred with any seriousness among Jews. Judaism emphasizes ritual practice and, traditionally, has been less concerned than Christianity about doctrine and theology. Judaism's principal conflicts with industrial society have been in the economic sphere, where the exigencies of the market may collide with ritual Sabbath observance, and in the social sphere, where an integrationist ethic may interfere with ritual dietary observances.

Other considerations affect Christian and Jewish attitudes toward healers. Among Protestants and Catholics the pastoral office is a significant ministerial function. As such, it may sense a challenge from the new psychiatric healers. In modern times a rabbinical pastorate has been important within the Hasidic sect of Jewish orthodoxy. This group is quite insulated against psychiatry. The pastorate has not been stressed among Jews who have adapted more radically to American and European society. Consequently, Jews are less likely than Christians to perceive psychiatry as usurping a religious function.

The above considerations apply to psychiatry in general. Among all schools of psychotherapeutics, however, the strongest attacks have been leveled at the Freudian. Again, the principal critique of Freudianism has been Catholic and Protestant rather than Jewish. The relative acceptance of Freud by Jews may bear some relation to the Jewish elements in his thought and his movement. He himself was a Jew, and most of the members of his immediate Vienna circle were Jews.[16] Admittance to the psychoanalytic movement requires analysis by a previous initiate, a sort of "apostolic succession." The original Jewish group tended to analyze Jews.[17] Unwittingly, psychoanalytic ideology may be couched in a Jewish ethic strange to individuals socialized in the Protestant ethic.[18]

These cultural, social, and psychological factors may make some

Christian ministers reticent about treatment by Jewish analysts. Nevertheless, under the impact of the mental health movement, they have come to accept the principle of a scientific approach to personal problems, especially as this approach is developed in psychoanalysis. As a result psychoanalysis may tend to become an ambivalent reference group for them (not to be confused with our usage of "double reference group" to refer to an individual taking his standards from two groups). They are attracted to certain of the standards of psychoanalysis and repelled by others. Establishing a Christian psychotherapy is a partial response to the dilemma. Therapeutic services are provided not by Jewish analysts but by Christian clergymen.

This conjecture will be supported by evidence that over the years the growth and peregrinations of the ministerial part of the religio-psychiatric movement have paralleled those of Freudianism rather than of psychiatry in general. We will not prove, thereby, that Freudianism is both a positive and negative reference group for Christian ministers, but will demonstrate an occurrence which would be expected were the contention true. Table 17 examines the location of the Protestant ministerial part of the movement at various times.[19]

Table 17—Proportion of Writings by Protestant Ministers on Religion and Psychiatry in Several Countries During Various Time Periods

Countries	TIME PERIODS (in Per Cent)			
	to 1932	1933 to 1947	1948 to 1957	Total
Germany, Austria, German Switzerland	80	—	20	100 (15)
Great Britain	16	34	50	100 (38)
United States, Canada	10	22	68	100 (403)

Freudianism was developing in Vienna and Berlin from the turn of the century until its curtailment by Hitler. During this period psychoanalysis was relatively uninfluential in England and the United States. English and American psychiatry, however, did not lag. Almost all the German Protestant ministerial writings appeared during the heyday of German-speaking psychoanalysis. Few of the

English and American Protestant ministerial items had appeared. Jewish analysts fled Germany and Austria during the Hitler period. Initially, England, where ground had been prepared by men such as Ernest Jones, was a principal reception center. Freud himself found shelter there in 1938. Immigration of analysts to the United States, some after an English stopover, developed during the thirties.[20] No German, but a sizeable proportion of English and American, ministerial items were written during this second period. Freudianism continued to grow in England and, especially, in the United States during and after the Second World War. A good deal of the English and the bulk of the American ministerial material appeared in this last period.

The temporal and geographic correspondence of Freudianism and Protestant ministerial religio-psychiatric literature may merely imply that both were the products of the same underlying cause. Were this the case, however, Jewish and Christian clerical writings might be similarly influenced by this cause and their participation would follow a similar chronology. If, on the other hand, Christian clerical interest is, in part, a reaction to the Jewishness of psychoanalysis, then Catholic and Protestant clerical participation in the movement would precede rabbinical participation. Table 18 compares Protestant, Catholic, and Jewish interest over time.

Table 18—Proportion of Protestant, Catholic, and Jewish Ministerial Items Published in Each Time Period

Clergymen	to 1932	TIME PERIODS (in Per Cent) 1933 to 1947	1948 to 1957	Total
Protestant	14	25	61	100 (374)
Catholic	9	16	75	100 (142)
Jewish	—	8	92	100 (26)

Thirty-nine per cent of all works by Protestant ministers, 25 per cent of the Catholic, and 8 per cent of the Jewish clerical literature appeared before 1948. Since psychoanalysis emerged in Catholic Austria, why were Protestants earlier to respond than Catholics? Perhaps Catholics, with separate school systems and professional associations, are more insulated from psychoanalytic influence.

Freud was especially careful to avoid a religious encounter in Catholic Vienna during the early years.[21] Further, the Swiss developments led by Carl Gustav Jung and Oskar Pfister engaged European Protestant interest. The reception accorded the movement in the United States by G. Stanley Hall, James J. Putnam, Morton Prince, and Adolf Meyer involved American Protestants more than Catholics. Religio-psychiatric literature among Jews seems less a direct response to psychoanalysis than an imitation of the Christian literature. All Jewish clerical contributions have been made in the United States, and predominately by Reform rabbis. Reform, more than Orthodox or Conservative Judaism has been influenced by the Protestant conception of the clerical role and has most seriously attempted to evolve a pastorate. The Jewish literature has accompanied this development. We must be careful to note that some of the Protestant literature appeared before psychoanalysis was known and, even later, a good part of it does not speak directly to questions raised by psychoanalysis.

So much for the ecology of the literature. Up to this point we have been concerned with interest in the field as expressed by publication as such. What about the attitudes of these authors toward psychoanalysis in particular? Information was sufficient for classifying some authors as propsychoanalytic, accepting and using Freudian ideas, and others as antipsychoanalytic, explicitly critical of these ideas. Among the ministers and psychiatrists whose position could be ascertained, 71 per cent (118) of the Catholics, 35 per cent (224) of the Protestants, and 10 per cent (48) of the Jews were antipsychoanalytic. The antipsychoanalytic authors approve of other types of counseling.[22] The greater unanimity of Catholic than of Protestant criticism of psychoanalysis may be due to the more clearly stated doctrinal position which enables Catholics to scrutinize the implications of psychoanalysis. Catholic and Protestant criticism along with overwhelming Jewish support for psychoanalysis, despite an equivalent possibility of theological clash, and despite favorable attitudes toward counseling, is what we would expect were psychoanalysis an ambivalent reference group for Christians.

The religio-psychiatric movement has followed the passage of psychoanalysis westward from Europe. The movement attracted Protestant and Catholic clerical attention considerably before it awoke Jewish interest. Opposition to psychoanalysis has been primarily Christian. Psychoanalytic practitioners and patients tend to be Jewish. Calls for a Christian psychotherapy appear in the religio-psychiatric literature.[23] These facts suggest that the religio-psychiatric movement may be, in some measure, a Christian response to psychoanalysis. This is not to say that the Christians in the movement do not use psychoanalytic concepts. As we analyze the recommended norms for therapy it will become abundantly clear that they adopt and adapt Freudian notions. The acceptance of psychoanalytic ideas and psychological services accompanied by the blocking of access to analytic services is one basis for the emergence of psychological pastoral counseling.[24] Even when a minister takes a psychiatric reference group, he may do so ambivalently. Why, however, would an individual change his reference group in the first place? We turn now to this question.

CHOOSING A NEW REFERENCE GROUP

We have observed the effect of choosing a new reference group upon the direction of variation and upon the type of therapeutic goals advocated. The reference group has been treated as an independent or intervening variable. What, however, influences an individual to select one or another reference group? What leads a minister to evaluate his work according to psychiatric standards? Under what conditions will a psychiatrist judge his practice by religious standards? The reference group will be treated as a dependent variable to answer these questions.

Three types of factors seem related to a minister's or psychiatrist's choice of a nonmembership group as a reference group. If the nonmembership group is approved in its own right by the membership group, there will be a greater tendency to take it as a reference group. Second, the greater the interaction with members of the approved group, the more likelihood of its becoming a reference group. Finally, the greater the "inconsistency" of an individual's status in his membership group, the more likely he will be to choose a nonmembership group as a reference group. Status inconsistency seems to have this effect when it involves a discrepancy among an individual's ranks in several statuses, or a discrepancy among norms applicable to a single status.

Institutional Approval of a Potential Reference Group

If there is a tendency to vary from the norms and goals of one's membership group, an individual is more likely to adopt norms and goals of a nonmembership group which his colleagues otherwise approve than of one they reject. This would be a line of least resistance. Colleagues' acceptance of that group's values would minimize their opposition to adopting them. An individual is also more likely to have been exposed to, and so learned, the values of an approved than of a disapproved group. Since, as shown in the previous section, psychoanalysis and, in some measure, psychiatry in general, receive differential approval among Jews, Protestants, and Catholics, this thesis may be tested by comparing the reference groups selected by members of these faiths. Table 19 shows that the selection of a reference group is influenced by the religious affiliation of the ministers and psychiatrists.

Table 19—Religious Affiliation of Ministers and Psychiatrists According to Reference Group (Double Reference Groups not Shown)

Reference Groups	RELIGIOUS AFFILIATION (in Per Cent)		
	Jews	Protestants	Catholics
Ministers (474)			
Psychiatric	54	30	2
Religious	12	24	58
	(24)	(336)	(114)
Psychiatrists (136)			
Psychiatric	80	41	23
Religious	—	6	22
	(27)	(53)	(56)

Over half of the rabbis, but less than a third of the Protestant ministers, and almost no Catholic priests, select a psychiatric reference group. No Jewish, few Protestant, but about a fifth of the Catholic psychiatrists select a religious reference group. The tendency among clergymen of each faith to select one or another reference group differs only in degree from the tendency among psychiatrists of that faith. Selection of a psychiatric reference group seems related to the extent that psychiatry is institutionalized as an appropriate way of dealing with emotional problems in each of these three religious communities. Studies have shown Jews to be most likely, and Catholics least likely to seek psychiatric aid when in distress.[25] Conversely, the tendency to select religious reference groups seems related to the acceptance of religious healing as a part of the clerical role. Religious healing has played a part in all of these traditions. Today, however, the rabbi retains almost no healing function. The Protestant minister, in some cases, may hold healing services. The individual practitioner of religious healing, such as Oral Roberts, is best known among Protestants, especially among fundamentalists. The healing function of the Catholic confessional and penitential remains significant. Catholics alone maintain the tradition of healing shrines, such as Lourdes. Thus, the more psychiatry is institutionalized, the greater the likelihood that a variant will select a psychiatric reference group. Conversely, the more religious healing is institutionalized, the greater the chance that the variant, minister or psychiatrist, will elect a religious reference group in the counseling area. It is an old truism that approval of a nonmembership group increases the probability that its values will penetrate the membership group.

This finding need not be restricted to groups with which the individual is affiliated. Groups of orientation, such as the audience for whom he writes, should have a similar influence on selection of a reference group. Psychiatry is more institutionalized or approved as a way to meet emotional problems among professionals and the highly educated than among the general public.[26] Consequently, authors writing items for professionals should have a greater propensity to select a psychiatric reference group than authors of items directed to the general public. The books and articles in this study were classified according to whether they were directed either to psychological or religious professionals or to lay audiences. The judgment was based on the technical level of the writing, the specialization of its content, and, if it appeared in a journal, the primary audience to which that journal is directed. Of 1,328 items which were classified in this way, 53 per cent were directed to professionals in religion and 20 per cent were written from a religious point of view but directed to laymen. Another 19 per cent were written for professional psychologists or psychiatrists, and 4 per cent were written from a psychological point of view but directed to a lay audience. The remaining 4 per cent of these items were directed to various other audiences. The profession of the authors as well as their reference groups is known for slightly less than half of these items. Among these we may test the relation between the type of audience and reference group. Among ministers writing for a professional audience, whether religious or psychological professionals, 28 per cent (326) choose a psychiatric reference group, while 13 per cent (134) of those writing for a lay audience do so. Similarly, among psychiatrists, 44 per cent (112) of those writing for professionals and 26 per cent (27) of those writing for laymen choose a psychiatric reference group. This positive correlation between orientation to a professional audience and selection of a psychiatric reference group holds even when the professional audience is a theological one. In sum, if a nonmembership group enjoys legitimacy on the part of an individual's membership group, or on the part of the audience to which he is oriented, there is a greater likelihood of its becoming his reference group.

In the face of incipient variation, the offering or withholding of approval by one group of other groups has a social function. It enables the group to control the types of variation which occur among its members. There is little chance, for example, that an American Catholic priest will take Communists as a reference group or that American psychiatrists will take voodoo or mediums as their reference group, since both of these are disapproved in their membership groups. It is as if the group says, if you must vary, do it in the least disturbing way. It does not follow, however, that if the church approves of psychiatry *qua* psychiatry, that it also approves of its clergymen adopting psychiatric standards for their pastoral office or becoming practicing psychological counselors. In fact, the response of the church to variant clergymen, and of medicine to variant psychiatrists, indicates the limits of the approval enjoyed by the nonmembership group. This situation is similar to that of a minister encouraging his congregation to join with neighbors of another religion for a Thanksgiving service but reproving a parishioner who accepts this other faith.

Interaction with Members of a Potential Reference Group

It is not necessary for a minister ever to meet a psychiatrist or for a psychiatrist to come face to face with a minister for a shift in reference groups. The climate of opinion in a group could influence individuals to look toward another group. However, an increased opportunity for interaction with the members of an approved non-membership group might increase the likelihood of its being selected as a reference group. Given a tendency to accept the standards of another group, interaction facilitates learning those standards.

The various work settings in which ministers are employed provide differential opportunities to interact with psychiatrists.[27] The ministers in the sample are employed in a variety of institutional settings. Of the ministerial authors whose work-setting could be ascertained (553), 18 per cent are primarily parish ministers, 21 per cent are engaged primarily in hospitals or clinics, 22 per cent teach pastoral subjects in seminaries, and 39 per cent are teachers of traditional religious fields (nonpastoral) or are in church or seminary administrative capacities. Ministers in a parish and in nonpastoral teaching have relatively less opportunity to interact with psychiatrists than those in clinics or pastoral teaching. The psychiatrists are also found in several settings. Of the psychiatrists whose work-setting could be ascertained (257), 37 per cent are engaged primarily in teaching and administration, 21 per cent serve in hospitals and clinics, and 42 per cent engage solely in private practice. Those in hospital clinics interact little with ministers. (The clinic situation with one or two ministers among dozens or even hundreds of physicians is a high interaction situation for the former and a low one for the latter.) Psychiatrists in private practice would have normal community relations with ministers, and those in academic settings (in this sample they are largely Catholic psychiatrists in Catholic schools) would have most opportunity.

Are ministers who have greater opportunity to interact with psychiatrists more likely to take a psychiatric reference group? Are psychiatrists with more opportunity to interact with ministers more likely to select a religious reference group? Table 20 shows the proportion in each institutional setting selecting each type of reference group. Individuals who choose the nonmembership group for a reference group are combined with those having a double, that is, partly nonmembership, reference group.

If the assumption is correct that opportunity for interaction with the opposite profession increases from the left to the right side of the table, then the data support the hypothesis. Opportunity to

Table 20—Ministers and Psychiatrists in Each Institutional Setting According to Reference Group (Religious Reference Groups of Ministers and Psychiatric Reference Groups of Psychiatrists not Shown)

	INSTITUTIONAL SETTINGS (in Per Cent)			
Reference Groups	Nonpastoral Teaching	Parish	Pastoral Teaching	Clinical
Ministers: Psychiatric or Double	66 (138)	78 (67)	84 (83)	90 (60)
	Clinical	Private Practice	Academic	
Psychiatrists: Religious or Double	48 (27)	52 (59)	74 (14)	

interact with members of a nonmembership group is associated with increased tendency to take it as a reference group. This finding remains substantially the same with religion held constant, so that it is not a function of the different proportions of Catholics, Protestants, or Jews in the various settings. It is a common sociological generalization that people who interact tend to become alike if they are initially well disposed toward one another.[28]

The classification by institutional setting, though suggestive, is not firm evidence of the direction of influence. Perhaps individuals with a nonmembership group as their reference group choose situations which allow greater opportunity for interaction with that group. Whatever the direction, however, interaction with a group and selecting it as a reference group are associated.

Ministers and psychiatrists who contribute to the religio-psychiatric literature and those engaged in religio-psychiatric activities are a small proportion of their professions. Most ministers in an environment where psychiatry is an approved approach to emotional problems are satisfied to stay within the traditional framework and do not elect a psychiatric reference group. Many psychiatrists approve of religious interest in healing and interact intensively with ministers without orienting to a religious reference group. What determines which individuals are more likely to do so? The following section discusses influential factors to which some individuals are exposed more than others.

Low Status Consistency and
Change of Reference Group

A single individual occupies a number of statuses and is ranked within each one. A parish minister has a community position and rank and may occupy a status and rank in an academic institution. A minister's rank among his clergymen colleagues and in the community may depend, in part, on the social prestige accorded his denomination. Education may influence his desirability as a minister and be a basis for ranking him in the community and in academia. The relation among his ranks in these spheres may be termed his "status consistency."[29] A minister having both high academic and high community ranks would enjoy consistency among his ranks in these two statuses. High education coupled with belonging to a low prestige denomination would give him inconsistent ranks or low status consistency. Individuals may seek status consistency by raising their lower ranks to the level of their higher ones. If a minister's or psychiatrist's lower rank derives from his professional status, he might look to a nonmembership profession, which he perceives as according prestige, as his reference group. A less frequent solution might be to withdraw into the lower ranking status and assert its virtues.

The relation of status consistency to the choice of reference group may be examined in the case of Protestant ministers. Ministers in this movement are generally highly educated and enjoy high educational rank in their denominations. A highly educated minister who belongs to a denomination with low social prestige would suffer low status consistency. The tendency to select a psychiatric reference group by ministers of variously ranked denominations is examined in Table 21.

The denominations are presented in descending order of the socioeconomic position of their adherents from the left to the right

Table 21—Protestant Ministers of Various Denominations Who Choose Psychiatric Reference Group

DENOMINATIONS (in Per Cent)			
Episcopalian	Congregational Presbyterian	Methodist Lutheran	Baptist
17	18	46	50
(58)	(71)	(74)	(28)

side of the table. Since in all cases the minister's educational rank is high, lower socioeconomic status of his denomination means greater status inconsistency. The table shows that the lower the rank of the denomination, the greater the tendency to select a psychiatric reference group.[30]

These findings are particularly significant because the ministers of the high-ranking denominations have the greater tendency toward variation as measured by participation in the movement. Some four out of five of the variants are nonconformists. Nonconformist variation, in turn, is positively associated with selecting a psychiatric reference group. (Compare with Table 9, page 42.)

We do not have the data for a parallel examination of the relation of low status consistency and the selection of a religious reference group among psychiatrists. It is possible, however, to speculate that the situation among psychiatrists complements that among ministers. Ministers may enjoy high rank, based on education, in their own institution, and low rank, based on denominational prestige, in the broad community. By identifying with psychiatry they seek to raise their general community prestige. Significantly, the religio-psychiatric movement is interdenominational. Thus, it allows ministers from lower ranking denominations to escape their denominational rank. Psychiatrists, on the other hand, as physicians are highly regarded in the general community. The psychiatrist, however, has a low rank among other medical specialists. By identifying with religion, he does not raise his position among physicians but rather enters a new environment, that of the religious institution, where his specialty is accorded a degree of respect which he cannot claim among his colleagues. Since status inconsistency would be a general problem among psychiatrists, and yet very few of them adopt a religious reference group, we would expect that other psychiatrists find other ways of handling the problem.

Multiple Socialization and
Change of Reference Group

The status consistency just discussed concerns the relations among the status ranks. Presumably the strain experienced by the individual is a result of the differential power he may exert in several situations. An inconsistency in status ranks implies a discrepancy in the given and received deference behavior from one institutional context to another and a discrepancy in the levels of society to which he may be admitted by virtue of each rank. Another sort of status consistency relates to the compatibility of behavioral expectations built into the same status. This may derive from "multiple socialization," that is, having been socialized in several prior statuses all with some relevance to the present one.[31] Inconsistent behavioral expectation may also derive from a conflict within his "status set." Several statuses which he occupies may provide conflicting directives for action in a single status. For example, a military chaplain may be committed to opposing war by virtue of his church status and of accommodating to it by virtue of his military status.[32]

As one type of "multiple socialization" let us examine the effect of a varied program of formal schooling on the ministers' choice of reference group. The more varied the curriculum, the more the student may be subjected to competing behavioral and attitudinal possibilities. This type of status inconsistency may well increase the probability that he will look to a nonmembership group for guidance when he becomes a minister. The authors indicated their major fields of study as graduate and undergraduate students, in the personal questionnaires returned by a number of them. Of 521 ministers supplying such information, 78 per cent listed theology, 40 per cent philosophy or the humanities, 30 per cent psychology, 26 per cent personal counseling (included as a field study), 14 per cent combined religion and psychology courses, and smaller proportions other fields.

These ministers may be classified into those who report having studied one, two, and three or more major fields, irrespective of what they were. Of ministers who report but a single field 50 per cent (26) have either a psychiatric or ambivalent reference group. This is the case with 73 per cent (119) who reported studying two fields, and with 79 per cent (135) of those reported having studied three or more fields. The additional fields often included psychological ones. It is not, however, the educational exposure to psychology as such which here predisposes to selecting the psychiatric nonmembership group as a reference group. Those who studied psychology in this sample have no more of a tendency to select a psychiatric reference group than those who studied any other single field. Studying a number of fields presents the potential minister with a wide array of behavioral and attitudinal possibilities. This widening of his horizon reduces the liklihood that he will remain with an exclusively religious reference group.

The problem of multiple socialization may be pinpointed with respect to the fields of religion and psychiatry. We find that a psychiatric or ambivalent reference group is elected by 55 per cent (76) of those ministers who report having studied only theology or only subjects in the humanities. (Some of these studied more than one such subject, or theology together with a field such as philosophy.) However, of those who studied a religious and/or a humanities field, on the one hand, and a psychological field, on the other hand, 79 per cent (158) select a psychiatric or ambivalent reference group. Of those who studied religion and psychiatry or psychology as a single combined course of study, 87 per cent (46) have a psychiatric or ambivalent reference group. The evidence is similar for psychiatrists. Among those who, beyond medicine, report having studied only psychiatry, 59 per cent (106) have a religious or ambivalent reference group, whereas 77 per cent (24) of those who combined psychiatry with work either in the humanities or theology have a religious or ambivalent reference group.[33] Thus multiple socialization increases the probability of shifting reference groups. If this combination of studies includes a psychological field for the ministers or a humanistic field for the psychiatrists, the probability of shift is further increased.

Nothing in this evidence supports a causal relation. Individuals who studied many fields may have done so because they were already searching for different sources for behavioral standards. Ministers who elect to study psychology as well as religion may already have been ambivalent about their reference groups. Despite the fact that the direction of influence cannot be fixed, the association between multiple educational socialization and the selection of a nonmembership group as a reference group is clear.

CONCLUSION

The previous chapter analyzed pressures toward change, the push away from tradition. This chapter has explored the reasons determining the direction of variation; why, in response to these strains, some ministers elect to move toward psychiatry and some psychiatrists to move toward religion. The reference group was found to be a powerful intervening variable. Individuals who, under pressure, maintain their membership group as a reference group reassert their institutional allegiance and appear as militant conformists. Those who shift to a nonmembership group as a reference group appear as nonconformists. The attitudinal change involved in nonconformity might only lead ministers to seek psychiatric services for themselves and their parishioners. That some establish their own services seemed related to the role of psychoanalysis as an ambivalent reference group for them. The elements attracting ministers to psychoanalysis provide a drive which is thwarted by the elements repelling them from it. In the conduct of their own services, they may select the elements to be admitted.

What, however, leads ministers to look to psychiatry or psychiatrists to look to religion for their standards, to select a nonmembership group as a reference group in the first place? The probability that individuals will look to a nonmembership group is increased if that group is approved, within its own sphere of competence, by members of the individuals' home institution. An opportunity for interaction with the members of that group further increases the chances of its becoming a reference group. Why, however, when the nonmembership group is approved and when there is interaction with its members do some and not other ministers and psychiatrists change their reference groups? Apparently the most likely to do so are those experiencing status inconsistency. This may be due to a lack of balance among their social ranks which they try to equilibrate, at least perceptually, by changing their reference group. It also may be due to multiple socialization, having been exposed to conflicting possibilities for behavior and attitudes in counseling.

Until now militant conformists and nonconformists have been studied as the two variant types constituting the religio-psychiatric movement. The emphasis has been on the relation of the individual to his institution. The next two chapters turn to the meaning of nonconformity for the counseling relation. Three types of nonconformists will be delineated. These types differ in the degree to which they depart from traditional counseling forms. Their institutional dissidence will be shown to be concomitant with departure from tradition in the counseling relationship.

NOTES

1. Reference group theory in this study follows Robert K. Merton, *Social Theory and Social Structure*, Chaps. VIII and IX. "Reference group" is used to denote that group which an individual uses as a standard of comparison as well as the group to which he looks as a source of attitudes or norms. See Harold H. Kelly, "Two Functions of Reference Groups," *Readings in Social Psychology*, ed. Guy E. Swanson, Theodore M. Newcomb, and Eugene L. Hartley, pp. 410–414; and Herbert Hyman, "Reflections on Reference Groups," *Public Opinion Quarterly*, pp. 389–396.

Ministers and psychiatrists differ in their emphasis on these two reference group functions. For the ministers, psychiatry is important as a standard of comparison. It is an ego ideal, an image of what he would like to be. For psychiatrists, religion is primarily a source of attitudes. It is a model of desirable behavior, an element in the superego. These psychiatrists are relatively less likely to see themselves as "priest-like" than the ministers are to see themselves as "psychologist-like."

2. This is the phenomenon of "anticipatory socialization" as described by Robert K. Merton, *Social Theory and Social Structure*, pp. 265–268.

3. This is what Charles H. Cooley observed in saying that "One is led to a mode of life different from the people about one, partly by intrinsic contrariness, and partly by fixing his imagination on the ideas and practices of other people whose mode of life he finds more congenial." *Human Nature and the Social Order*, p. 298. See also Tamotsu Shibutani, "Reference Groups as Perspectives," *American Journal of Sociology*, pp. 562–569; and Alberta E. Siegel, "Reference Groups, Membership Groups and Attitude Change," *Journal of Abnormal and Social Psychology*, pp. 360–364.

4. See, for example, Albert Cohen, *op. cit.*, where identification with middle-class values figures in an explanation of working-class delinquency. In Robert K. Merton, *Social Theory and Social Structure*, pp. 227 ff., the concept of "relative deprivation" is used to explain soldiers' "satisfaction in the military." Martin Patchen, "The Effect of Reference Group Standards on Job Satisfaction," *Human Relations*, pp. 303–314, uses the reference group concept to explain job satisfaction; Norman Kaplan, "Reference Group Theory and Voting Behavior" applies the concept to predict voting.

5. This is not to be confused with our use of the notion of "double reference group." The classification of "double reference group" is used when the standards of two groups are applied in a single role or situation. The concern here is with what has been termed in the literature "multiple reference groups," the use of different reference groups in different roles or situations.

Ralph H. Turner, "Reference Groups of Future Oriented Men," *Social Forces,* pp. 130–136, points out that groups are segmentally rather than totally relevant to an individual's values and that one group may be more relevant for evaluating occupational success and another for evaluating ethical and moral behavior. See also Lewis M. Killian, "The Significance of Multiple-Group Membership in a Disaster," *American Journal of Sociology,* pp. 309–314.

6. "Legitimacy of authority" is used here in a sense similar to Max Weber's concept of the "validity of an order." See *Theory of Social and Economic Organization,* pp. 134ff.

7. Assent to the ideological statements of a group is not merely a cognitive conviction. It also expresses commitment to the people constituting that group. Loss of religious belief involves a social strain between a minister and his church. Questioning basic psychiatric doctrine (though not specific ideas and techniques) is accompanied by strain between the psychiatrist and his institution. This social strain leads colleagues to withdraw from the variant, pushing him farther way. This has been referred to as the "vicious circle" of variation. Culturally, the increasing variation reflects a strain to consistency among values. When one value, such as the attitude to mental health, is changed, changes ensue in other values in an effort to restore equilibrium.

8. For present purposes nonconformists may be distinguished from militant conformists according to whether they are the authors of statements cited in the previous chapter critical of or defensive of their institutions. Actually, the classificatory criteria were more specific. Nonconformists are those who advocate either means or goals for counseling which are appropriate to the other institution. The militant conformists advocate counseling procedures and goals appropriate to their institutions. These indicators will be presented in the following chapter.

9. The sharp differences revealed in Table 15 might be due to a lack of independence between the indicators used for non- and militant conformism and those used for reference groups. Perhaps classifying a minister, for example, as a nonconformist because he uses psychiatric language to describe what he does in counseling (see Chap. V) is the same as saying that he uses psychiatric standards, or has psychiatric reference group, to evaluate counseling. Were this so then almost all ministerial nonconformists would have to be classed as having a psychiatric reference group and almost all militant conformists as having a religious one. One type of evidence for the independence of the indicators is that only 56 per cent (151) of ministers with a religious reference group were also classified as militant conformsits and only 32 per cent (56) of the psychiatrists with a psychiatric reference group were classified as militant conformists.

There is, however, a more rigid way of dealing with the question of independence. A reference group has been defined as the group to which an individual looks for standards of evaluation. A nonconformist is one who departs from either the institutional means or the cultural goals of his group. Since we are studying a closed system, ministers, for example, who reject the cultural goals of religion for therapy replace them with the cultural goals of psychiatry. Does this overlap with taking psychiatry as a reference group? In order to obviate this difficulty, the association of reference group with innovation will be examined. The innovators are those nonconformists who reject the institutional means but not the cultural goals of their membership group. (For examples of indicators for innovation see Chap. V). If there is a lack of independence between "cultural goals" as used to determine variation and "standards of evaluation" as used to classify reference groups, then those classified as innovators should be those classified as taking their membership group as a reference group. That is, innovating ministers would all have religious and innovating psychiatrists would all have psychiatric reference groups. Table 15A examines this possibility.

Table 15A—Innovating Ministers and Psychiatrists According to Reference Groups

| | REFERENCE GROUP (in Per Cent) | | | |
	Psychiatric	Double	Religious	Total
Ministers	28	55	17	100 (254)
Psychiatrists	45	55	—	100 (18)

Eighty-three per cent (28% + 55%) of the innovating ministers (advocating religious goals for therapy) have a psychiatric or double reference group (evaluate their work, at least in part, on the basis of psychiatric standards). Similarly, 55 per cent of the innovating psychiatrists (those advocating psychiatric goals for their practice) have a double reference group (in part, base their evaluations on standards derived from religious groups). Measures for "cultural goals" and for "standards of evaluation" seem essentially independent.

10. On this distinction between "shame" and "guilt" see I. Piers and M. Singer, *Shame and Guilt.*

11. On this contrast between religious and scientific world views, see Ernst Cassirer, *The Philosophy of Symbolic Forms,* Vol. I.

12. Meaning goals may be either immediately sought or they may be considered the ultimate outcome of the achievement of more immediate instrumental goals. That is, adaptation to the environment may be considered

a precondition for coming to terms with problems of meaning. The instrumental goals may either be immediately sought or they may be considered an ultimate consequence of attaining more proximate meaning goals. That is, a sense of purpose or a clear value position may be considered prerequisite for instrumental adaptation. The present analysis is concerned with the type of ultimate goal advocated.

13. We may exclude from the table the individuals who pursue meaning goals through prior instrumental goals and those who pursue instrumental goals through prior meaning goals. This provides purer types who seek immediate meaning or instrumental goals. The differences become even more striking in this case, as can be seen in Table 16A. (Though there are few psychiatrists in this group, they are percentaged for comparison with the ministers.)

Table 16A—Proportion of Those with Various Reference Groups Seeking Immediate Meaning Rather than Immediate Instrumental Goals

Reference Groups	Immediate Meaning Goals (in Per Cent)	Total
Ministers		
Psychiatric	7	(53)
Double	39	(23)
Religious	98	(60)
Psychiatrists		
Psychiatric	7	(29)
Double	75	(8)
Religious	83	(6)

14. Table 16B shows the relation between reference groups and therapeutic goals among nonconformist variants.

15. See S. N. Eisenstadt, "Studies in Reference Group Behavior: Reference Norms and the Social Structure," *Human Relations*, pp. 191–216, especially p. 197.

16. See the remarks by Ernest Jones on efforts to prevent psychoanalysis from becoming a Jewish movement and on the relation between the Jewish Viennese and Aryan Swiss analysts in *The Life and Work of Sigmund Freud*, II, 33f., 69f., 148f.

17. Ethnic matching between physicians and patients has been noted by Jerome K. Meyers and Leslie Schaffer, "Social Stratification and Psychiatric Practice: A Study of an Outpatient Clinic," *American Sociological Review*, pp. 307–310; and Stanley Lieberson, "Ethnic Groups and the Practice of Medicine," *American Sociological Review*, pp. 542–549. Homogeneous grouping among physicians is studied by Hall, *op. cit.*, pp. 30–44. Selective

**Table 16B—Ministerial and Psychiatric Reference Groups
According to Whether Meaning or Instrumental Goals
are Advocated as an Outcome of Therapy Among
Nonconformist Variants**

Reference Groups	THERAPEUTIC GOALS (in Per Cent)			
	Meaning Goals	Meaning and Instrumental Goals	Instrumental Goals	Total
Ministers				
Psychiatric	22	17	61	100 (107)
Double	33	40	27	100 (164)
Religious	50	31	19	100 (48)
Psychiatrists				
Psychiatric	14	35	51	100 (31)
Double	28	50	22	100 (57)
Religious	50	30	20	100 (10)

recruiting of analytic candidates may result from differential institutionalization of analytic culture in the various sectors of society. See Charles Kadushin, "Social Distance Between Client and Professional," *American Journal of Sociology*, pp. 517–531. This phenomenon might also be related to the "transference" phenomenon. Transference, the projection of parental and other images upon the analyst, seems easier to establish when analyst and analysand have similar cultural backgrounds.

18. On the Jewishness of psychoanalysis and its relation to Protestant culture, see these recent works by social scientists: David Bakan, *Sigmund Freud and the Jewish Mystical Tradition*; Richard La Piere, *The Freudian Ethic: An Analysis of the Subversion of the American Character*; and Philip Rieff, *Freud: The Mind of the Moralist*.

19. This chrono-ecology is difficult to trace among Catholics since most of their writings in our sample are relatively recent. Part of the Catholic critique of psychoanalysis during its early stages did not qualify for inclusion in the religio-psychiatric movement.

20. This migration may be followed from the residences of the membership of the International Psychoanalytic Society, as published in the *International Journal of Psychoanalysis* during these years.

21. On this, see Freud's remarks in *Moses and Monotheism*, pp. 66ff.

22. Antipsychoanalytic Catholics tend to adhere to a Thomistic psychol-

ogy. Protestants and Jews with this attitude tend to be attracted to learning theory or to more somatically oriented psychiatric conceptions.

23. Some examples are included in the indicator citations of the following chapters.

24. The pull toward psychiatry, combined with a blocking of the possibility of going to psychiatrists, would not eventuate in the religio-psychiatric movements without some opportunity for ministers to learn psychology. In some measure, psychology may be learned from books. Ultimately, however, clinical practice requires personal counseling experience. An available structure to facilitate ministerial socialization is provided by psychiatrists who include among them a number of Jewish analysts. This should be of interest to students of the history of ideas as a latter-day instance of reciprocal influences of Judaism and Christianity.

25. See, for example, Gerald Gurin, Joseph Veroff, and Sheila Feld, *Americans View Their Mental Health*, pp. 334ff.; and Leo Srole *et al.*, *Mental Health in the Metropolis*, pp. 317ff.

26. See tabulations on education and interest in psychiatry in Gurin, Veroff, and Feld, *loc. cit.*; and Srole *et al.*, *loc. cit.*

27. Richard A. Cloward, "Illegitimate Means, Anomie, and Deviant Behavior," *American Sociological Review*, pp. 164–176; Edward H. Sutherland (ed.), *The Professional Thief.*

28. George C. Homans, *The Human Group.*

29. This notion has been referred to as "status congruency," and "rank consistency." When the ranks are not "equilibrated," the individual is subjected to strain. See, for example, Gerhard Lenski, "Status Crystallization: A Nonvertical Dimension of Social Status," *American Sociological Review*, pp. 405–413.

30. The argument is based on the assumption that all the ministers are highly educated. Actually, the various denominations differ in the proportion of ministers with high education. Examining the relation in Table 21 only for those holding the doctorate, the finding remains essentially the same. (See Table 10, page 43.)

The findings are clearer still with Congregationalists separated from Presbyterians and Lutherans from Methodists and with form of church polity held constant. Thus, among those with an episcopal polity, the proportions of ministers with a psychiatric reference group are Episcopalians 17 per cent, Lutherans 29 per cent (14) and Methodists 63 per cent (40). Among those with a congregational polity we have Congregationalists 11 per cent (28), Presbyterians 26 per cent (39), and Baptists 50 per cent.

31. The "status sequence" leading to a present status may differ among status occupants. See Robert K. Merton, *Social Theory and Social Structure*, pp. 368ff.

32. On the general problem of status sets, see *ibid*. For this example see W. W. Burchard, "Role Conflicts of Military Chaplains," *American Sociological Review*, pp. 528–535.

33. These questionnaire responses probably do not adequately reflect premedical majors for the psychiatrists. Personal acquaintance with psychiatrists writing on religion and psychiatry provides the impression that they are more likely than other psychiatrists and considerably more likely than physicians in general to have studied philosophy or the humanities before entering medical school.

Chapter IV

A Changing Counseling Relationship

OUR INTEREST in institutional variation arises, in part, from an assumption that it influences the way a pastor counsels his parishioner or a psychiatrist his patient. We turn now to an analysis of the meaning of the content of the counseling procedures for the relationship of a therapist to his client. The procedures with which we are concerned are given by the norms which guide this relation.

An analysis of counseling norms is a step toward answering a poignant question. Does it matter whether an individual presents his problem to a minister or to a psychiatrist? Do the norms mediating these counseling relationships differ, or does the difference reside only in their institutional settings? A description of counseling norms is an aid in answering still another question. Does the counseling advocated by ministers and psychiatrists in the religio-psychiatric movement differ from that advocated by their nonparticipating colleagues? If so, how does it differ?

We shall classify norms in a relatively generic fashion, since it would be endlessly complicated to compare norms for many concrete counseling situations. This chapter presents a four-fold classification of norms and some examples of indicators used to categorize items according to their author's advocacy of these norms. The distribution of each counseling norm among nonconformist and militant conformist ministers and psychiatrists will be presented and discussed briefly. The chapter concludes with a discussion of two principal types of counseling relationships based on the clustering of these norms.

The next chapter extends this discussion by attempting to show that departure from traditional norms in the counseling role is correlative with the broader institutional variation. The militant conformist-nonconformist dichotomy will be extended by a typology of institutional nonconformists. This correspondence of general institutional with role variation will make it unnecessary for us to account separately for the social conditions underlying the latter. Changes in counseling orientations would presumably be related to the same kinds of factors as underlie institutional variation.

COUNSELING NORMS OF THE "IDEAL TYPICAL" MINISTER AND PSYCHIATRIST

Indicators for Counseling Norms

Change must be measured with reference to an initial base line. In the case of normative change, such a base line may be constructed conceptually. For example, to compare empirical political states one could begin by imaging an "ideal type" of state.[1] This "ideal" state might be defined as, among other things, a political organization which monopolizes the means of violence in a territory. No existing state ever controls all means of violence in its territory. However, the extent to which several empirical states depart from this "ideal" of complete control may be measured and this measure used to assess them relative to one another. Empirical states could be compared on several such relevant dimensions either taken separately or as a pattern.

In this way the norms expected to guide the relationship between a psychiatrist and his patient, and that between a pastor and his counselee may be "ideally" conceptualized on the basis of norms general to the medical and religious institutions respectively. The referent of the "ideal" conceptualization might not exist in pure form. We ask how a "typical minister" and a "typical psychiatrist" would be expected to behave and state the extremes of the normative trends.

"Ideal types" will be constructed with the Protestant minister and the analytically-oriented psychiatrist in mind. The norms which constitute this "ideal type" will be described in terms of Parsons' "pattern variables."[2] The "pattern variables" represent norms guiding a set of five dichotomous choices of an actor orienting his role

partner. The pattern formed of these five decisions characterizes
the role.[3] Each pair of "pattern variables" will be defined and the
"ideal type" minister and psychiatrist counseling norms expressed
in terms of it.

Norms of Doing and Being

Should an actor orient to another person in terms of an inherent
quality possessed by that person, or in terms of what the person
does, that is, the functions he performs in that or some other
relationship? That is the *quality-performance* dilemma. The King
of England, for example, assumes his throne on the basis of an
inherent quality—royal birth. His performance may characterize
him as a good or bad king, but up to a point, it is not relevant to
his legitimacy. The right to be a teacher, on the other hand, is
achieved through performances attested to by an academic degree.
In American society the inherent qualities of sex, religion, and race
induce controversy when they are considered relevant criteria for
teacher selection.

The ministerial role is not assumed directly on the basis of the
incumbent's training or performance, but consequent to his "call,"
a *quality* inherent in his being.[4] In counseling he is expected to
make this quality or "charisma" available to the parishioner who
may or may not avail himself of it. The psychiatrist assumes his
role following certain academic *performances*. This orientation is
generalized to the counseling relationship in his expectation of
cooperative performances from his patient, which, if not forth-
coming on a conscious level, become reason for terminating the
relationship.

An author was classified as advocating a performance orientation if he required that the therapist or patient actively follow
procedures in counseling. For example, Jeshaia Schnitzer says it is
the responsibility of the spiritual leader to apply techniques in
helping people solve their own problems (1129). F. S. M. Bennett
calls upon ministers to make use of faith (90). Russell Dicks lists
attentive listening as a technique of the counselor (340). William
Hulme advises the counselor to give the troubled soul an incentive
to continue talking by indicating that he has been understood
(616).

The patient may be expected to be the active one in the

counseling. Lewis Sherrill expresses a basis for this in reminding the individual that responsibility for the solution of his conflict lies within himself (1155). Lawrence Kubie states that psychoanalysis demands confidence in the analyst and intellectual willingness to cooperate and to produce material freely and honestly (741). William Rogers would have a bereaved person repeat the story of his loss time after time (1093). Glenn Clark describes seven baths of immersion to health: washing outer skin, washing inner skin, washing blood vessels with exercise, washing lungs with fresh air, and washing emotions, mind, and soul (268). John Gasson recommends the spiritual exercises of St. Ignatius in retreat (453). The patient may be expected to act instrumentally upon the environment or upon himself. Otto Riecker says repentance must be supplemented by restitution to the people who have been wronged (1076). Fritz Kunkel speaks of eradicating the distinction between the conscious and the unconscious through confession (744).

Several transitional positions between the performance and quality orientations are classified as quality norms. A performance, for example, may be advocated because it leads to a quality. According to Hugh Crichton-Miller, if a person chooses to make an adjustment in the right way, spiritual resources are available to him (265). Cure may reside in an inherent quality which may or may not be manifested. Carroll Wise states that it is not what the counselor does to or for the counselee but it is what happens between them that is important (1313). Reuel Howe writes of the Holy Spirit of God bringing the gift of *agape* (598). The quality may be considered inherent in the situation. Performance of either patient or therapist would be considered irrelevant to the presence of the quality and to the cure. Carl Gustav Jung refers to Rudolph Otto's concept of "numinosum" which seizes and controls the human subject who is always its victim rather than its creator (662). Maryse Choisy concurs that God comes to us when He pleases (260).

The "ideal type" minister is expected to advocate a quality and the "ideal type" psychiatrist a performance orientation. Table 22 shows the empirically observed distribution of militant and non-conformist ministers and psychiatrists on this dimension.

Over half of the militant conformist ministers do not correspond to their postulated "ideal type." This may reflect the strong

Table 22—Militant Conformist and Nonconformist Ministers and Psychiatrists Who Advocate Quality Rather than Performance Orientations for Counseling[a]

Variant Types	MINISTERS		PSYCHIATRISTS	
	Per Cent	Number	Per Cent	Number
Militant Conformist	43	82	10	19
Nonconformist	24	337	11	82

a. This and the following tables are to be read as stating, for example, that 43 per cent of 82 militant conformist ministers advocate a quality orientation while the remaining 57 per cent of these 82 advocate a performance orientation.

bias in favor of a performance orientation in their cultural context. Some religions may be so pervaded by a performance orientation that the quality characterization is not appropriate for them. Performance is relatively more significant in Judaism with its emphasis on the "good deed" and Catholicism with its "acts of penance" than it is in Protestantism. Even in Protestantism the performance orientation intrudes in the acts of faith healers and in some recent instrumental interpretations of religious worship. Though nonconformist ministers adopt psychiatric performance norms, nonconformist psychiatrists do not move in the quality direction. In passing from militant conformists to nonconformists, the proportion of ministers and psychiatrists differing in orientation is reduced from 33 per cent to 13 per cent.[5] This is almost entirely due to change in the orientations of ministers.

Norms of Impulse and Restraint

The second dilemma concerns the actor's control of the motivational energy with which he cathects or invests his object of orientation. If an actor is expected to release his impulse and gain immediate gratification from the relation, the orientation is termed *affective*. The counselor might become emotionally involved with the patient. The relationship tends to be an end in itself. If an actor is expected to inhibit his feeling in favor of delayed gratification, the orientation is termed *affective-neutrality*. Counselor and patient remain in detached objectivity. The relationship tends to be considered in the context of other relationships. A love relationship is guided by affective norms—emotional expression is legitimately expected. A business relationship is characterized by affective-neutrality—the salesman is not expected to be emotionally involved with his customer.

The minister, "ideal typically," is expected to be *affectively* oriented, to take a personal and emotional interest in his parishioner. The psychiatrist, on the other hand, is expected to be *affectively neutral,* not to become emotionally involved with his patient. Control of his countertransference, his feelings for the patient, frees him to elect procedures in terms of long-range benefits to the patient.

Items were classified as advocating affective norms if they recognized an emotional involvement even though it was based on the counselor's office or status. Edgar Jackson, for example, recommends that preachers speak from a belief in the meaning and power of God's healing love (625). Authors were also classed as affective if they advocate expressing love personally even though passively. Don Shaw, a chaplain in a mental hospital, says he provides the ministry of assurance when he shows that God loves the mentally ill as they are (1148). Others recommend more active loving. Oskar Pfister asks that mercy be shown in response to atonement (1023). Glenn Clark phrases the requirement as creative love (268). Wesley Schrader describes how he becomes emotionally and spiritually involved with people whom he helps (1157).

Items were classified as supporting an affectively neutral position if, for example, they call for observing the patient to gain insight into him. Edith Weigert looks at unconscious impulses as something to be investigated (1282). R. Hudson looks to the psychiatrist for diagnosis and case management (606). A second type of affective neutrality recommends active control by the therapist over his own and the patients' emotions. Seward Hiltner warns the counselor against the sort of empathy that leads him to become so emotionally involved that he loses perspective (565). Sandor Rado advises against responding to the depressed with kindness (1062). A third type of item classed as supporting affective neutrality refers to emotional control by the patient as a therapeutic outcome. G. A. Ellard says that both sanity and sanctity require control of the emotions and rational choice (390). Caroll Wise says that postponing present satisfaction for long-range goals is a rediscovered Biblical insight (1316).

"Ideal typically" ministers would be expected to advocate affective and psychiatrists affectively neutral norms for counseling. Table 23 shows the distribution of these norms for our sample for militant and nonconformist ministers and psychiatrists.

Table 23—Nonconformist and Militant Conformist Ministers and Psychiatrists Who Advocate Affective Rather than Affectively Neutral Orientations Toward Counselees

Variant Types	MINISTERS		PSYCHIATRISTS	
	Per Cent	Number	Per Cent	Number
Militant Conformist	41	61	—	19
Nonconformist	22	285	13	81

Almost half of the militant conformist ministers are affectively oriented. All of the militant conformist psychiatrists are affectively neutral. In the case of the psychiatrists, the actual situation coincides with the "ideal type." The fact that 59 per cent of the militant conformist ministers do not conform to the "ideal" pattern may reflect the influence of the predominantly affectively neutral culture of industrial society upon religion in general and upon this sample in particular. Nonconformist ministers depart from the ideal in the affectively neutral direction and nonconformist psychiatrists move slightly toward an affective orientation. The proportions of militant conformist ministers and psychiatrists having the same orientation differs by 41 per cent. Nonconformist ministers and psychiatrists differ by but 9 per cent. This suggests a convergence in the advocated orientation to clients concurrent with the emergence of nonconformism.

Norms of Lawful and Personal Relations

The third problem is whether the actor is to evaluate his object of orientation by standards applicable to all objects possessing similar attributes, or whether the object is to be judged in terms of its relationship to the actor. The first is termed a *universalistic* and the second a *particularistic* orientation. A teacher is expected to be universalistically oriented toward his pupils. He is enjoined against favoritism in being expected to treat all according to the same rule.[6] A parent, on the other hand, is expected to assume a particularistic orientation toward his child with respect to nonfamily members. While the child may be evaluated as a criminal or a madman by the community, the parent is expected to consider their common family membership as primary.

The minister's relation to his parishioner tends "ideal typically" to be *particularistic*. He is expected to relate in singular individuality to each parishioner who, in turn, expects to be treated as a special case by virtue of his relation to the minister or their common membership in the church. The prisoner may seek solace from the prison chaplain despite his sin in the eyes of the community. The psychiatrist is expected to follow *universalistic* norms. One patient may present an instance of paranoia and another a case of hebephrenia. In each instance the psychiatrist is guided by medical principles for treating cases of a similar nature under similar conditions.

Classified as advocating a universalistic orientation in counseling were authors who indicate the need for general rules or who expound a principle for deriving them. Hugo Munsterberg writes that the physician diagnoses and treats the patient in terms of the general standards of medicine (931). Carl Gustav Jung writes of replacing immediate experience by suitable symbols (662). Robert Brinkman would acquaint the student with a large number of patients (186). J. Berkeley Gordon would base norms on the authority of the priest (505). Louis Beirnaert takes his cue from the Pope (80) and Charles Kemp prefers to depend on experimentation to reveal certain principles (687). Others specify the character of the standards. Thomas Moore selects standards for their effectiveness in handling problems in the field of mental hygiene (908). William Hulme is concerned with rules fixing suitable hours and places for counseling (612).

A quasi-particularistic orientation is evolved by individualizing the universal or by maintaining a universalistic relation in a particularistic context. For example, J. R. Oliver asks priests to learn the basic syndromes but nevertheless to see people as individuals (999). Closer to a true particularism are notions of an abstract relatedness such as the relationship of faith or communion. Oliver Huckel, for example, writes of the need for faith and prayer (600). Kenneth Irving Cleator speaks of man reuniting with God (273). Paul Tillich conceives of a state of being grasped by the ultimate (1231). A mediated communion with God may be expressed in transcendental terms. Otto Riecker writes of the sinner relating to God through his confessor (1076). In more immanent terms, George Pratt sees the clergyman providing a link to the outside world for the hospital patient (1051). The "personal" relationship may be expressed in role terms. C. J. O. Corcoran says that it is the hope and confidence in the confessor that effects the cure (293). In pure particularism, the role notion disappears. Hans Prinzhorn describes one's opening himself to another person (1054). David Roberts reflects on a continual return to the I-Thou relationship (1085).

The "ideal type" minister is expected to be particularistically and the "ideal type" psychiatrist universalistically oriented. What are the empirically observed orientations in this sample? Table 24 classifies militant conformist and nonconformist ministers and psychiatrists according to whether they call for a universalistic or a particularistic orientation in counseling.

Table 24—Militant Conformist and Nonconformist Ministers and Psychiatrists Who Advocate Particularistic Orientations Toward Counselees

| | MINISTERS | | PSYCHIATRISTS | |
Variant Types	Per Cent	Number	Per Cent	Number
Militant Conformist	67	64	—	18
Nonconformist	45	279	26	85

All of the militant conformist psychiatrists correspond to the universalistic "ideal type." Two-thirds of the militant conformist ministers correspond to their particularistic "ideal type." The departure of as much as a third of the ministers from the "ideal typical" particularistic orientation may be related to the universalistic culture in which these authors find themselves. Nonconformist ministers depart substantially more from their "ideal type" in the direction of psychiatric norms and nonconformist psychiatrists move somewhat in the religious direction by adopting particularistic norms. In moving from militant conformism to nonconformism the proportions of ministers and psychiatrists differing in their therapeutic orientations are reduced from 67 per cent to 19 per cent. This is again evidence of convergence in the norms advocated for governing the relationship between therapist and patient concomitant with the emergence of institutional nonconformism.

Norms of Inclusiveness and Exclusiveness of Concern

A fourth choice concerns the scope of the actor's interest in the object of orientation. Should an actor be involved with a broad range of the attributes of or relationships with another actor or should he limit his concern to a few aspects or relationships? In the former case, the orientation is termed *diffuse,* in the latter, *specific.*[7] Norms governing the relation of a parent to his child are diffuse in that the parent is interested in the child's work at school, the friends he keeps, and the church he attends. Norms guiding the relation of a merchant to a customer are specific. Only behavior in the segmented merchant-customer relation is relevant.[8]

Traditional ministerial roles are *diffuse.* A minister's relation to his parishioners is not limited to a single segmented role. He is interested in his parishioner as a father, as a congregant, and as a counselee. Norms guiding the psychiatrist-patient relation are *specific.* The psychiatrist's interest is confined to the individual's status as a patient. He may inquire into the patient's other statuses only insofar as they are relevant to his progress as a patient.[9]

Indicators of a diffuse orientation include, for example, Joseph Fletcher's recommendation of a "multiple field" where the clinical pastoral student can have many types of meetings with parishioners (413). Carroll A. Wise relates to pastoral candidates as a researcher, teacher, supervisor, and counselor for problems of personal adjustment (1311).

Indicators for specificity are illustrated by Ernest Bruder's belief that a chaplain has an advantage in not being involved in parish relationships (197). Rollin Fairbanks advises counselors to visit patients only in the role of a clergyman to avoid confusion (400). Joseph Mullen, a psychiatrist, asks the confessor to limit his work to cases of genuine temptation and leave the outpourings of morbid obsession to the psychiatrist (928).

"Ideal typically," the ministerial orientation has been posited as diffuse and the psychiatric as specific. The empirically observed distribution of ministers and psychiatrists on this dimension in our sample is shown in Table 25.

Consistent with the "ideal type," almost all ministers in this sample advocate a diffuse orientation. Better than three-fourths of

Table 25—Militant Conformist and Nonconformist Ministers and Psychiatrists Who Advocate Diffuse Rather than Specific Orientations Toward the Counselee

| | MINISTERS | | PSYCHIATRISTS | |
Variant Types	Per Cent	Number	Per Cent	Number
Militant Conformists	87	68	23	22
Nonconformists	85	317	44	89

the militant conformist psychiatrists advocate a specific one. Non-conformist ministers do not differ from the militant conformists on this dimension. For psychiatrists, however, nonconformism is accompanied by an increase in the proportion advocating a diffuse orientation. The difference between the proportions of militant conformist ministers and psychiatrists with the same pattern variable here is 64 per cent. The respective nonconformists differ by only 41 per cent. In this case the change is due to a shift in the position of the psychiatrists. Again, institutional variation is accompanied by a convergence in the type of counseling norms advocated.

Norms of Responsibility and the Collectivity

The fifth problem is termed the *self-collectivity* dilemma. It hinges upon identity, or lack of it, between the goals of two actors. If ego grants primacy to realization of alter's goals, the relationship may be said to be collectivity-oriented. Ego's and alter's goals overlap as both strive to realize alter's objectives. If the goals of alter are but a means or condition for the attainment of the ego's goals, the action may be said to be self-oriented. An entrepreneur is expected to be self-oriented, to orient himself to a situation in terms of profit opportunities. Customer satisfaction is but a means to the attainment of this goal. The storekeeper who distributes his wares freely to the poor is a variant. Norms guiding ministerial behavior are *collectivity-oriented*. The minister is expected to be more interested in the welfare of his flock than in his salary. A physician is also expected to be *collectivity-oriented*. If treatment is made contingent upon the fee, he will be regarded with opprobrium by the community. This attitude suggests that a norm is being violated.[10]

TWO COUNSELING RELATIONSHIPS: THE INTEGRATIVE AND THE INSTRUMENTAL

The observed orientations of the writers on religion and psychiatry, especially those of the militant conformists, are in the direction of the "ideal types." Relative to psychiatrists, ministers are more likely to advocate affective, particularistic, quality, and diffuse counseling norms. Relative to ministers, psychiatrists tend to be guided by norms of affective neutrality, universalism, performance, and specificity. These two clusters of norms define the

contrasting therapeutic approaches of the traditional minister and
the traditional psychiatrist. The ministerial approach may be termed
integrative and the psychiatric approach *instrumental* therapy.

What sort of client expectations might these approaches engender? A parishioner presenting his problem to an affectively
oriented minister would expect a sympathetic response. Since an
affective norm does not in itself define the quality of the feeling
released, the parishioner would not be assured against a hostile
response. The content of the statements classed as affective, however, suggest that manifest hostility would be unlikely. The particularistic orientation would lead the parishioner to anticipate a
personal relationship rather than a diagnosis. The instrument of
therapy would be the person of the minister rather than therapeutic
technique applied in accord with specialized knowledge. The quality
element releases the relationship from dependence upon the responses of the parishioner. The minister would be expected to be
continuously ready to offer himself and his help. Guided by diffuse
norms, he would not be expected to limit his availability to a
counseling hour. He might work with the parishioner through his
Sunday sermon and pastoral calls, and might even meet with other
members of the parishioner's family. These norms united with a
collectivity orientation imply that, if necessary, the minister would
be prepared to sacrifice himself for his parishioner. Both minister
and parishioner would be expected to change in their encounter.[11]

A psychiatrist's patient would expect the affectively neutral
orientation to be expressed as a "detached concern"[12] for him and
his problem. Based on the universalistic norm, the patient would
expect the psychiatrist to seek objective information by which to
diagnose his condition. With the syndrome defined, a performance
orientation would require implementation of the therapeutic procedures indicated by psychiatric theory and practice for dealing
with this type of condition. The patient, for his part, would expect
to actively cooperate by following the doctor's "orders." The psychiatrist's manipulation of rewards, especially his attitude of approval and disapproval, help the patient learn appropriate behaviors.
Norms of specificity make the therapeutic a special relationship
limited to the therapeutic hour, and distinct from the patient's and
the psychiatrist's usual social network. A collectivity orientation
requires the psychiatrist to be concerned more with the patient's

recovery than with remuneration. The collectivity orientation in this universalistic context may require that for the patient's recovery the psychiatrist be prepared to sacrifice time and money as objective and nonpersonal rewards. In this context norms of specificity limit, for example, the abuse he need accept from the patient and the extent of his financial sacrifice. Change is expected in instrumental therapy as a result of the application of empirically based knowledge. Change in the patient would, by far, exceed that in the therapist.[13]

These "ideal type" descriptions of integrative and instrumental therapy are closest to what the militant conformists in our sample advocate. Nonconformist ministers and psychiatrists tend to differ from the "ideal" on one or more dimensions.[14] As nonconformist ministers and psychiatrists diverge from their respective "ideal types," they seem to converge with one another, the ministers accepting some psychiatric norms and the psychiatrists accepting some ministerial ones. As part of the transition, one minister might combine norms of diffuseness with norms of universalism, meeting his parishioner in several contexts but guiding his relation in terms of psychological principles or, if he retained religious norms, of "eternal verities" applicable in all similar situations. A psychiatrist might combine specificity and affectivity, restricting the meetings to the therapeutic hours but in those hours expressing sympathy for the patient or implementing "direct analysis" through impulsive action in a focused relationship instead of detachedly diagnosing the problem.[15]

At this point it would be appropriate to analyze forces which induce ministers and psychiatrists to change their counseling orientations.[16] We could inquire into the factors leading ministers to move from a particularistic to a universalistic orientation, or influencing psychiatrists to abandon affective neutrality and adopt an affective orientation. We have already found that the shift in counseling norms corresponds with the shift from institutional militant conformity to institutional nonconformity. Consequently, in lieu of approaching this question of norms in isolation, in the following chapter we will try to establish in a more precise fashion that change in the norms guiding interaction in the counseling role and variation at the institutional level are parallel phenomena and, therefore, need not be accounted for independently. This approach not only avoids a recapitulation of the argument regarding the emergence of variant types, but also demonstrates the pervasiveness of the process underlying variation.

NOTES

1. A discussion on the use of the "ideal type" construct will be found in Max Weber, *The Methodology of the Social Sciences*, pp. 89ff.; and in Talcott Parsons, *The Structure of Social Action*, pp. 601ff.

2. For a description of the pattern variables, see Talcott Parsons, *The Social System*, pp. 58ff. A critical exchange concerning the pattern variables is found in Robert Dubin, "Parsons' Actor: Continuities in Social Theory," *American Sociological Review*, pp. 467–482.

3. With two choices on each of the five variables, thirty-two patterns are theoretically possible. Empirically, however, some of the combinations are incompatible. They produce unstable patterns which do not persist. Parsons describes four significant clusters which develop in meeting the functional exigencies of social and personality systems in "phase movement in a Theory of Action," *Working Papers in the Theory of Action*, Talcott Parsons, Robert F. Bales, and Edward A. Shils (eds.).

4. See the discussion on charisma and religious leadership in Joachim Wach, *op. cit.*, pp. 337ff. Practically speaking, American middle and upper class churches are tending to require performances as prerequisites for ordination.

5. A perfect fit between the "ideal type" and the empirical observation should not be anticipated. That the empirical contrast between ministers and psychiatrists corresponds to the "ideally" posited contrast justifies using the "ideal type" as a heuristic for comparing them. Where a discrepancy between actual and "ideal" is such, however, so that not even half of a population conforms to the "ideal type," the usefulness of that particular ideal concept for characterizing the population may be questioned. Part of the discrepancy here may be accounted for in terms of the transitional character of some of the indicators used above. This possibility may be examined.

The performance category here includes both instrumental performances, oriented toward environmental manipulation, and expressive performances, oriented toward control of the self. Only the former are "true" performance orientations. The expressive performances are acts of self-control which

**Table 22A—Militant Conformist Ministers and Psychiatrists
According to Whether Their Performance Orientation
is Instrumental or Expressive**

| | PERFORMANCE ORIENTATION (in Per Cent) | | Number |
	Instrumental	Expressive	
Militant Conformist Ministers	7	50	82
Militant Conformist Psychiatrists	85	5	19

appear overtly as states or qualities. Table 22A separates performances among militant conformists into the instrumental and expressive types.

Few of the militant conformist ministers but almost all the militant conformist psychiatrists are actually oriented in the instrumental or "true" performance direction. If the instrumental performances alone were considered, few militant conformist ministers or psychiatrists would be found to depart from their respective ideal types. The 50 per cent of the militant conformist ministers advocating expressive performances are but equivocally categorized as performance oriented. This more detailed analysis suggests that the discrepancy between the observed and "ideal types" is related more to a problem of what to place in a category than to error in conceptually defining the categories.

6. Universalism does not imply egalitarianism. Different students may receive different grades. The giving of the grades, however, must be based on the same rule.

7. In any concrete situation, diffuseness-specificity does not appear as an all-or-none affair. Complete diffuseness, in which the person is caught up in an "oceanic feeling" or a mystical oneness, is a polar extreme. On the other hand, facing a completely differentiated world is but a theoretical possibility. The question is whether a differentiated sector of concern to the actor shall be oriented to as a whole or shall be further differentiated.

8. The family relationships of the customer would be relatively unimportant for the merchant. The fact that the customer is a father would enter the picture only insofar as he becomes a potential buyer of children's clothes or as an extenuating circumstance explaining delay in paying his bill.

This dilemma of specificity-diffuseness is equally applicable to the organization of objects within the self. The reference there, however, is not to norms and values but to the internalized aspects of these norms and values. Internalized, they become foci of energy or motivation. What appears externally as an expectation that one behave in a certain way appears internally as a complementary need to behave in that way. The motive patterns may be diffuse or specific. In the parent-child relationship, the parent responds to the child with a broad spectrum of motives. In the case of the merchant-customer relationship, the customer only engages a small sector of the merchant's motivational interest.

9. The expected degree of personality involvement on the part of the actor is a corollary of these social expectations. The psychiatrist only becomes segmentally involved with the patient. In therapy his ego splits into experiencing and observing aspects. The patient's problems are not to intrude on the psychiatrist's other roles, such as his own family life. The minister, on the other hand, is expected to meet the parishioner with his "whole being." He cannot legitimately restrict the relationship to specific times and places.

10. Since both minister and psychiatrist are collectivity-oriented, this dichotomy will not be treated here. Below, however, reference will be made to the changed meaning of a collectivity orientation when it is embedded in otherwise different normative clusters.

11. This type of therapeutic relationship is described by Martin Buber, "Distance and Relation," *Psychiatry*, (1957). It is also illustrated in another context by Robert Freed Bales, "The Therapeutic Role of Alcoholics Anonymous as seen by a Sociologist," *Quarterly Journal of Studies in Alcohol*, pp. 267–278. These are "ideal type" expectations. The "real" situation diverges from them in varying degrees.

12. On this term see Robert K. Merton, G. G. Reader, and Patricia L. Kendall (eds.), *The Student Physician.*

13. This is the type of therapeutic or social control relationship described by Talcott Parsons, Robert F. Bales, *Family: Socialization and Interaction Process.*

14. Variation is measured in terms of departure from the norms institutionalied in a group. "Ministers" and "psychiatrists" constitute two different interaction groups. The ministerial, and to a lesser degree the psychiatric, interaction group is apt to be religiously homogeneous. This is pointed out, for example, by Gerhard Lenski, *The Religious Factor*, pp. 266ff. Behavior considered variant for a Catholic priest might not be considered so among rabbis. Separate base lines are needed for each faith (and, perhaps, for other subcommunities as well). The following table provides base lines in terms of distributions on each pattern variable for the entire sample of ministers and psychiatrists of each faith. Since the ministerial "ideal types," were constructed with the Protestants in mind, it is not surprising that they advocate norms closest to these ministerial "ideal types." Priests are more divergent and rabbis the most divergent (except in affectivity) from this type. Among psychiatrists the Jews are closest, the Catholics more divergent, and the Protestants most divergent from the psychiatric "ideal type." A rabbi advocating universalistic and performance norms

Table 25A—Proportion of Ministers and Psychiatrists of Each Faith According to the Counseling Norms they Advocate (Only One Pole of Each Pattern Variable Given)

Religions	Quality	Affectivity	Particularism	Diffuseness	Number
		COUNSELING NORMS (in Per Cent)			
Ministers					
Protestants	30[a]	30	53	93	249
Catholics	27	12	45	78	75
Jews	—	24	21	76	19
Psychiatrists					
Protestants	29	25	27	56	36
Catholics	11	13	19	36	29
Jews	5	12	6	43	17

a. These figures are to be read, "30 per cent of 249 Protestant ministers advocate quality norms while 70 per cent of these ministers advocate performance norms," etc. The numbers vary slightly for each pattern variable. Those given at the right of the table are modal.

would be less of a variant from his group than the Protestant minister would be from his group were he to advocate the same norms. On the other hand, a Jewish psychiatrist who advocates quality and particularistic norms would be more variant from his psychiatric co-religionists than a Protestant psychiatrist advocating these norms would be with respect to his co-religionists. It would be more exact for us to establish base lines for each geographic area and time period. The same behavior might be more or less variant at each time or place. We do not have enough cases to consider these relatively more exact base lines in the following analyses.

15. According to Talcott Parsons, in Parsons, Bales, and Shils, *op. cit.*, a social or personality system must solve four problems, which he denotes as the Adaptive, Goal Attainment, Integrative, and Pattern Maintenance problems. Each of the above therapeutic approaches focuses principally on one of these functional problems. Instrumental therapy, characteristic of psychiatrists, deals mainly with the Adaptive problem. Integrative therapy, characteristic of ministers, seems more concerned with system integration. The combination of specificity and affectivity, especially if it is also combined with performance and particularism, seems related to the Goal Attainment problem. The approach of John Rosen seems to border on this type. See his *Direct Analysis*. The combination of universalism and diffuseness, especially if it is also combined with affective neutrality and quality, seems to focus on the Pattern Maintenance problem. See the discussions of the "life theme" in Rollo May, Ernest Angel, and Henry F. Ellenberger (eds.), *Existence, A New Dimension in Psychiatry and Psychology*.

16. We are assuming that a given individual begins as a nonvariant conformist and becomes a variant nonconformist or militant conformist, and

that the counseling norms advocated by the militant conformist are the same as those of the nonvariant conformist. The data are actually drawn from several individuals at a single point in time who are more or less variant. As we discuss the problem of becoming variant in the following pages, the reader should remember this limitation.

Chapter V

The Correspondence of Institutional Variation and New Counseling Relationships

THREE SUBTYPES OF NONCONFORMIST MINISTERS AND PSYCHIATRISTS

OUR EARLIER DISCUSSION distinguished militant conformists from nonconformists in general. To correlate shifting counseling norms with the process of becoming a variant, three subtypes of nonconformist variants will be described.[1] Merton, it will be recalled, is concerned with variant behavior which emerges in response to a malintegration of culturally induced aspirations or cultural goals and the availability of effective and socially legitimate institutional norms or means for realizing these goals. A nonconformist variant adapts to his inability to attain his goals either by departing from his group's legitimate institutional means or rejecting its cultural goals or doing both of these.

Merton distinguishes five forms of adaptation, one conformist and four conconformist.[2] The conformist, faced with the malintegration of the culture and the social structure, persists in his attempt to achieve the cultural goals in the institutionally prescribed manner. Conformist ministers and psychiatrists do not appear in the present study because they tend to be indifferent to the relation between their institutions. In this sample the advocates of traditional means and goals tend to be militant conformists who are concerned enough to attack the nonconformists. The militant conformist is actually ambivalent toward the means and goals of his own group and, overreacting, holds to them tenaciously and assertively.[3]

Merton terms the nonconformist types innovators, ritualists, rebels, or retreatists according to the way they combine acceptance or rejection of the goals or means of their institutions. Participants in the religio-psychiatric movement who reject means or goals of their membership group substitute those of the nonmembership group.[4] Innovators adhere to the cultural goals of their own group, but adapt the other group's means for attaining these goals. Ritualists relinquish the goal to which they have been taught to aspire in favor of a goal proposed by the nonmembership group, but retain the means for goal attainment traditional in their own group. Rebels, like militant conformists, are ambivalent about both goals and means of their own group. Unlike militant conformists, however, rebels choose to respond by substituting both the goals and the means of the nonmembership group.[5]

Classification of the items according to whether their authors are innovators, ritualists, or rebels rests upon whether the terms by which they refer to counseling means or goals are selected from psychological or religious discourse. Each subtype of variant is defined by the relation between the author's recommended means and goals and those institutionalized in his membership group. A minister citing "salvation" as his goal would not necessarily be a nonconformist variant. A psychiatrist with this as his counseling goal would be. The following are a few examples of indicators used to classify the ministerial and psychiatric authors as ritualists, innovators, and rebels.

Ritualist Ministers: Substituting Psychiatric Goals

Ministerial ritualists advocate traditional religious practices in the pastoral relationship, but these appear in the service of goals phrased in mental health language.[6] Their stated psychiatric goals fall into four groups. The first type of goal is to increase rationality. Edmond Rochedieu, for example, aims for the "conquest of the personality" through cognitive control (1087). A second goal is to enable the parishioner to accomplish concrete tasks or to meet psychological need. W. E. Hulme, for instance, believes the satisfaction of human psychological needs is the duty of religion (611). A third type of goal concerns the parishioner's social adjustment. Carrol Wise describes the function of religion in producing healthy relationships (1310). Samuel Southard sees the social as an intermediate goal in describing how sectarianism prevents psychoses by redeeming isolated individuals socially (1174). A fourth type of goal is to enable the parishioner to attain psychological health, relief from anxiety, or physical health. Leslie Weatherhead contends that religion relieves mental disharmony (1278). The term anxiety, though appearing in theological literature in the nineteenth century, re-enters the pastoral field through psychology. Paul Johnson (643) and others write of religion relieving anxiety in the psychological sense (500, 925, 954, 978). Such terms as "cognitive control," "psychological needs," "psychoses," and "mental disharmony" belong to psychological rather than religious discourse. The means of ritualist ministers are religious, but they tend, more than those of other ministers, to have an instrumental character.[7]

Innovating Ministers: Substituting Psychiatric Means

Innovating ministers advocate the techniques of psychiatry to achieve the goals of religion. Four types of statements appear in the discussion of techniques. The first type makes general reference to psychological techniques. K. J. Saunders writes of relating the adventures of the Christian soul to physiological processes and applying the inductive methods of science to religion (1116). R. Dalbiez believes that methods of psychiatry could be useful in aiding priests in detecting psychotic, and therefore not responsible, parishioners (313). A second group of statements recommends selection of specific techniques. Louis Beirnaert says the Pope condemned the pansexualists but that Catholics may use the nonpansexual methods of Adler, Jung, Horney, and Rogers (80). A third group of innovators discusses the procedures themselves. Seward Hiltner would probe underlying feelings rather than urge parishioners to action (570). Paul Irion discusses "working through" to release the emotion of grief (623). A fourth type of innovator is concerned with techniques for ordering the counselor-counselee relation. Robert Leslie discusses the role of the minister in group therapy (765). The religious goals which innovating ministers seek are influenced by these techniques.[8]

Rebellious Ministers: New Psychiatric Goals
To Accompany New Means

Rebellious ministers reformulate both the techniques and the goals of counseling in psychological terms. They do not entirely abandon the goals of religion, but change them more drastically than do the ritualists. Their psychological means, however, are essentially those of the innovating ministers and so there is no need to repeat examples of them. Rebels may be classified according to the nature of the goal change.

Religious goals may be reconceptualized psychologically. Mark May defines religious conscience as an internalization of the authority of God over man (836). Seward Hiltner formulates Freud's "constructive theology." It consists in the awareness that life is truth, human freedom comes through an awareness of determinism, and bringing together conscience, impulse, and reason (575). Some ministers psychologize only certain religious activities. Johannes Neumann considers piety a matter of the emotions (950). E. S. Waterhouse thinks of prayer, conversion, guilt, and temptation in psychological terms (1271). A few ministers would have the pastor pursue the goals involved in nontraditional roles. Ralph Lankler calls upon ministers to cooperate with psychiatrists in setting up local clinics (749). Ministers are summoned to research roles. Paul Maves studies older people (834a). John Thomas evaluates clinical pastoral training (1226). Ministers who replace rather than merely reconceptualize religious goals are more deeply alienated. Clifford Barbour observes that the New Psychology with its deterministic view is questioning the Christian doctrine of sin. If determinism is true, the church must accept it even at the expense of the most cherished ecclesiastical dogma (55).

Ritualist Psychiatrists: Substituting Religious Goals

Ritualist psychiatrists retain the techniques of psychiatry while reformulating psychotherapeutic goals in religious terms. One type of religious goal is attaining general spiritual orientation. Karl Stern seeks to adapt the psychological insights of Freud to a spiritual philosophy of man (1190). J. R. Cavanaugh, a Catholic psychiatrist, attacks psychiatry based on materialism and advocates consideration of the existence of the spiritual nature of God, will, and moral duties (256). Moral and spiritual development of the individual is a second type of goal of psychiatric ritualists. Wladimir G. Eliasberg writes that psychiatry can reveal the type of religious instruction which can lead to moral development (384). A third group of ritualistic psychiatrists suggests that psychiatry enter more directly into religious activities. Joseph Mullen suggests that psychiatry could assist the confessor by illuminating problems of scrupulosity (928). A fourth

type of goal consists of attaining a religious relationship. Rhaban
Liertz contends that the image of the physical father projected into
a psychological conception of God can distort the relation of man to
God. Treatment can improve this relation (782). John Blake believes that therapy means restoring a relationship to some exalted
power outside of man (122).

Innovating Psychiatrists: Substituting Religious Means

Innovating psychiatrists describe their means in religious terms
and their goals in psychiatric ones. Few psychiatrists directly introduce religious ceremonials into their practice. Rather, they recommend cooperation with clergymen or the participation of their patients in religious rites. Some statements of innovating psychiatrists
refer to religion in general as a therapeutic means. Thomas Moore
says religious experience gives strength, conviction, and confidence,
and has a mental hygiene value peculiarly its own (909). Robert
Felix writes of the contribution of religious faith to maintaining
mental and emotional health (410). Specific religious means are
suggested by some psychiatrists. Albert Stunkard lists aspects of
Zen he considers important for psychiatry: meditation, brief dia-
logue between master and disciple, and presentation of a problem
insolvable on an intellectual level as a basis for meditation (1212).
Some innovating psychiatrists invite clergymen to aid them in
therapeutic activity. J. Berkeley Gordon looks to the authority of the
religious leader to bring to light painful and confidential material
needed by the therapist (505).

Rebellious Psychiatrists: New Religious Means
To Accompany New Goals

Rebel psychiatrists introduce both religious goals and means
into therapy. Their religious goals are not very different from those
mentioned by ritualists. Their means, however, do differ a bit from
those of the innovators, so these will be illustrated here. Three types
of statements refer to new religious means. The first considers the
therapeutic experience as basically religious. W. Bernet holds that
Jung's description of the archetype verges upon a transparent epiph-
any of the "other worldly" (102). Others, like Smiley Blanton,
refer to specific religious means. Writing jointly with Norman
Vincent Peale, he says man's difficulties will be answered if he im-

merses himself in the Bible. For every problem, faith is the answer (124). Carl Gustav Jung traces neuroses to lack of an adequate world view and says that only religion can supply a viable world view (666). Religion itself may be treated as a technique. Thomas Moore looks to the ideal of duty to block the lower outlets of the libido aiding the individual to arrive at religious sublimation. This is conscience triumphing in the conquest of the libido (913).

Distribution of Variant Subtypes

Differences in the pressures to which individuals are exposed and in the constraints the institution places upon them would affect the relative proportion of the variant subtypes. This sample, by definition, consists almost entirely of variants; but, as shown in Table 26, ministers and psychiatrists differ in the subtype of variant

Table 26—Distribution of Militant Conformist and Nonconformist Variant Types among Ministers and Psychiatrists

	Militant Conformists	NONCONFORMIST VARIANT TYPES (in Per Cent)			
		Innovators	Ritualists	Rebels	Number
Ministers	21	55	15	9	509
Psychiatrists	16	14	43	27	141

adaptation preferred. Innovation for ministers and ritualism for psychiatrists are the most common subtypes of variant adaptation. This may be understood in terms of the foci of social control in these two institutions and in terms of the influence each institution exerts on the other. An institution will exert the strongest censure to control variation from those elements it considers most fundamental. Other considerations being equal, an individual under stress may well choose the form of variation which brings the least censure. As discussed in Chapter III, religion emphasizes purpose and values. Worship is not empirically related to these ends, but symbolically expresses them. Ritualists, who disclaim these ends or goals, are more likely to be censured than innovators, who claim goal adherence or support doctrinal positions while modifying some practices.[9] Consequently innovation, being less severely censured than ritualism or rebellion, becomes the adaptation of choice.

Applied science, on the other hand, stresses means; it is essentially a method. The psychiatric community is more likely to look askance at an innovator who adopts unorthodox therapeutic procedures than at a ritualist who "does the right things" through importing strange terms to describe the purposes of therapy.[10] It seems paradoxical that science should discourage experimentation with new means, since discovery is almost part of the definition of science. Science carefully defines the channels through which new procedures may enter. Religion is not a legitimate source of scientific procedures.[11] Consequently, the psychiatrist under stress is more likely to elect ritualism than either innovation or rebellion.

These choices may also be a result of the influence of each institution on the other. Science offers religion a set of procedures and so encourages ministerial innovation, while religion offers psychiatry a value or goal orientation and so encourages psychiatric ritualism.

Nine per cent of the ministers, but 27 per cent of the psychiatrists, become rebels. Rebellion has a different meaning in each institution. A rebel pastor substitutes some of the means and goals of psychiatry for those of religion. Some go so far as to leave the parish for the private practice of pastoral counseling where, superficially, they seem indistinguishable from psychologists. A rebel psychiatrist, on the other hand, does not assume the cloth nor appear to do so. The psychiatric rebel continues to treat patients in his office setting, though he speaks of "faith" and of "existential" problems. A rebel minister's break with his institution is considerably sharper than that between the psychiatric rebel and his field. This variant subtype would encounter more resistance in the church than it would in medicine, and consequently ministers would be more reluctant than psychiatrists to elect this adaptation.

About one militant conformist minister appears for every four nonconformist ministers and one militant conformist psychiatrist for every five nonconformist psychiatrists. If it is true that the militant conformist shares the ambivalence of the rebel, but is expressing it in an opposite fashion, then the argument advanced above to explain the distribution of rebels may also hold here. Since rebellion has more serious implications for ministers than for psychiatrists, they are more likely to resolve the ambivalence by overasserting tradition than by risking departure from it. Further, religion encourages militant conformism because of its link to traditional styles of legitimation.

RELATING ADAPTATIONAL TYPES
AND ORIENTATIONAL TYPES

The Empirical Correlation Between
Variant Types and Role Orientations

The subtypes of variants have been delineated to provide a way of studying different degrees of variation and the correspondence between institutional variation and change in counseling norms. Each variant subtype is associated with a particular orientation toward the client.[12] Table 27 shows these associations between role orientations and institutional variation among ministers and psychiatrists.

Table 27—Orientations to Clients among Ministers and Psychiatrists Classified According to Variant Subtype[a]

Variant Subtype	Quality	Affectivity	Particularism	Diffuseness
Ministers (385)				
Militant Conformists	43	41	67	87
Ritualists	27	23	55	86
Innovators	22	23	38	83
Rebels	11	18	30	98
Psychiatrists (110)				
Rebels	29	22	31	76
Innovators	16	6	42	65
Ritualists	5	11	12	40
Militant Conformists	10	—	—	23

ORIENTATIONS (in Per Cent)

a. Only one side of each pattern variable dichotomy is shown. Thus, reading the upper left of the table, 43 per cent of the militant conformist ministers are quality oriented. The unwritten implication is that the complementary 57 per cent are performance oriented. Variant subtypes of psychiatrists are presented in the reverse order of the ministerial types to keep with the generally declining magnitudes of percentages in the columns.

Moving from militant conformists to rebels among both ministers and psychiatrists, the proportions supporting most of the orientations change progesssively. Forty-three per cent of the conformist ministers are quality oriented, while 27 per cent of the ritualists, 22 per cent of the innovators, and only 11 per cent of the rebels are. This steady decrease in the proportion of quality oriented ministers is, *pari passu*, a steady increase in the proportion of the performance oriented. Similarly, there is decreasing support for affective and particularistic norms. There is little difference regarding diffuse norms excepting for the increased proportion of rebels advocating them. Practically all ministers in the sample retain a diffuse orientation.[13] If we assume a quality, affective, particularistic, and diffuse orientation as typifying the norms of the ministerial status, it appears that the militant conformists are closest to this pattern, the ritualists slightly removed, the innovators even more divergent, and the rebels, excepting as regards diffuseness, most distant from it.

Reading upward in Table 27, we find a similar phenomenon among psychiatrists. If we assume a performance, affectively neutral, universalistic, and specific orientation as ideal typical of the psychiatric status, then moving from militant conformism to rebellion corresponds to decreasing adherence to this pattern.[14]

The magnitude of the proportions changing orientation between militant conformists and rebels differs for each norm. For ministers the greatest change is in quality and particularistic norms. For psychiatrists it is in particularistic and diffuse norms. The near unidirectionality of the change from one to the other variant subtype suggests a progression from greater to greater variation. The variant types may not simply be qualitative permutations of adaptations but may be ordered according to the extent to which they are variant.

The Scale Order of Variation

We may define "extent of variation" as the proportion of ministers or psychiatrists in each subcategory departing from the "prevailing" norms of their respective institutions for therapist-patient interaction.[15] Observing, for example, that 55 per cent of the ritualist ministers support particularistic norms but only 30 per cent of the minister rebels do, it is possible to say rebels tend to be "more variant" than ritualists with respect to this norm. This may be stated in terms of the probability that a person classified according to his variant type will conform to a given interaction norm. The probability is .55 that an observed ritualist minister will support a particularistic position. For a rebel, the comparable probability is only .30.

It is possible to be more variant with respect to one norm and less variant with respect to another. We need a way of ordering the types that will consider the entire pattern variable cluster at once. This may be done by constructing a scale to order the variant types according to the clusters of pattern variables associated with each type. The general unidirectionality of the changes in norms advocated with each variant type suggests that they might be ordered on a Guttman-type scale. This would imply that they differ in degree along a single dimension, "extent of variation."[16] The successively more variant scale types would be defined by the clusters of pattern variables associated with each adaptation.

Scaling has a further value. Were over 50 per cent of the militant conformist ministers quality oriented and over 50 per cent of the ritualists performance oriented, then militant conformists could simply be called a quality and ritualists a performance oriented type. The entire distribution, however, is skewed in the direction of performance rather than quality orientation. This skew may be due to the criteria of classification or to the impact of the broader milieu on the sample. in either case it obscures the contrast between relatively performance and relatively quality oriented types. Scaling establishes "cutting points" separating the relatively-quality from the relatively-performance oriented.[17] We may take the mid-point of the probabilities which associate each pattern variable and a variant type. On the quality performance norm, for example, the probabilities of each type being associated with a quality orientation vary from .43 for the militant conformist ministers to .05 for the ritualist psychiatrists. The mid-point between these figures is .24. This probability of .24 may be taken as a new zero point established by the distribution itself. All variant types having 24 per cent or more quality oriented individuals may be termed relatively quality oriented. The extent of their quality orientation is given by their excess over .24. Those having less than 24 per cent quality oriented individuals may be termed relatively performance oriented.[18] The extent of their performance orientation is given by their distance below .24. In this way ministerial conformists and ritualists and psychiatric rebels are characterized by quality and the remaining types by performance orientation. This procedure is followed for each of the pattern variables.[19] The results of performing this transformation on Table 27 are shown in Table 28.

Each variant type is associated with a particular configuration of pattern variables. Pattern variables on each side of the "cutting

Table 28 (Transformation of Table 27)—Scaled Orientations to the Client of Ministers and Psychiatrists Classified According to Variant Subtypes*

Variant Subtypes	Orientations with Probabilities of Their Association with the Respective Variant Types							
Ministers								
Militant Conformists	Quality	.19	Affectivity	.21	Particularism	.33	Diffuse	.27
Ritualists	Quality	.03	Affectivity	.03	Particularism	.21	Diffuse	.26
Innovators	Performance	.02	Affectivity	.03	Particularism	.04	Diffuse	.23
Rebels	Performance	.13	Neutrality	.02	Universalism	.04	Diffuse	.38
Psychiatrists								
Rebels	Quality	.05	Affectivity	.02	(Universalism)[a]	.03	Diffuse	.16
Innovators	Performance	.08	Neutrality	.14	Particularism	.08	Diffuse	.05
Ritualists	Performance	.19	Neutrality	.09	Universalism	.22	Specific	.20
Militant Conformists	Performance	.14	Neutrality	.21	Universalism	.33	Specific	.37

* The order of norms from left to right follows the tradition of showing the first "cutting point" in the left column.

a. The universalistic orientation of psychiatric rebels has been placed in parenthesis to indicate that this is a scale error which, in view of the particularism of the otherwise less variant innovators, would have been a particularistic orientation were there perfect reproducibility.

points," reading vertically, are stated complementarily. Three distinctive clusters or scale types emerge. Militant conformists and ritualists are associated with the same pattern variables among both ministers and psychiatrists. Minister militant conformists and ritualists tend to advocate quality, affective, particularistic, and diffuse orientations toward clients. The norms psychiatric militant conformists and ritualists advocate for orienting toward patients are defined in terms of performance, neutrality, universalism, and specificity.[20] These correspond to the "ideal type" orientations of their institutions. Ritualists and militant conformists do, however, differ in their probabilities of association with each norm within the scale types. Ministerial ritualists are considerably less quality, affectively, and particularistically oriented than the militant conformists. This is to be expected. Though they retain what are classified as religious practices, these tend to be magical in character, to be instrumental applications of religiously conceived acts. As such, they move toward a performance orientation. The detailed procedural rules associated with magic type acts lead toward a universalistic orientation. The need for restraint and control during the preparation for magic pulls in the direction of affective neutrality.[21] Psychiatric ritualists, for their part, are less likely to be affectively neutral, universalistic, and specific in orientation than the psychiatric militant conformists. These ritualists reformulate their goals in religious language but do not change their practices. In fact, they may even compensate by stressing traditional procedures and so show little change in the performance dimension. Their goal change, however, tends to be influenced by Protestant theology, particularly by its concern with spontaneous love and relatedness. These considerations press in an affective and particularistic direction. The decreased specificity of the psychiatric ritualist may reflect a general instability in the differentiation of the healing role. The healing of emotions tends to draw the healer into the client's network of disturbed human relations. In most nonwestern societies the role tends to be diffuse.[22]

The move from ritualism to innovation is associated with a change in the pattern variable cluster. The shift toward universalistic norms among ministers may be associated with the innovators' readiness to classify parishioners' problems according to syndromes to justify one or another psychiatric procedure. Among psychiatrists innovation and ritualism also differ in scale type. The sharpest changes are toward quality, particularistic, and diffuse orientations. The normative difference between ritualist and innovator psychiatrists is greater than that between any other adjacent types. The decrease in performance orientation may reflect the fact that the religious means of the psychiatric innovator tend to be noninstrumental insofar as they involve faith or meditation. This argument would not hold for psychiatric innovators who have a magical view of worship or of their priest-type charisma. The increase in particularistic orientations would follow from the innovators' concern with the "meeting" of personalities as a therapeutic means.

The normative orientation of ministerial rebels is similar to that of conformist psychiatrists (excepting on the diffuse-specific dimension). Rebel ministers differ from the innovator ministers in their increased advocacy of performance and universalistic orientations. In so doing ministerial rebels assume the significant norms of the psychiatric approach, the application of techniques according to objectively designated principles. Considering universalism as a scale error, psychiatric rebels advocate a traditional ministerial-type orientation. The quality and affective orientations imply the reduction of conscious instrumental effort and the freeing of feeling for response which is so characteristic of the religious approach. Ministerial and psychiatric rebels are more diffusely oriented than the respective innovators. By clouding the role boundaries they avert being "defined" out of their institutions by virtue of their new specializations.

Further Confirmation of the Order of Variation

We have found that the subtypes of institutional variants correspond to specifiable clusters of interaction norms. Further, these subtypes may be ordered from least to most variant on the basis of extent of change in their associated normative orientations. This finding is further confirmed by evidence that these subtypes assume the same order when correlated with other indicators of variation which distinguish militant conformists from nonconformists. A shift from a membership to a nonmembership reference group is such an indicator. Table 29 shows the proportions of each variant subtype who select their membership group as a reference group.

Table 29—Proportion of Each Variant Subtype with Membership Group as Reference Group (The Complementary Percentages Have a Double or Nonmembership Group as a Reference Group)

Variant Subtype	Ministers with Religious Reference Group	Psychiatrists with Psychiatric Reference Group
	(in Per Cent)	
Militant Conformists	83	86
	(101)	(22)
Ritualists	28	48
	(72)	(56)
Innovators	17	44
	(254)	(18)
Rebels	—	6
	(45)	(35)

The proportion of individuals of each variant subtype who take their own membership group as a reference group progressively decreases (or the proportion with a double or nonmembership group progressively increases) in moving from militant conformists to ritualists to innovators and to rebels. However, the difference between psychiatric ritualists and innovators is small, despite the great difference in interactive norms between these types. The innovators advocate religious means in the service of psychiatrically phrased goals while looking to psychiatry as a source of standards. These standards are likely to judge their religious type behaviors harshly. The psychiatric innovator consequently would be a rather unstable type. This further helps us understand why innovation is the rarest adaptation among psychiatrists (see Table 26).

Commitment to the core of institutional ideology, as given by our religious and psychiatric belief indices, also discriminates between militant conformists and nonconformists. Table 30 shows the proportion of each variant subtype scoring high on each of these indices.

Table 30—Proportion of Each Variant Subtype High on Psychiatric and Religious Belief Indices

Variant Subtype	HIGH RELIGIOUS BELIEF		HIGH PSYCHIATRIC BELIEF	
	(in Per Cent)			
	Ministers	Psychiatrists	Ministers	Psychiatrists
Militant Conformists	77	4	2	74
	(99)	(23)	(100)	(23)
Ritualists	45	8	14	21
	(78)	(59)	(77)	(57)
Innovators	34	15	11	5
	(261)	(20)	(263)	(20)
Rebels	9	26	34	3
	(47)	(38)	(47)	(37)

For both ministers and psychiatrists, the progression from militant conformists to ritualists to innovators to rebels corresponds to decreasing commitment to the ideological statements of their membership group and increasing commitment to the beliefs of the nonmembership group. (Excepting that the move from ritualist to innovator among ministers and from innovator to rebel among psychiatrists involves little change in psychiatric belief.) Commitment to the beliefs of the membership group is reduced more drastically than the commitment to the nonmembership group is increased. Variation in these terms seems to be less a conversion to a new group than a process of becoming peripheral to one's own group.

The Parallel Between Institutional Dissidence and Counseling Norms

Why is one rather than another set of norms of interaction associated with each variant subtype? Why is the move from ritualism to innovation among ministers associated with a change from a universalistic to a particularistic relationship? A few *ad hoc* hypotheses were advanced above to account for some of the major shifts. We shall examine the changes step by step.[23] Let us assume that the clusters associated with the ministerial and psychiatric militant conformists are equilibrated or harmonious patterns. If undisturbed by outside forces, nothing intrasystemic would happen to change the pattern.[24] The initial change in norms in each case may be understood with reference to an external factor introducing a new norm into therapy. Then, as the therapist and patient find themselves exposed to incompatible expectations, an internal strain develops between the newly introduced norm and the other norms of therapy. Pressure for further normative revision ensues. This subsequent revision may be accounted for with reference solely to an internal adjustment among the norms in the direction of a new equilibrium.

How does this come about among ministers? Minister innovators are more likely than either the militant conformists or ritualists to take psychiatry as their reference group. They also have more varied educational backgrounds. Both their concern with psychiatry and their wider education expose them to performance orientations. These pressures toward a performance orientation supplement those to which almost all ministers in our society are subject. The performance orientation is institutionalized in the statuses which link ministers as individuals to economic institutions. As family heads, they participate as consumers in the economy. By accepting salaries (in addition to fees) in their ministerial status, this status becomes less of a free profession and more of an occupation. Thus, they enter the economy as "producers" and are evaluated by their "productive" success.[25] The performance norms encountered in these and other statuses come to be accepted as relevant to their religious functions. This influence is abetted by the diffuse role orientation which militates against segregation of the ministerial from other statuses.[26] Ministers who agree to evaluate their ministry in terms of its "effectiveness" as measured by church or congregational size soon judge their pastoral success by problems solved or cures achieved. Thus, the performance orientation replaces the quality orientation in therapy. With performance as a legitimate role requirement, they seek to meet this requirement through psychological training and personal counseling. The training and counseling experiences fix the performance norm in the pastoral repertoire.

The introduction of a performance norm produces an imbalance in the otherwise *gemeinschaft* cluster. Ensuing normative changes are in the direction of a new equilibrium. These changes may be understood with reference to the internal relations among the norms themselves. The traditional minister with a quality orientation is not especially concerned with judging the appropriateness of the quality since it is, by definition, beyond the therapist's control.[27] Performance norms, however, invite evaluation of their appropriateness and effectiveness. Universalistic norms may then be introduced to classify the client, to choose therapeutic techniques, and to evaluate the therapeutic outcome.

This combination of universalism and performance makes an affective orientation difficult to maintain. An affective orientation presses toward an expression of feeling uninhibited by rules. When patient performances are evaluated, some may be found inappropriate. To indicate inappropriateness and encourage the patient to abandon these performances or adopt others, the therapist may withhold emotional rewards. Rules for withholding feeling signify an affectively neutral orientation. Thus, the introduction of the performance orientation draws in its wake univeralism and affective neutrality. These orientations help discriminate between situations where one or another technique is feasible and so limit the scope of the relationship. Under these conditions the diffuse orientation gives way to a specific one. Thus, an original normative change introduced from without induces further changes within the interaction pattern until the relation is guided by a newly equilibrated *gesellschaft* pattern of norms associated with the ministerial rebel.[28]

A parallel sequence of normative changes accompanies institutional variation among psychiatrists. Initially (see Table 28) the psychiatrist does not drop his performance for a quality orientation. The psychiatric ritualist incorporates the conception of a religious goal into his empirical framework as something to be attained by effort. Subsequently the religious elements, such as "prayer" and "faith," introduced by the innovators may continue to be treated as instrumental techniques. These religious means, however, since they involve a conscious reaching for "love," tend to encourage a particularistic and diffuse relationship. The nature of the psychiatric relationship contributes to this. As an isolated dyad, client and therapist are constantly under pressure to see their relation as taking precedence over external rules governing it, as being one of mutual faith and confidence. Therapeutic rapport is stressed. These factors account for the initial change from universalistic to particularistic and from specific to diffuse orientations. The decline of universalistic principles removes some of the criteria for evaluating performances. There is less likelihood that one or another therapeutic technique will be considered more effective. The discussion turns more to the nonspecific and noncontrolable role of the therapist's personality. With this emphasis a quality orientation tends to emerge in place of the performance orientation. There is now less justification for withholding affective rewards to assure certain performances. In addition, the particularistic character of the relation, which now stresses rapport, works against the withholding of affect. An affective replaces an affectively neutral orientation. The original introduction of particularistic and diffuse orientations among psychiatric innovators through exposure to religion has led to quality and affective orientations among psychiatric rebels.[29]

SUMMARY

The previous chapter opened by positing "ideal type" minister and psychiatrist relations in counseling. A classification of writers in our sample showed that the militant conformists of both groups do indeed advocate norms comparable to their "ideal types." Militant conformist ministers, relative to psychiatrists, advocate quality, affective, particularistic, and diffuse norms for counseling. Militant conformist psychiatrists, relative to ministers, tend toward their "ideal type" normative cluster of performance, affective neutrality, universalism, and specificity. Ministers and psychiatrists who are institutional nonconformists also tend to depart from traditional orientations in the counseling role.

To show the steps by which variation progressively increases in both the institutional and role relationships, the nonconformists were divided into three subtypes: ritualists, innovators, and rebels. When the norms were mapped on these types, they formed a Guttman-type scale indicating that the variant subtypes may be considered, in that order, as increasingly variant. This ordering and the normative clusters corresponding to each step permitted speculation about the mechanisms involved in the emergence of new counseling norms. The initial normative change was attributed to influences external to counseling, the ministers' participation in industrial society and the psychiatrists' friendliness toward religion. The remaining changes toward the norms of the nonmembership group were accounted for in terms of internal adjustments of the normative pattern in the direction of a new equilibrium.

These findings imply that individuals whose allegiance to their institution weakens may be expected to change their role behavior within that institution. Further, the increasing extent of variation from one to the other subtype suggests that the "vicious circle of deviance" may be viewed as a sequence of steps in a determinable direction. On the level of norms, once some salient element in the stable normative pattern is changed, a process is set in motion which, if social control mechanisms do not intervene to suppress the new element, produces further changes. Relations within the system are restructured until a newly equilibrated pattern is reached.[30] On the interaction level, once an individual begins to change, increased interaction with members of the new group and decreased interaction with his old colleagues, and perhaps censure on their part, may push him toward greater and greater variation.[31]

APPENDIX

The Scale Based on Individual Clusters of Norms

The scale presented in this chapter was constructed by mapping the pattern variables on variant adaptational types. These variant types are not individuals but classes of individuals. The traditional way to construct a Guttman scale would be to arrange the individual ministers and psychiatrists according to some attributes, such as their associated pattern variables. Those with the same pattern variable clusters would be designated as one scale type. The variant adaptational types could then be mapped on the already determined scale types as a way of studying the correlation between the two. This appendix presents the Guttman scale constructed in this way. The ministers are assembled according to clusters of three pattern variables: affectivity-neutrality, universalism-particularism, performance-quality. Diffuseness-specificity is deleted since almost all ministers choose diffuseness. Further, there is little need for the additional scale type based on this dimension, since the intent is to

Table 31—Guttman Scale Constructed from the Various Combinations of Pattern Variables of Individual Ministers and Psychiatrists

Scale Type	Number	PATTERN VARIABLE TYPES			PER CENT OF EACH VARIANT SUBTYPE ASSOCIATED WITH EACH PATTERN VARIABLE CLUSTER				
					Militant Conformists	Ritualists	Innovators	Rebels	Total
Ministers									
I	20	Quality	Affectivity	Particularism	44%	15	31	10	100%
	19	Quality	(Neutrality)	Particularism					
II	42	Performance	Affectivity	Particularism	26%	19	41	14	100%
IIA	60	Performance	Neutrality	Particularism	20%	23	40	17	100%
III	23	(Quality)	Neutrality	Universalism	10%	10	42	38	100%
	125	Performance	Neutrality	Universalism					
	10	Performance	(Affectivity)	Universalism					
	4	(Quality)	(Affectivity)	Universalism					
Total cases =	303								
Errors		(27)	(33)	(—)					
					Reproducibility = .93				
Psychiatrists									
I	64	Performance	Neutrality	Universalism	29%	35	17	19	100%
	4	(Quality)	Neutrality	Universalism					
	4	Performance	(Affectivity)	Universalism					
II	15	Performance	Neutrality	Particularism	—%	18	53	29	100%
	4	(Quality)	Neutrality	Particularism					
IIA	5	Performance	Affectivity	Particularism					
III	2	Quality	Affectivity	Particularism	—%	25	25	50	100%
	1	Quality	Affectivity	(Universalism)					
Total cases =	99								
Errors		(8)	(4)	(1)					
					Reproducibility = .96				

correlate only four variant adaptational types with pattern variable clusters. Three dichotomous pattern variables may be clustered in eight possible ways, four of which are Guttman-scale types.

The scale is presented in Table 31. The scale types are defined in such a way as to minimize error. All of the eight possible clusters appear. The four defining clusters are designated by Roman numerals to their left. Among ministers scale type I is identified by the cluster affectivity, particularism, quality. It includes 20 individuals with exactly this pattern of norms and 19 who advocate quality and particularistic norms but are affectively neutral in orientation instead of affective. These 19 instances of neutrality are shown in parentheses to indicate that this is a scale error. Of these 39 individuals of this scale type, 44 per cent are militant conformists. This is a higher proportion of militant conformists than appears in association with any of the succeeding types. Consequently, ministers who advocate quality, affective, and particularistic norms tend more than others to be militant conformists. Inspection will show that the militant conformist ministers in Table 28 are associated with the same pattern variable cluster. The other types are defined similarly, with the Roman numeral adjoining the principal scale types and the error categories in parentheses in each case. An additional type, designated as IIA, appears here, but not in Table 28. For ministers, ritualists, and innovators share this type. Since there are so few of types IIA and III among psychiatrists, the variant adaptational types of both of these have been combined. These correlate with the rebel type. The reproducibility of the minister scale is .93 and of the psychiatrist scale .96. Scalability shows that the variant types may be ordered on a single dimension of "degree of variation" and that variation from the broad institutional norms is correlative with variation in the specific counseling role.

NOTES

1. This specification of variant subtypes is indebted to Merton's *Social Theory and Social Structure*, pp. 121–194.

2. For a discussion of this typology see Robert Dubin, "Deviant Be-

havior and Social Structure, Continuities in Social Theory"; Richard A. Cloward, "Illegitimate Means, Anomie, and Deviant Behavior"; and Robert K. Merton, "Social Conformity, Deviation, and Opportunity Structures: A Comment on the Contributions of Dubin and Cloward," *American Sociological Review*, pp. 147–188.

3. Though defined with reference to Merton's paradigm, the militant conformist is similar to the conformist described by Parsons in *The Social System*, pp. 256–280.

4. Rejection and substitution is clear in this study, since only two institutions, religion and psychiatry, are considered. Actually, this must occur in all cases of variation except where the individual opts out of the "game." (See Chap. II, footnote 13.)

5. Merton's retreatist does not appear in this study because he rejects the means and goals of his own group and ceases striving without substituting those of the other group. He simply withdraws without producing religio-psychiatric writings.

6. Merton's use of ritualism should not be confused with the religious sense of the term. As a variant adaptation, ritualism refers to compulsively abiding by institutional norms despite failure to attain cultural goals. The term may be used in any institutional context.

7. The religious means advocated by ritualist ministers to accompany their psychological goals fall into four groups. Religion may be seen as providing a general resource. George Muedeking reminds us that the Bible has an answer to all situations (925). Religious ritual as a therapeutic device is a second type of religious means. Elwood Worcester speaks of the application of prayer (1326). Preaching is suggested as an instrument of group therapy by Edgar Jackson (625, 626). Elwood Worcester, in his later years, supplements prayer and suggestion by the use of a medium. An individual diagnosed as schizophrenic appears to be "possessed" by "discarnate personalities." A medium is able to reveal the identity of the spirit and induce it to quit the possessed person (1327). Religious fellowship may be used as a means. Paul Johnson describes the cathartic value of worshipping together (643). For a fourth group of ministers, being in the church with its ideals or allowing Faith or Grace to enter is therapeutic. Hadfield (532), McKenzie (862), and M. Gregory (516) stress the purpose and ideals provided in the church. Faith is the key for Rochedieu (1087). Goldbrunner adds Hope and Charity (500).

Every one of the four types of psychological goals may be found in conjunction with every one of the religious means. These combinations produce 16 types of ritualist ministers. Too few cases, however, appear in this study for analysis of each type. The succeeding analysis collects them all under the heading of ritualists.

8. Following are some examples of four types of religious goals of innovating ministers. Broadly stated, religious goals of innovating ministers are illustrated by John Bonnell's belief that psychological methods lead to a healing of the soul (154). Augustin Leonard says that through Jung's therapy one may be led to spiritual perfection (755). More specifically, Joseph Fletcher preaches the philosophical advantages of clinical training in making religious doctrines meaningful to the student (413). Accomplishing religious tasks as a goal is exemplified by John McKenzie, who sees psychotherapeutic techniques as an aid in his evangelism (863). E. F. Latko recommends psychological methods as a way of treating scruples (751). Noel Mailloux finds in the methods a road to freedom of the will, enabling man to live by moral conscience and judgment (813). Attaining religious relationships as a goal is illustrated by Lewis Sherrill's expectation that psychological techniques lead to *agape* love between parishioner and pastor (1155).

Each of the four types of psychological techniques might be combined with any one of the four types of religious goals, producing sixteen types of innovating ministers. Too few of the subtypes appear in this sample, however, for separate analysis.

9. Religion has traditionally considered heretical doctrines more dangerous than heretical cultic practice. Cultic changes, themselves, may be associated with new views on doctrine. See Wach, *op. cit.*, pp. 190–193.

10. On this contrast between religion being concerned with purpose and of science with procedures, see Chap. III, pp. 96ff., and footnote 11 of that chapter. Empirical evidence is needed on the truth of this contrast between contemporary religious institutions. Some religions, e.g., Hindu Yoga, do place more stress on means. This differs, however, from the scientific orientation in that the efficacy of the means is not held to be empirically testable.

11. Social psychological factors influencing the readiness of scientists to accept new means are studied by Bernard Barber, "Resistance by Scientists to Scientific Discovery," *Scientific Manpower*, pp. 36–47.

12. The indicators used for the two classifications are essentially independent. Despite the clustering of the pattern variables in defining ministerial and psychiatric "ideal type" counselors, a particular pattern variable has no necessary or inherent connection with either a religious or a psychological orientation. The statement that the therapist would transmit "Divine love" reflects an affective orientation. The expression belongs to religious discourse and was coded as reflecting institutional norms of religion. Since variation is departure of an individual from the expectations institutionalized in his own membership group, this expression has different implications for ministers and psychiatrists. A minister claiming this as his means could be classified as a conformist if his goal were also selected in religious terms. He

would be a ritualist were his goal phrased psychologically. A psychiatrist citing "Divine love" is selecting a means discrepant from the institutionalized expectations of his membership group. He would be classed as an innovator if his goal were stated psychiatrically or a rebel if he joined "Divine love" as a means to a religiously phrased goal. One further illustration may be in order. A statement that the therapist should "not control his countertransference" reflects an affective orientation and is couched in psychiatric language. A minister making this statement could be either an innovator or a rebel with an affective orientation. A psychiatrist adhering to the same idea could be an affectively oriented conformist or ritualist. Note that he could be a conformist despite the fact that the content of the statement runs counter to the weight of contemporary psychiatric opinion. He would join the debate on countertransference within his group's frame of reference.

13. The increased diffuse orientation of the rebel ministers may be due to the fact that by advocating both the means and the goals of psychological counselors they are in danger of losing their clerical identity. At the same time, they seek acceptance among secular counselors. Consequently, they emphasize both identities and relate to patients as clergymen as well as psychologists. Were they to be specific in orientation, relating to clients as psychologists, they would become "retreatists" with respect to their clerical status. This need to affirm both statuses may be an aspect of what Merton has noted as the ambivalent character of the rebel adaptation.

14. Table 27 shows three discrepancies or reversals of order among the psychiatrists. The reversals in the quality and affectivity columns are small enough so that, given the number of cases involved, they may well be due to "chance." The high proportion of psychiatric innovators with a particularistic orientation is due to psychiatrists who stress personal relationship as a general therapeutic means almost irrespective of the psychodiagnosis.

15. The argument may be made in terms of departure from the respective "ideal types" or from the pattern set by the conformists as a rough indicator of the institutionalized norms. The conclusions are the same in either case.

16. On the theory of Guttman scaling see Samuel Stouffer *et al.*, *The American Soldier: Studies in Social Psychology in World War II*, Vol. III: *Measurement and Prediction*.

17. On the problem of the zero point in scaling see *ibid.*, pp. 33f., 41f.

18. This is the same as saying that a type will not be termed relatively performance oriented unless 76 per cent of the associated individuals advocate a performance norm. The procedure is the common one of evaluating a sample distribution taking the population marginals into consideration.

19. This scale is related to the Guttman type. The traditional way of

constructing a Guttman scale would have required an ordering of the individual cases according to their associated sets of pattern variables and then an examination of the proportions of militant conformists or ritualists associated with each pattern. The probabilities would then be attached to the variant subtypes rather than the pattern variables. This is done in the appendix to this chapter. Substantially the same relations with variant subtypes appear. Following the traditional procedure the ministerial scale has a reproducibility of .93 and the psychiatric scale a reproducibility of .96. Such coefficients of reproducibility suggest that we are justified in treating the four discrepant figures in Table 27 as scale errors. That is, the discrepancies are not frequent enough to cause rejection of the hypothesis of unidimensionality.

20. Were the pattern variables not dichotomous, ritualists and militant conformists might have emerged as distinct types rather than differing in degree on the same type.

21. These types of distinctions between magic and religion are made by Bronislaw Malinowski, *Magic, Science and Religion*, pp. 17–92.

22. Modern psychotherapeutic literature is replete with warnings against being "seduced" by the patient. See, for example, Karl Menninger, *The Theory of Psychoanalytic Technique*, pp. 116ff. A statement of this problem within a general paradigm of social control is given by Parsons, *The Social System*, pp. 322ff. On the character of the healer or leech in other cultures see Rivers, *op. cit.*

23. The following model remains conjectural, since the inferences are made from different individuals who are more or less variant rather than from the same individuals who move through stages of increasing variation.

24. This assumption has some basis since these normative patterns persistently characterize the *gemeinschaft* and *gesellschaft* forms of social relationship. The use of an equilibrium model for analysis is illustrated in W. B. Cannon, *The Wisdom of the Body*. For the application of an equilibrium model in the theory of social and personality systems, see Talcott Parsons and Edward A. Shils, *op. cit.*, pp. 107f.; and Robert F. Bales, "The Equilibrium Problem in Small Groups," *Small Groups: Studies in Social Interaction*, A. Paul Hare, Edgar F. Borgatta, and Robert F. Bales (eds.), pp. 498–515. For a statement relating the equilibrium problem to the problem of system integration, see Edward E. Devereux, "Parsons' Sociological Theory," *The Social Theories of Talcott Parsons*, Max Black (ed.), especially pp. 33f.

25. See F. Ernest Johnson and J. Emory Ackerman, *op. cit.*; and Joseph H. Fichter, *Religion as an Occupation*.

26 See Robert K. Merton, "The Role Set: Problems in Sociological Theory," *The British Journal of Sociology*, pp. 106–120.

27. This applies to the quality orientation within therapy where treatment rather than admission to the status is the problem. In a broader context, standards to judge the possession of a quality may be important, as, for example, a religious initiate may demonstrate his qualifications for election to the group.

28. This particular sequence of normative changes toward a new equilibrium is peculiar to the psychotherapy system. A minister influenced by a performance norm but less oriented to science might become a faith healer instead of becoming a pastoral counselor. In faith healing performance, affective and particularistc norms, would be an equilibrated cluster. Or he might become an evangelist guided by performance, affective, and universalistic norms. The compatibility of norms can only be evaluated with respect to the goal of the system and of the role relationships within the system.

We have attempted to account for changes in the interaction system which accompany the shift from one to another variant subtype. The change may also be traced in the variant subtypes accompanying a shift in orientation. Why does a minister who changes the norms guiding his counseling relationship, say from quality to performance, tend to become institutionally more variant? The development may be as follows: The first step for ministers is some flirting with psychiatric goals. This may come about as part of the general trend in industrial society toward a scientific approach to problems as indicated in Chap. II. Interest in the performance orientation might follow. He seeks training in psychology and perhaps personal counseling to improve his technique. As he absorbs these, he moves toward innovation. This involves him with psychologists and psychiatrists. With this increased exposure he tends to take psychiatry as his reference group and to accept the standards of evaluation and cultural goals of psychiatry. "Improving patient functioning" takes precedence over otherworldly "salvation." This consequence is peculiar to the Western world. In the East an instrumental orientation is quite consistent with religious cultural goals. Both psychiatry and pastoral counseling appear only in Western culture.

29. The process also may be analyzed from the vantage of the variant types. Why is this interactional change accompanied by a move from ritualism to rebellion? Innovation is accompanied by acceptance of a particularistic norm. This is understandable, since the psychiatric innovator, though defining his goal psychiatrically, has imported religious procedures which are, by their nature, relational. The particularistically oriented psychiatrist becomes less concerned about following theoretical principles and selecting one or another technique. He reduces his involvement in professional psychiatric training and attends fewer meetings with his col-

leagues, who, in turn, begin looking upon him as a variant and withdraw from him. Gradually his interest increases in reading theology and attending meetings with ministers. Already being kindly disposed toward religion, he tends to adopt a religious reference group for his professional work. This draws him closer to a religious view of counseling and to adopting religious goals. As the cultural goals of religion, which the ritualist may have already accepted in a broad sense, become significant in counseling, the innovator becomes a rebel.

(The explanation for changes in counseling orientation has been given in terms of the malintegration of norms, a cultural type explanation. The change in adaptational types has been explained in terms of interaction, a sociological type explanation.)

30. See Talcott Parsons' discussion on the "tendency to polarization" of ideologies in *The Social System*, p. 358.

31. On this type of process see *ibid*, pp. 222–227.

Chapter VI

Justification Before Institution and Conscience

THE RELIGIO-PSYCHIATRIC MOVEMENT emerges amidst pressures and counterpressures. Ministers and psychiatrists attempt to reduce dissonance within their roles by shifting their reference groups and their counseling orientations. Nonconformism conjures up its own antithesis, militant conformism, a pressure for return to conformity. Under this pressure some nonconformists relinquish their new behavior and attitudes. They appear once or twice in our literature and then disappear from the movement. Others hold their ground, and still others become increasingly dissident. Ritualists are replaced by innovators and innovators by rebels. The variant adaptations which were designed to reduce pressure within their counseling roles precipitate them into conflict with their institutions. To mitigate the consequent institutional pressure, they try to explain and justify their actions. A trace of an earlier conformist remains within each nonconformist. The explanations are also intended to soothe this uneasy partner within.[1] These explanations and justifications will be termed rationales. Rationales attempt to mollify the outer and inner pressures by symbolically referring the new behavior and attitudes to acceptable values. This chapter analyzes the rationales which ministers and psychiatrists offer to explain their departures from tradition and their attractions to another institution.

A rationale expresses a motive or reason for an act. When the motive appreciated by the individual differs from his "real"[2] or latent motive we speak of a rationalization. Rationalization interests psychologists as an intrapsychically determined mechanism of defense.[3] An individual behaving, thinking, or feeling in a way inconsistent with his ego-ideal or super-ego may suffer, respectively, feelings of shame or guilt. To pacify the ego-ideal or super-ego and ward off these feelings, he may cathect an ego-syntonic explanation for his act, thought, or feeling. The psychologist inquires into the personality conditions underlying this disposition to rationalize rather than to employ an alternative defense. Alternatively, the individual might, for example, deny what he is doing or, by projection, attribute it to someone else. The sociologist observes the rationalization and asks after the social conditions influencing an individual to formulate his rationalization in one way or another.

The term rationale will be retained here to signal our interest in the conscious content of the proffered justification. The rationales in the religio-psychiatric literature have been published for all to see. They are formulated so as to be consistent with group norms and values,[4] to be sociosyntonic. Their content is as diverse as the situations to which the group values may be applied. To reduce this variety, rationales will be subsumed under a few headings. A first type consists of nonconformist arguments that religion and psychiatry are essentially the same and that therefore these individuals are not variants. These will be called "consolidating rationales." A second type of rationale explains that religion is concerned with the spiritual side of man and psychiatry with the natural side of man. The fields are separate but complementary. Such justifications will be termed "complementing rationales." A third type argues that psychiatry leads to religion or religion contributes to psychiatry. This type recognizes the systems of ideas as distinct but relates them as precursor and successor. Justifications of this type will be termed "harbinger rationales." The harbinger rationale is an affirmation that the two fields complement each other in time, and so is a special case of the complementing rationale. Consolidating, complementing, and harbinger rationales all justify action by appeal to ideas, principles, concepts, norms, or values. Together, they will be termed "rule oriented rationales." Rule oriented rationales may be distinguished from a fourth type of justification in which the individual refers his behavior to that of present or former heroes of the group. These will be termed "socially oriented rationales."[5] Indicators for rationales are statements which the ministers and psychiatrists offer to justify their behavior or attitudes. Some of these overlap with the statements which were used as a basis for the reference group classification. As indicators of a reference group, the question was whether these justificatory statements expressed religious or psychiatric standards. As indicators of rationales, our attention is upon the form of relation implied between the fields and whether they refer to rules or to the behavior of people. Each book or article was given a single classification according to the predominant type of rationale appearing in the abstract. The following pages present examples of indicators for each type of rationale.

SOME INDICATORS FOR RATIONALES

Rule Oriented Rationales

Consolidating rationales: the relation of identity between religion and science. Some ministers justify the adoption of psychological methods because, despite the difference in terms used to refer to them, they are identical with the methods of religion. Paul E. Johnson lists psychotherapeutic methods directly translatable into methods of Christian healing: catharsis is confession; empathy is compassion; relationship therapy is Christian love; insight is revelation; action therapy is Christian service; group therapy is Christian fellowship; spontaneity and productivity are Christian joy; and emotional security is faith (647). Alfred B. Haas identifies congregational singing with group therapy and prescribes psychological guides for choosing hymns (529).

The concepts of religion and science, rather than the methods, may be considered identical. Clifford E. Barbour considers the religious notion of "absolute perfection" identical with the psychologist's value of a completely integrated personality (55). Victor White associates the concept of the unconscious with the idea of God (1297). Ernest White says that in the reference to Christ dwelling in the heart through faith, heart is equivalent to mind in modern psychology (1291). Edward T. Sandrow compares the Jewish concept of the struggle between the evil and the good inclinations to the idea of the ego-libido conflict (1111).

Psychiatrists also identify religious and scientific techniques and concepts. William B. Terhune, identifying Christ as the first and

greatest psychiatrist, says both religion and psychiatry teach understanding, forgiveness, love, loyalty, courage, acceptance, direction of
the instinct toward socially acceptable goals, and a life of unself-
seeking service (1217). Karl A. Menninger says that both aim to
re-establish a sense of relatedness, of self-dignity, and of self-
acceptance in man (875). James H. Van der Veldt and Robert P.
Odenwald argue that since Truth is one, the valid teachings of psychiatry cannot fail to harmonize with Christian ethics (1252).
Joseph J. Mullen identifies scrupulosity with anxiety neurosis (928).
Smiley Blanton and M. H. Ross equate sin and symptoms (123).

*Complementing rationales: the separate but complementary re-
lation between religion and science.* Religion and psychiatry are
held to be separate but complementary on the institutional and on
the role levels. Charles Baudouin, presenting the Jungian view to
Catholics, hopes religious symbols will conciliate the religious and
psychological worlds, forming an ideal passage transcending the
conflict (61). For Robert A. Preston, psychiatry deals with the
stresses and strains of life and religion provides meaning and purpose (1052). Granger Ellsworth Westberg, concerned with religious
and scientific statuses, contends that total cure is effected only
when physicians and ministers work in conjunction (1286). Paul
Tillich writes of existential anxieties as the province of the minister
and pathological anxieties as a problem for the physician (1234).
Erich Franz Steinthal describes man's being as including animal,
social, and spiritual elements requiring cooperation between physicians, psychologists, and spiritual counselors (1188).

Harbinger rationales: the relation of precursor and successor.
Ministers state that psychiatric techniques and values will realize
religious values, help meet the parishioners' needs, or aid in the
fulfillment of the pastoral role. Everett C. Herrick, for example,
writing on clinical training contends that the new psychological
methods make theology come alive (551). Seward Hiltner hopes
pastoral counseling will make basic contributions to our understanding of ethics (571), illuminate theological doctrine (572), and
point the way toward truth (573). Immanuel B. Schaier feels that
the solution of emotional difficulties prepares a person to accept the
full Trinity (1121). Noel Mailloux tells the skeptic that freedom of
will, moral conscience, and judgment become possible through clear-
ing away anxieties (813). According to H. Walter Yoder counsel-

ing leads to a sensitivity to the Holy Spirit (1337). Russell L. Dicks foresees that ministerial authority will be restored through psychiatry (340). Israel J. Gerber attests that his counseling experience gave him a new perception of his responsibilities as a rabbi (474).

Psychiatrists argue that introducing religion into therapy helps realize the goals of psychiatry. Thomas Verner Moore would draw closer to religion because love of God enriches human love (914). Gotthard Booth says that through the symbols and services of the church man transcends his physical consciousness in a relatedness to all being, therefore, the Christian religion is good for the health of modern man (161).

Socially Oriented Rationales: Relating Own Behavior to That of Heroic Colleagues

Some individuals justify their variant behavior by referring it to the activities of other members rather than to the values, norms, or ideas of their group. Seward Hiltner notes that there are more chaplains in clinical settings than ever before (559). Anton T. Boison points to Paul as a successful explorer of the inner world and compares his own experience to that of the prophets of old (136). Paul E. Johnson describes Jesus as a practicing psychologist (648). Sol W. Ginsburg is encouraged because Fromm, Menninger, and Zilboorg tend toward religious interests (482). Viktor E. Frankl quotes Hippocrates as saying that the doctor who is also a philosopher is like unto the gods (437).

APPEAL TO RULE VERSUS APPEAL TO PERSON

What determines whether ministers or psychiatrists justify their behavior or attitudes by a rule or by a socially oriented rationale? Table 32 shows the frequency of each type of rationale among ministers and psychiatrists.

Both ministers and psychiatrists prefer to explain themselves by appeal to concepts, norms, or values rather than by appeal to the behavior of others. The rule oriented rationale may generally be the more popular form of justification in universalistic societies. These societies may consider the rule of law a more legitimate guide than the rule of personal example. The intellectual concern of the professional circles from which these authors came provides an

Table 32—Proportion of Items by Ministers and Psychiatrists
Employing Each Type of Rationale
(in Per Cent)

Ministers (265)		
Rule Oriented Rationales		85
Consolidating Rationales	31	
Complementing Rationales	25	
Harbinger Rationales	29	
Socially Oriented Rationales		15
Psychiatrists (74)		
Rule Oriented Rationales		78
Socially Oriented Rationales		22

intense universalistic ethos. Perhaps in a more particularist society, such as that of Arab bedouins or of Mexican villagers, socially oriented justifications might be more frequent. This interpretation assumes consistency between the type of rationale and the group's ethos. This should be so almost by definition, since a rationale appeals to some accepted value to justify behavior.

That ministers show relatively more preference for rule oriented rationales than do psychiatrists is the reverse of what the particularistic ethos of religion and the universalistic ethos of science would lead us to expect. This suggests that factors other than consistency with the ethos may influence the choice of rationales. For example, the type of rationale might well be sensitive to the degree of variation which individuals are called upon to justify. Entering this movement involves more variation from tradition for the minister than for the psychiatrist. No psychiatrist abandons his primary counseling role. He incorporates religious elements within the same role structure. Some of the ministers, however, leave the parish minister's position to specialize in pastoral counseling. Socially oriented rationales may be most useful for the psychiatrists justifying a slight variation, while rule oriented rationales are needed by the ministers to justify a greater variation. Let us pursue this hypothesis.

Degree of Dissidence and the Choice Between Social and Rule Oriented Rationales

It seems reasonable that individuals might justify relatively slight variation by pointing to the actions of others, but appeal directly to the values when a sharp divergence is to be explained.

For instance, a man charged with hiking his expense account by a few dollars might ask for release because others also violate regulations. If this violation is either slight or known to be common, the violator might receive a willing ear from others embarrassed to single him out for rebuke. A man caught embezzling large funds would be less likely to point to others to justify his behavior. He might criticize the basis for the regulation—that is, appeal to a higher norm—or he might argue that he was "borrowing"—that is, ask that his behavior be interpreted according to a more acceptable norm. Two kinds of considerations contribute to this situation. First, a marked departure from the rules forces itself on the attention in its own terms. The discrepancy itself must be dealt with by appealing to the rules which define it as discrepant. Second, the slight variant more easily discovers variant associates than the extremely divergent person. Few members of a group are likely to be extremely variant. A large number of extremely variant individuals would be, in the long run, incompatible with the maintenance of the group in the same form.

This hypothesis may be tested by comparing the rationales of ministers and psychiatrists who do or do not conform to their group's norms, as described in Chapter IV, for orienting toward the client. The comparison will be made on the basis of the extent of departure from the norms institutionalized in their group as described by three pattern variables: affectivity-affective neutrality, universalism-particularism, and performance-quality. Among ministers who do not vary from the institutionalized type at all or who vary on only one of the pattern variables, 74 per cent (84) employ rule rather than socially oriented rationales. Among those varying on two or three variables, 86 per cent (179) use rule oriented rationales. Among psychiatrists the comparable proportions are 54 per cent (39) and 73 per cent (11).[6] The more an individual varies in relating to clients from the norms institutionalized in his group, the more he is likely to explain his variation by a critique of the norms themselves. Contrariwise, the less variant individual tends to point to the actions or opinions of others to justify his behavior.

The hypothesis may be subjected to another test. Ministers and psychiatrists may support criteria for admitting individuals to the counseling roles which diverge from the criteria institutionalized in their groups. It will be found later that ministers emphasize inherent ascriptive criteria such as personality or grace, while psychiatrists stress achievement, especially training, as prerequisites for becoming a therapist. We find that among ministers supporting their institutional position, 79 per cent (39) offer rule rather than socially oriented rationales, while 88 per cent (116) of those varying from the position offer rule oriented rationales. Among psychiatrists the comparable proportions are 69 per cent (32) and 86 per cent (7).[7]

In the two instances above, rule oriented rationales are associated with a relatively greater divergence from tradition and socially oriented rationales with relatively less divergence. This pattern does not hold when we compare rationales with such indicators of variation as reference group, adherence to psychiatric or religious beliefs, and variation based on the selection of institutional means and cultural goals. What is the difference between divergence in these areas and departure from norms relating a professional to a client and criteria of role allocation? The reference group and belief indices measure institutional identification. Classification as a ritualist, innovator, or rebel hinges upon use of religious or scientific forms of discourse—upon the individual's identification with the linguistic symbolism of his group. All three of these classifications refer to an individual's relation to his group or institution as a whole: of the minister to the church and of the psychiatrist to psychiatry. The cases where the findings hold concern variation from specific role norms, those governing the relation between client and professional, and those governing admission to this role. Thus, the choice between a rule and a socially oriented rationale is influenced by these more specific positions taken within an institution. The individual's relation to the institution as a whole is reflected in the type of rule oriented rationale he uses.[8] The subtypes of rule oriented rationales reflect various ways of stating the relations between the institutions. Let us turn to the analysis of these types of rationales.

Personal Attitudes and the Choice Between Consolidating and Complementing Rationales

Given that an individual, responding to a universalistic ethos and justifying a relatively large behavioral or attitudinal variation, has decided to advance a rule oriented rationale what determines whether it will be consolidating or complementing in form?

Under what conditions do individuals argue that there is little or no difference between religion and psychiatry, or that the fields are different but complementary? Lacking enough cases of psychiatrists, this analysis will be limited to ministers. Further, since harbinger rationales are a special type of complementing rationale, considering the fields as separate but sequentially complementary, we include them along with the other complementing rationales. In the following discussion our 100 per cent base is the total of rule oriented rationales, so that by and large, the percentage of ministers using a consolidating rationale will be presented with the understanding that the remainder use complementing rationales. We shall show that the type of rule oriented rationale selected is a function of identification with the institution. This has been suggested above. In addition, we will find that this decision is influenced by the individual's relative rank in the institution and his role attitudes toward the client. Let us begin with this last.

The attitudinal components of the minister's orientation toward his clients are given by the pattern variables of affectivity-affective neutrality and diffuseness-specificity.[9] Of those advocating norms of affectivity 55 per cent (38) use consolidating rationales as compared with 20 per cent (71) of those advocating norms of affective neutrality. Among those advocating diffuse norms, 40 per cent (113) use consolidating rationales, but only 19 per cent (16) of those advocating specific norms do so. This is understandable since, on the one hand, consolidating rationales deny distinctions between religion and psychiatry and, on the other hand, affective and diffuse orientations militate against status distinctions. An affective relation tends toward a merging of egos; a diffuse one mutually involves counselor and client in many facets of their personalities. Attitudinally resisting distinctions between themselves and their clients may be one aspect of ministers' reluctance to segment the world in general or the fields of religion and psychiatry in particular. Contrariwise, complementing rationales and the attitudes of affective neutrality and specificity express such distinctions. The attitude of affective neutrality objectifies the role partner, places him outside the self, and restrains emotional involvement. Specificity restricts the scope of personality engagement between counselor and client.

Rationales are also conditioned by the minister's religious affiliation. Consolidating rationales are offered by 27 per cent (33) of the Catholic priests, 37 per cent (112) of the Protestant ministers, and 47 per cent (17) of the rabbis. This may be related to the ontological doctrines of the respective groups. Catholic doctrine supports a dualistic view of the realms of nature and the soul which clearly distinguish between the two healing professions. A priest would find it difficult to gloss over these differences. He offers complementing rationales which refer to the need to heal both the body and the soul. Protestants, while in principle maintaining a similar ontological doctrine, have often tended toward monistic conceptions of being. On a concrete level they are concerned with concepts such as the "priesthood of all believers." The principle of the equal status of laymen and clergymen, when generalized, is conducive to consolidating rationales. This is also the case in Judaism where the rabbi, being a teacher rather than a priest, is not religiously distinguished from laymen.

With the relation of these rationales to attitudes regarding segmentation of the environment and the self in mind, let us return to the issue of institutional identification. The minister's institutional identification may be thought of as segmented or not. An individual's reference and his membership group both contribute to the establishment of his personal identity. Among ministers with a psychiatric reference group, 50 per cent (42) use consolidating rationales, as compared with 34 per cent (92) of those with a double reference group, and 28 per cent (18) of those with a religious reference group. A minister's identity is divided when he has a psychiatric reference group. The consolidating rationale minimizes the meaning of the differences between these two sources of identity—his religious membership group and his psychiatric reference group. He does not face this problem when his reference group and membership group are identical. Thus, rationale is correlated both with role attitude and with institutional identity. However, the correlation is explained in a different way for each of these. The type of rationale is formally consistent with the type of role attitude. A rationale may be thought of as a direct manifestation of the role attitude. A "consolidating" role attitude is paralleled by a consolidating rationale. The rationale is not formally consistent with the sources of institutional identifications, but arises to solve a problem presented by these identifications. The rationale seems to be an indirect function of the problem of identification. A split identification and its correlative, divided personal identity, call forth a consolidating rationale to symbolically resolve the division.

This problem-solving consideration in the choice of rationale also seems operative with respect to orientation to the institutional doctrines as given by the religious and psychological belief indices. A curious curvilinear relationship exists here. Consolidating rationales are used by 50 per cent (2) of those high on the psychiatric belief index, 30 per cent (10) of those medium, and 39 per cent (31) of those low. Similarly, they are offered by 31 per cent (38) of those high on the religious belief index, 23 per cent (52) of those medium, and 39 per cent (44) of those low. Consolidating rationales are used by the highs and lows on both indices. A similar finding appears when we consider advocacy of institutional means and cultural goals of counseling as another measure of doctrinal adherence. It will be recalled that the degree of variation increases from ritualists to innovators to rebels. Consolidating rationales are offered by 47 per cent (17) of the ritualists, 28 per cent (67) of the innovators, and 49 per cent (41) of the rebels. Again the slightly and the extremely variant use consolidating rationales while those in the middle prefer complementing rationales. Consolidating rationales may function differently at the two ends of the continua. For the least variant, the consolidating rationale asserts what is actually the case. The behavior of the slightly variant minister is, by definition, comparable to that traditionally expected. He may support a few bland statements about the worthwhileness of science or assume mental health goals which are incorporable in a religious framework with scant difficulty. An extreme variant, on the other hand, may be caught in such a serious identity conflict that he employs the consolidating rationale to deny its uncomfortable existence. These interpretations assume that the individual chooses a rationale in terms of the way the relation between the fields appears from the perspective of his own behavior or attitudes. The rationale either simply expresses this relation or responds to a problem created by the relation.

The rationale may also function to solve a problem faced by an individual on account of his social rank. It will be recalled that some 77 per cent of the ministers in this sample of writers hold a doctorate. We discover that 39 per cent (72) of those with a doctorate but only 15 per cent (20) of those lacking it use a consolidating rationale. That is, the elite of the movement, the "ins," use the consolidating rationale. They are "melting pot" theorists whose identity is rooted in the movement and its ability to unify the two fields. Those lacking the high credentials for full role acceptance in this movement are more likely to use complementing rationales. Being in a sense outsiders themselves, they are differentiated from the mainstream of the movement. Their use of complementing rationales is a kind of "cultural pluralism" which admits of differences and then asks acceptance on the basis of them.

The rationale in its personal problem-solving function also is illustrated through a comparison of the rationales and the motives that led individuals into the movement. Of those for whom the movement was a solution to role or value conflict, 40 per cent (40) offer consolidating rationales, but only 28 per cent (46) of those who were concerned about the effectiveness of their role performance do so. Recalling that those experiencing role conflicts are the more "elite" or highly educated members of the profession, this is another example of the use of consolidating rationales by the "ins" to deny differences. Consolidating rationales also answer to the cognitive aspects of their value conflict by denying its existence. Those concerned with their competence recognize a difference in training between themselves and the psychiatrists. They deal with this discrepancy by appeal to a pluralistic brotherhood, that is, with complementing rationales.

The type of rationale preferred by different age groups may be similarly explained. Among ministers of age 45 or more, 50 per cent (30) use consolidating rationales as compared with 29 per cent (45) of those younger. The older minister, being better established professionally and again the elite "in," seeks to deny differences. The consolidating rationale allows him to maintain hegemony in his religio-psychiatric kingdom. On the personality level, his age may lead him to prefer syntheses which give unitary meaning to his life. The younger minister, on the other hand, anxious to establish his position, bases his claim on his special contribution. Again, it is the "outs" who press toward the pluralism implied in the complementing rationale.

Rationales are also related to the problems they set for themselves in the themes of their writing. Forty-five per cent (73) of those writing on the counseling relationship offer consolidating rationales, as compared with 23 per cent (35) of those writing about role relations between ministers and psychiatrists. A consolidating rationale may accompany descriptions of counseling to justify a minister's approach to his counselee by identifying it with the client's image of a similar service offered by psychological workers. Those writing of role relations prefer complementing rationales because in their argument their theme challenges them to delineate the contributions peculiar to each profession.

This finding suggests that in choosing a rationale, the ministers consider the audiences for whom their works are intended. The point may be pursued with respect to whether their audiences are psychologically or religiously oriented. Among ministers writing to a psychologically oriented audience, whether professional or lay, 52 per cent (25) offer consolidating rationales, as compared with 33 per cent (136) of those who write for a professional or lay religious audience. When facing a psychologically oriented audience, they claim acceptance on the basis of doing work similar to that accepted as legitimate by the audience. When facing a religious audience, complementing rationales justify their claims to special status as those able to contribute something beyond what the psychiatrists offer.

SUMMARY

The choice between offering a complementing or a consolidating rationale has been related to the attitudinal component of the professional's orientation to the client, the doctrinal position of his religious group, the nature of his institutional identification, his rank within the movement, the subject matter treated in the writing, and the audience to which it is directed. This superficial diversity of correlates is united by a single theme. Each type of rule oriented rationale states a way of organizing the relation between religion and psychiatry, and by implication, the individual's position in that organization. The consolidating rationale is associated with the individual's desire to belong as one of a homogeneous mass, on the basis of what he has in common with other members of the group. The complementing rationale is associated with belonging on the basis of a special contribution to the group, being a distinct individualistic member with a special function.[10] The rationales appear either as a direct manifestation of those attitudes or as attempts to resolve a disparity between the individual's actual position and the one he strives to realize.

Looking at the rationales in this light, we observe that a consolidating rationale is employed by a minister anxious to avoid distinctions between himself and his client. It is also the preferred rationale of the individual with a clear group identification who, thus, is not anxious to distinguish himself from the others in his group, and by the individual with weak identification who is anxious to deny the significance of the rift. The individual holding a high rank in his institution favors consolidating rationales as a way of maintaining his position in the group and gaining its support. Consolidating rationales are also bids to members of the other profession for acceptance on the basis of commonality.

Complementing rationales are offered by those who stress the role segregation of the professional from his clients. For those unclear about their group identity, the complementing rationale provides them with a special position slightly on the outside. Those who have low rank claim recognition on the basis of a promised special contribution. Similarly, ministers writing about role relations claim a special status for ministers among the healers. Ministers addressing a religious audience seek acknowledgement for their contribution to counseling. It is significant that in accounting for the choice between rule and socially oriented rationales, it was sufficient to refer to degree of variation from the norms. The explanation was given on the sociological level. The rationale served to resolve an interpersonal problem. In accounting for the choice between consolidating and complementing rationales, the questions of attitudes and personal identity were raised. Psychological components were included in the explanation. The form of the rationale seemed linked to a projection of the condition of the self. Perhaps our first dimension of classification catches the justifications offered to the voice without and the second classification catches the justification offered to the voice within.

In relating the choice of rationale to the social position and to the problems of the minister and psychiatrist, we have not judged the substantive validity of those rationales. The motives for proffering one or another rationale are not relevant to the correspondence of the rationale with "reality." Whether religion and psychiatry really use two languages for the same thing, or are separate but complementary must be resolved through a philosophical analysis. Our findings, however, serve to caution us against accepting the arguments for the movement at face value. Rationales are integral parts of the ideology of the movement and have consequences for its future development. Those who support complementing or consolidating rationales are not only trying to express and to manage their past and present problems, but also have different images of the future structure of the movement.

NOTES

1. A theoretical statement of the way earlier, less differentiated levels of the personality continue beneath later differentiations is found in Parsons, Bales, and Zelditch, *Family: Socialization and Interaction Process*, Chaps. III–V.

2. A methodological discussion of "real" reasons is found in Charles Kadushin, *Paths to a Psychiatric Clinic*.

3. Anna Freud, *The Ego and the Mechanisms of Defense*.

4. Since the ego ideal and the superego are formed from the internalization of these norms and values, psychological rationalizations and these public rationales will overlap. They will not be identical, however, because the ego ideal and the superego were formed in many earlier interactions, while the public rationales are offered primarily to a present group.

5. The classification of rule and socially oriented rationales follows the pattern variable distinction of universalism versus particularism. In the literature on voting, for instance, this is similar to the distinction between issue and party identification. See Angus Campbell, Gerald Gurin, and Warren E. Miller, *The Voter Decides*.

No fixed genus-species relation is implied by defining the rule and socially oriented rationales as the types and the consolidating and complementing rationales as subtypes. We might just as well have described consolidating and complementing rationales as the types with rule and socially oriented subtypes. Only the empirical exigency of too few socially oriented rationales for partitioning led to the present classificatory order.

6. Behavior or attitudes which are variant for the ministers are conforming for the psychiatrists. A psychiatrist advocating affective, par-

ticularistic, and quality norms would vary on all three counts from the pattern variables institutionalized among psychiatrists. A minister advocating the same norms would be conforming on all three counts. Thus, we find that ministers who are affective, particularistic, and quality oriented to clients, who diverge on none of the dimensions, tend more than other ministers to use socially oriented rationales. Psychiatrists with this same orientation, who diverge on all three dimensions, tend more than less variant psychiatrists to use rule oriented rationales. It is not the specific content of the orientation which determines the rationale here but the amount of divergence from the institutionalized orientation, whatever it may be.

7. The conforming position for psychiatrists is a variant position for ministers and vice versa. Ministers advocating achievement criteria tend to offer rule oriented rationales. Psychiatrists advocating the same position tend toward socially oriented rationales. Again, it is the divergence from the institutionalized position which counts rather than the context of that position. The number of psychiatrists upon which these figures are based is so small that the percentage differences, though in the expected direction, are no more than suggestive.

8. Presumably, institutional relations would also be reflected in the comparable subtypes of socially oriented rationales, were we to have enough cases to partition them in this way.

9. These two pattern variables are primarily concerned with the organization of motivation within the actor, while universalism-particularism and quality-performance are more concerned with the objects of action. See Parsons, *The Social System*, p. 105.

10. These manners of belonging are the social-psychological analogs of what, on a social system level, Emile Durkheim termed mechanical and organic solidarity. See *The Division of Labor in Society*.

Chapter VII

Relations of Pastors and Psychiatrists:
The Jurisdictional Question

THE PRECEDING CHAPTERS have shown how a change in the relations of ministers to the church and of psychiatrists to psychiatry implies a change in their counselor-client relations. Changes in institutional and role relations in religion complement those in psychiatry. This complimentarity is due to the fact that the changes are, in part, a consequence of one institution's impact upon the other. We have touched only peripherally upon the minister-psychiatrist relation through which this influence travels. What are the attitudes of these ministers toward psychiatrists and of these psychiatrists toward ministers? Specifically with respect to healing, how does each define his own special province for action and the legitimate competence of the other profession? This chapter describes some ways these ministers and psychiatrists divide their jurisdictions[1] and analyzes some factors underlying each form of division. The form of the "division of labor" is a key to the types of social relations possible between the professions.[2] Two themes will be developed at the same time in this chapter. On the one hand, there will be analysis of the technical problem of structural differentiation; on the other hand, the implications of various structural arrangements for pastor-psychiatrist relations will be specified.

TWO ASPECTS OF THE JURISDICTIONAL QUESTION: WHAT IS TO BE DONE AND WHO SHALL DO IT?

Indicators for Four Jurisdictional Positions

The ways in which responsibility for counseling is divided will be classified with respect to the counseling task and the counseling role.[3] First, the counseling task may be conceived[4] by an author as simply psychological or simply religious, or it may be conceived as involving both psychological and religious elements.[5] This is the problem of "task differentiation." Second, the author may maintain that counseling is to be carried out by a single practitioner, either a minister or a psychiatrist, or that counseling requires the cooperation of both types of practitioner.[6] This is the problem of "role differentiation." Together these form four conceptions of counseling jurisdictions or, if they are effected in practice, forms of "structural differentiation." These may be diagramed as follows:[7]

		ROLE DIFFERENTIATION	
		One Role	Two Roles
TASK DIFFERENTIATION	One Task	Material Reductionists Spiritual Reductionists	Alternativists
	Two Tasks	Dualists	Specialists

Reductionists see no reason for either task or role differentiation. Personal problems may be subsumed under a single rubric, and one type of therapist is sufficient. Material reductionists believe that personality and the problem of counseling are exhaustively analyzable in terms of scientific psychology. Psychiatrists in this group tend to believe that they alone should do psychotherapy. Ministerial material reductionists tend to accept psychiatric therapy but believe that a psychologically trained minister would be a self-sufficient counselor. Spiritual reductionists grasp personality and counseling solely in religious terms. Ministers in this group tend to believe that they alone should counsel. Psychiatrist spiritual reductionists accept pastoral counselors but believe a religiously oriented psychiatrist alone could counsel as well.

Dualists believe that a disturbance of personality has both religious and psychological aspects but do not see the need for two types of practitioners. Ministers and psychiatrists in this group believe that each alone would be a self-sufficient counselor if he were doubly qualified.

The alternativists are opposite to the dualists in their conception. They support role differentiation but retain an undifferentiated concept of the task area. Minister and psychiatrist roles are considered functional alternatives for meeting the same, usually psychological, problem. The specialists recognize task differentiation and role differentiation. Religious and psychological problems are placed in different, in this sample usually complementary, categories for which the pastoral and psychiatric roles are respectively competent. Following are a few illustrations of authors' positions used as indicators for classifying their writings.

The spiritual reductionist position is exemplified by Hugh Chrichton-Miller who says religion provides the symbols for a total attitude toward life and the clue to the adjustment of any individual must make (265). Albert C. Outler affirms that a single human predicament, a declination away from God's purpose, accounts for the tragedy of human life (1005). Though these individuals address themselves to task rather than role differentiation, it was possible to infer from their general orientation that they consider a pastoral-type role alone sufficient for counseling.

The material reductionist position is illustrated by Johannes Neumann who says spiritual sickness stems from a feeling of worthlessness and insecurity. Piety is a matter of human emotions (950). David Forsyth says religion is the product of an infantile mind. A belief in God, the Trinity, the intercessor, etc., is a colossal projection of the family relationship (425). Even without direct reference to the counseling role, an inference was made from these types of positions that a single psychologically oriented counselor would be adequate without assistance from religion.

The dualist position, accepting task but not role differentiation, is exemplified by Samuel Moore Shoemaker who shows how Christ as a psychologist, and as an example for modern practitioners, dealt with three levels of life: the level of instinct, the level of conscience, and the level of Grace (1156). Eric S. Waterhouse states that the clergy are eminently qualified to engage in mind healing by combining psychology and curing of unhappy souls (1271). A. T. Mollegen would have psychoanalysts become Christians while ministers become psychoanalysts (904). Alexander Allen Steinbach says Hillel, the Talmudic Rabbi, provided both a religious and psychiatric therapy (1187).

Alternativists accept role but not task differentiation. Seward Hiltner, for example, says there is not a generic type of malady of which one can say that this is only for the psychiatrist or only for the clergyman (559). Robert A. Preston claims that in actual clinical experience the psychiatrist and the man of religion confront the same set of facts (1052).

Specialists accept or advocate both task and role differentiation. Cyril Edward Hudson, for instance, describes differences between psychoanalysis and confession. The repressed cannot be confessed, the analyst has no patience with repeated confession which does not cure Confession, on the other hand, aims at absolution and does not depend on transference (601). Rollin J. Fairbanks supports development of specifically pastoral skills but warns students not to try to function as psychiatrists (400). The relationship of referral is common. Eric S. Waterhouse, in a work following the one cited above to illustrate dualism, says ministers should have a grasp of psychological problems, realize their own limitations, and know when to recommend psychotherapeutic attention (1272). Louis Beirnaert separates guilt consciousness as a religious fact needing a religious solution from guilt as a pathological phenomenon (79, 81). For John Sutherland Bonnell the pastoral psychiatrist enables people to choose between good and evil. The medical psychiatrist directs his efforts to the regulation of feelings, emotions, and thoughts (154). H. Flanders Dunbar points out that the clergyman is concerned with purpose and the psychiatrist with causality. Muddy therapy results when one and the same person tries to combine treatment by two approaches (368).

Frequency of Each Jurisdictional Position

The reader must sense that some positions on the division of labor are more characteristically ministerial and others are more favored by psychiatrists. Table 33 shows the distribution of each

Table 33—Proportion of Ministers and Psychiatrists Advocating Each Type of Role and Task Differentiation

Role and Task Differentiations	Ministers	Psychiatrists
	(in Per Cent)	
Material Reductionists	13	9
Spiritual Reductionists	20	10
Dualists	33	23
Alternativists	1	2
Specialists	33	56
Total	100	100
	(427)	(126)

form of role and task differentiation among members of each profession.

We find that 33 per cent of the ministers and 19 per cent of the psychiatrists tend to be either material or spiritual reductionists.[8] This contrasts with 33 per cent of the ministers and 56 per cent of the psychiatrists who prefer specialism. These preferences are consistent with their orientation to their clients within their roles. Ministers, it will be recalled, tend to orient diffusely in counseling, to be concerned with a broad range of parishioner relations; psychiatrists tend to be specific, to limit concern to a narrow range of the patient's behavior. That the form of division of labor between the professions is consistent with the form of relation between each professional and his client is understandable. The practitioner involved in a broad range of relations with his client is less likely to feel a need for supplementary aid from another role. One who limits his relations to his client, while admitting that the client has other needs, would be more likely to seek the cooperation of another person.

Dualists are more common among the ministers than among the psychiatrists. This may be due to ministers who accept the validity of a psychological as well as a religious approach, but who are reluctant to relinquish the generally diffuse competence of their status. The finding might also represent a greater readiness of ministers to seek psychological competence than of phychiatrists to seek competence in religion. A psychiatrist who considers counseling as both religious and psychological tends to allocate the religious part to the minister, perhaps sensing a special charismatic character of the ministerial role. Since accession to a charismatic position tends to be by "call" rather than by training, he may be reluctant to assume the responsibility of it. These factors would, in part, also account for the psychiatrists' interest in specialism. The greater readiness of ministers to integrate psychological elements into their role than of the psychiatrists to assume religious tasks reiterates the fact that ministers in this movement shift more drastically in a psychiatric direction than psychiatrists shift in a religious direction.

Alternativism, though a theoretically possible position, seems to be empirically insignificant. Apparently, when one agrees that two different individuals are needed as counselors, it is difficult to deny that they have differing task competencies. The fact that the dualists, who agree to differentiate the task but accept the need for only a single counselor, are empirically frequent suggests that task differentiation may be almost a required antecedent to role differentiation.

THE CONDITIONS FOR STRUCTURAL DIFFERENTIATION AND ITS IMPLICATIONS FOR PASTOR-PSYCHIATRIST RELATIONS

The Influence of Institutional Variation On Jurisdictional Positions

The variant assumes some of the counseling means and goals of the opposite profession. The extent to which an individual accepts the characteristics of another profession might well condition his relation to members of that other profession, that is, his position on the jurisdictional question. The association between the jurisdictional positions and the variant subtypes is shown in Table 34.

As the extent of variation increases, we find a rather consistent change in the way of dividing up responsibilty for counseling. Each form of the division of labor, in its association with a particular variant type or stand on the means-goals question, has implications for interprofessional relations.

Beginning with the ministers and taking one jurisdictional position at a time, we find that militant conformist ministers, more than the others, tend to be spiritual reductionists, neither recognizing psychological aspects of human distress nor admitting the authority

Table 34—Ministers and Psychiatrists of Each Variant Subtype According to the Form of Role and Task Differentiation

	ROLE AND TASK DIFFERENTIATIONS (in Per Cent)				
	Spiritual			Material	
Variant Subtype	Reductionists	Dualists	Specialists[a]	Reductionists	Number
Ministers					
Militant Conformists	44	17	37	2	(75)
Ritualists	35	26	32	17	(72)
Innovators	10	37	42	11	(233)
Rebels	2	33	24	41	(46)
Psychiatrists					
Militant Conformists	—	—	71	29	(21)
Ritualists	8	21	65	6	(52)
Innovators	5	37	58	—	(19)
Rebels	24	32	38	6	(34)

a. Specialists include alternativists for the remainder of the discussion.

of psychiatric counseling. They advocate the ministerial as the only role competent for counseling. Similarly, psychiatric militant conformists are more likely than any other variant form of psychiatrist to be material reductionists. They recognize only psychological roots of problems and their own competence in dealing with them. That is, the individual who in his own role performance rejects norms of another status for counseling (the militant conformist position) is also likely to reject the right of the occupant of that other status to counsel on his own (the reductionist position). There is no basis for cooperation in counseling between these two types. Each militant conformist reductionist sees himself in fundamental competition with members of the opposite profession for the soul of the psyche, as the case may be, of man. These ministers preach against secular therapists and these psychiatrists seek legislation against lay therapists.[9] The militant conformist psychiatrists who support the specialist position are exceptions to this generalization. Their position is not to reject the validity of the spiritual but to reject it as a legitimate interest for themselves. They have a basis for cooperation with ministers.

Ritualist ministers, though advocating psychiatric goals for their own practice, are still quite likely to take a spiritual reductionist jurisdictional position. The ritualist reductionist would be in greater potential conflict with psychiatrists than would the militant conformist reductionist. Since, like the psychiatrists, he is interested in improving mental health, he would compete with the psychiatrists on their own ground. He claims to be the only one competent to employ the religious means needed to attain that objective. The ritualist reductionist minister is, however, less well defended against attack by the psychiatrist than is the militant conformist reductionist. These militant conformists are more likely to enjoy institutional support such as that provided the Catholic priest by the Church's critique of psychoanalysis. The ritualist, since he dissents from traditional goals, would have to establish his own legitimacy and perhaps appeal directly for popular support. This is the problem of the faith healer.[10]

Ritualists are also rather likely to be dualists and specialists. These positions, which involve elements of both fields, would seem more "natural" for them. The ritualist dualist might conflict with psychiatrists because he believes he can provide a full counseling experience, but he would not define psychiatrists as irrelevant or dangerous, as the spiritual reductionist might. He might complain that psychiatrists provide an incomplete therapy. This type of minister would enter training relationships with psychiatrists or psychologists in which he might have to commit himself not to become a therapist. If he explicitly intends to counsel, he would have to rely on individual supervision or special pastoral training programs. This would bring him into relation with psychiatrists who are themselves institutionally variant.

The ritualist specialist identifies with psychiatric goals but would advocate role differentiation based on their respective procedures. The ritualist specialist minister is in an excellent position to enjoy cooperative relations with psychiatrists. The ministers would apply religious means to complement traditional psychiatric procedures in the pursuit of the common goal of mental health. This is the situation of a minister on the staff of a psychiatric clinic or hospital.

Among ministers, specialism is even more strongly associated with innovation than with ritualism. Ministers who incorporate psychological procedures into their own repertoire seem to be the most ready to accept the differentiated healing competence of psychiatrists. Applying the same techniques but differing in goals this type of minister would, in effect, be saying to the psychiatrist, you heal his psyche or his body while I help save his soul. These ministers could participate in a training relationship with psychiatrists without posing a threat and could cooperate with psychiatrists in clinical settings.

Innovation is also asociated with dualism among minister. As a dualist, the minister recognizes both spiritual and psychological aspects of his parishioner's problem, but feels that he as a single practitioner is able to meet the need adequately. As an innovator he would advocate that this single practitioner use psychiatric methods. This type of minister tends to compete with the psychiatrist. His application of psychological procedures makes him a real alternative to a psychiatric counselor who might be serving within a church setting. Though more variant from the church than ritualist dualist ministers, they are less likely to encounter opposition from psychiatry or psychiatrists. Since they formulate their goals in spiritual terms, define their work as religious, remain within church settings, call themselves pastors, and do not claim the title of "psychotherapist," psychiatrists are less likely to recognize their competitive potential. A large number of the ministers in this study fall into this classification.

Among ministers, rebellion is associated with material reductionism. Thus, it has in common with militant conformism that both advocate reductionist positions on the jurisdictional issue. This reaffirms the earlier suggestion that rebels and militant conformists are similar in many formal ways despite their radical substantive opposition. A rebel minister who is a material reductionist may assume a psychological counselor-type role. He might practice as a special minister in a church or establish his own private office. As a counseling pastor, he would compete with psychiatrists but would maintain working relations with them during training, in meeting the legal requirements of clinics, and regarding committing a patient. This relation must be tenuous because, though denied legitimation by the legislative arm of the community, he would believe himself a competent psychotherapist. With less ambivalence he would apply to psychiatrists as consultants for psychosomatic problems, or when pharmacological or other medical-type therapy is indicated. Counseling pastors are denied admission to some organizations of therapists. At the same time, they are estranged from the traditional ministerial groups including some of those established for pastors. Enjoying the institutional protection neither of the church nor of psychiatry, their community position would tend to be weak. As a result, they would tend to establish their own organizations of psychologically oriented pastoral counselors.

Let us turn to the psychiatrists. Both militant conformist and ritualist psychiatrists are likely to advocate specialism. The specialist psychiatrist accepts the relevance of religion to health and so has a basis for cooperative relations with ministers. It does not follow, however, that he is prepared to have ministers deal with problems which he diagnoses as psychological. A militant conformist who is a specialist would not allow religious elements to intrude into his work, but might refer a patient who raises a spiritual issue to a pastor. This relation of referral is apt to be the common one. A ritualist who is a specialist might join with the minister to attain their common spiritual goal. He would contribute his psychological know-how to complement the minister's religious approach. The psychiatric consultant to religious organizations may function in this way.

The innovator dualist combination is common among psychiatrists. This type would consider himself a self-sufficient practitioner. He applies religious "know-how" to the combined religio-mental health problems of his patients. The kind of relationships he establishes with ministers would depend upon the extent to which he uses religious means. As long as he restricts himself to praying with a patient or encouraging the patient's spiritual life, his relations with the church will be comfortable. Ministers who do not themselves practice a psychologically oriented pastoral ministry would be anxious to establish a relationship of referral with this type of psychiatrist whom, they would feel, could deal with mental aberrations without destroying the individual's faith. Were the psychiatrist to present himself as religiously "intercessionary"[11] or to introduce unorthodox religious ways, he would encounter the traditional religious opposition to noninstitutional religious "virtuosos."[12] Few psychiatrists in this study behave in this way.

Among psychiatrists, rebellion and spiritual reductionism seem associated. The rebel reductionist would have little basis for stable cooperation with ministers in counseling, though he might relate to them in a traditional church setting. This type of psychiatrist is, in effect, providing pastoral-type services. Estranged from the traditional psychiatric organizations, he would seek special organizations for religiously oriented psychiatrists.[13]

The Basis of Counseling Specialism

Structural differentiation has been described as composed of task and role differentiation. Where task differentiation does not take place, there seems to be little chance of role differentiation and, as a consequence, little chance of developing cooperative relations between ministers and psychiatrists in the counseling area.

Once ministers and psychiatrists assert that personality has both spiritual and psychological aspects, that is, accept task differentiation, the possibility of their cooperation hinges upon whether they are dualists, who reject role differentiation, or specialists, who advocate role differentiation. A dualist tends to be self-sufficient, having only limited need for members of the other profession. Specialists, on the other hand, claim a more limited jurisdiction for themselves and grant the legitimacy of another professional counselor. This permits the specialist to establish a working relationship with members of the other profession. In the following pages we consider only those who choose either dualism or specialism, and inquire into influences upon this particular choice. As each factor is examined, the proportions choosing specialism will be presented, with the understanding that the complementary portion of 100 per cent choose dualism.

An individual's willingness to restrict his own jurisdiction and to work with members of another group, to be a specialist, would be related to his acceptance of the standards of that other group, that is, to taking that group as a reference group. It would seem that a cooperative working relationship must be built on some common assumptions about the enterprise. Comparing ministers and psychiatrists who have religious and psychiatric reference groups, we find that among ministers 57 per cent (64) of those with a religious reference group but only 37 per cent (61) of those with a psychiatric reference group are specialists. Among psychiatrists, 85 per cent (45) of those with a psychiatric reference group and 70 per cent (10) of those with a religious reference group choose specialism.[14] The findings are the reverse of the common-sense suggestion that it becomes easier for an individual to share an enterprise with members of another group when he is oriented to their way of doing things. An individual seems prepared to limit his own jurisdiction, to be a specialist, and cooperate with members of another group when he is solidly anchored in his own group as a reference group. A minister or psychiatrist who takes the opposite group as a reference group becomes like the members of that other group while remaining in his own. This may provide a basis for becoming a dualist rather than a specialist. A minister with a psychiatric reference group, for example, internalizes psychiatric standards and so comes to feel that he can fulfill both religious and psychiatric functions. Consequently, he has less tendency to share the field with psychiatrists and, in effect, becomes their competitor. The same may be said for the psychiatrist with a religious reference group. Being a specialist then, and, by implication, able to work with the other professions, is contingent upon taking one's own group as a reference group.[15]

The form of the division of labor would tend to be a function of the goal or purpose of that labor.[16] In Chapter III counselors were classified according to whether they set meaning or instrumental goals for counseling. Among ministers, 54 per cent (94) of those advocating meaning goals and 45 per cent (77) of those advocating instrumental goals support a specialist position. Among psychiatrists, the comparable proportions are 80 per cent (20) and 81 per cent (47). The type of goal advocated seems unrelated to the form of differentiation. This does not seem reasonable. Perhaps the influence of the goal of therapy is obscured because if its association with variant type. By relating counseling goals and form of role differentiation while holding variant subtype constant, we allow for this possibilty. This test cannot be made for psychiatrists, since there are too few in the sample. Among conformist and ritualist ministers, however, 76 per cent (17) of those advocating meaning goals and 29 per cent (21) of those advocating instrumental goals are specialists. Among ministers who are innovators or rebels, the respective proportions are 15 per cent (60) and 45 per cent (53). There is a marked association between goals and form of differentiation. However, the direction of the association is reversed among the less and more variant. Among the less variant ministers meaning goals are associated with specialism; among the more variant, instrumental goals are associated with specialism. Why might this be? Meaning goals, it will be recalled, are "ideal typically" associated with the ministerial role. A militant conformist or ritualist minister who advocates meaning goals would be identified with his institution on both of these counts: he describes his counseling in terms taken from religious discourse, and what he does is to help the parishioner with problems of value and purpose, an accepted religious pursuit. Those who are so identified tend to be specialists. This seems to repeat the previous finding that a solidary relationship with one's own institution permits cooperation as a specialist with representatives of another institution. We also find, however, that the innovators and rebels, those who support instrumental goals and so identify with their institution neither in their counseling language nor in pursuing a traditional religious goal, also tend to be the specialists. The above explanatory hypothesis about specialism and group solidarity apparently requires further specification. Both of these findings would be understandable were specialism related to a consistency in indentification. On the one hand, the individual who is either solidly within or solidly outside his membership group would be the one to support separate jurisdictions. On the other hand, those in an ambiguous position, either as less variant ministers who advocate instrumental goals or as more variant ministers who advocate meaning goals, would tend toward dualism.[17] Looking at the reference group finding in this light, the implication is that ministers, for instance, who have a psychiatric reference group would be better able to work with psychiatrists if they actually assumed a psychiatric (psychological) membership group as well, either by going to medical school or by becoming academically certified clinical psychologists. In this case his specialism parallels, instead of complementing, that of the psychiatrist. At the same time, the relation of complementary skills is possible for the minister with a religious reference group who remains wholeheartedly a minister. (Of course, he might be one of those few in the sample with recognized statuses in both institutions.)[18]

The suggested conclusion is that a clear identity may predispose an individual to specialism. Whether or not he becomes a specialist in practice depends on other factors. Education seems significant in the choice. Of ministers in this sample, 62 per cent (45) of those who did not complete doctoral education and 35 per cent (125) of those holding the doctorate are specialists. The greater tendency to dualism among the more highly educated suggests a "renaissance man" element. The highly educated are more anxious to handle psychological as well as religious problems. The less educated are reluctant to assert competency in both fields.

This finding points up two aspects of specialization. For Durkheim specialization is, in part, the result of a "struggle for existence" between "social segments." Individuals belonging to the segment losing out in this struggle maintain themselves by concentrating on and developing proficiency in a narrow portion of the task. They cooperate with other such specialists to accomplish the broader task. This is the type of specialization found on the assembly line where the simplified task is at a lower level of competence, as measured by the amount of training required, than the more complex task of the displaced artisan. Individuals belonging to the successful segment retain hegemony over the entire complex of tasks. In order to win the struggle, members of this social segment push their ability ahead and become another kind of "specialist." This second type of "specialist" results not from a partitioning of a job into simple elements, but from an accretion of elements through advanced work. The dualist of this study is of the latter type.[19] The few cases of individuals in this sample who are both ordained as clergymen and qualified in psychiatry would tend, in their own work, to be dualist "specialists."

Let us apply the Durkheim reasoning to our findings. The competition which generates the type of differentiation with which we are concerned is not that between traditional ministers and traditional psychiatrists. It is within religion and within psychiatry. An individual minister or psychiatrist may attempt to advance his professional rank by increasing his general competence. Education is a legitimate road to advancement. Some ministers do this by learning psychology and some psychiatrists by adding a religious approach to therapy. The "vanquished" ones with less education restrict themselves to their own bailiwick. The minister may recognize a psychological problem and refer his parishioner to a psychiatrist, and the psychiatrist may sense religious questions in therapy and refer his patient to a minister. In this way cooperative relations are established between members of the two professions. The "triumphant" ones with higher education are the dualists who remain self-sufficient social segments caring for both the religious and psychological elements. If they are psychiatrists, they may be appointed administrators of ministerial counselors. If they are ministers, they may be educators of pastors.

The choice between dualism and specialism is also influenced by the individual's religious membership. Among clergymen, 65 per cent (85) of the Catholics, 50 per cent (18) of the Jews, and 43 per cent (187) of the Protestants advocate specialism as opposed to dualism. Among psychiatrists specialism is advocated by 87 per cent (45) of the Catholics, 86 per cent (22) of the Jews, and 60 per cent (35) of the Protestants. The issue here may hinge on the relation between lay and religious roles in each group. It is not, as in the above case, the competition between the present roles which influences the division of labor. Rather, it is the way the competition was resolved long ago and embedded in the groups' cultural stances. Where the resolution was in terms of a "maximum type" religious organization, with a clerical class clearly set off from the laymen, the specialist relation would be preferred. The Catholic preference for specialism is consistent with the Thomistic recognition of the separate realms of Grace and nature. Catholics, for example, are often concerned with distinguishing between sacred confession of sin and secular compulsive neurotic scrupulosity. The role of the "consecrated" priest is radically separate from that of the layman. Protestants, on the other hand, are less concerned about the separation of these two realms and are more likely to observe that nature itself is a manifestation of the Divine. A Protestant "ordained" minister is not, except among maximal groups, such as the Anglicans, radically separated from the lay congregation. Protestants address their clergymen as Mister and preach the principle of the "priesthood of all believers." Jews are midway between the two. In one sense the rabbi is a layman. He is neither "consecrated" nor "ordained." By virtue of his profession of special knowledge he is set apart from laymen and "entrusted" as a teacher and judge. Since the source of his authority is a defined body of knowledge, the rabbi is less likely to claim a psychiatric function which is based on another body of knowledge.[20]

CONCLUSIONS

A Model of Structural Differentiation

We have discussed the affinities between the way an individual departs from institutional tradition and the position he takes on the jurisdictional question. At the same time, we have asked for the meaning to minister-psychiatrist relations when one or the other variant subtype assumes one or another particular combination of jurisdictional positions. The variant subtypes, it will be recalled, are ordered in terms of increasing variation. The association between these increasingly variant subtypes and the succeeding types of role and task differentiation suggests a tentative model of the process of structural differentiation in the religio-psychiatric movement.[21] For ministers, reading Table 34 from top to bottom and from left to right, we begin with an undifferentiated role. With increasing variation, there is first a bifurcation of the task. This is followed by advocacy of specialization, a recognition that each of these tasks is to be met by a separate compentency. As the minister becomes even more variant, he assumes the characteristics of the psychiatrist and advocates a material reductionism. In so doing, he revokes the task and role divisions and accepts the psychological as the only valid approach. Psychiatrists, reading Table 34 from top to bottom and from right to left, begin with a combination of specialism and reductionism. As militant conformists they either consider themselves the only required competency or they separate mental health as their preserve. With increasing variation, they dualistically absorb the characteristics of the ministerial role while still allowing that their patient may be presenting spiritual as well as psychological problems. If they become rebels, the accept a spiritual reductionism, no longer attending to the psychological aspects. This suggests that the schismogenetic model of role differentiation, which argues that new roles are formed through a bifurcation of a previous role, may not be complete. This model does seem to fit the development of specialists from dualists among ministers.[22] Two tasks originally handled by the same individual are partitioned as the specialities of two persons. New roles, however, may also be formed by a combination of elements from two previously separate roles. This occurs among psychiatrists, for example, who move from specialism to dualism.[23] They take the task performed by the minister and incorporate it within their own role. Other new roles are formed simply by requiring that the role occupants have some new accompanying statuses without changing the definition of the role. This occurs when, for example, a minister moves from spiritual to material reductionism or a psychiatrist from material to spiritual reductionism. The difference between a spiritual reductionist position occupied by a psychiatrist or a minister derives from the other statuses of the role occupant; from the context provided by the status and role sets in which it is embedded. For example, a minister who is a material reductionist may also be a preacher and a teacher of religion. He would not accompany his psychological-type counseling with outside medical activities as a psychiatrist would.

Optimum Conditions for Pastor-Psychiatrist Cooperation

The microcosmic process of structural differentiation presented in this chapter may conceivably recapitulate the historic macrocosmic differentiation of the scientific from the religious healer. Following Durkheim's reasoning, this split may have grown out of a struggle within the status of the priest-healer. The healing function, along with the "devil" theory of disease, remained principally within the priestly office while science specialized in the ways of the world of nature. With the approach of the modern era, the attention of the scientific medical healer was drawn to that aspect of man which he could include in the realm of nature. He and the religious healer found themselves again claiming the same jurisdiction. In this chapter, we have observed a new attempt to define their jurisdictions and conjectured about the social relations generated by each new division of labor. Some of these relations are or may become conflictual. One type of conflict negates the practice of the opposite profession. Militant conformist ministers who are spiritual reductionists and militant conformist psychiatrists who are material reductionists both lay claim to the entire province of mental healing. Each insists that what the other offers as therapy is invalid. A second type of conflict arises when the individuals seem to pre-empt the province of the opposite profession. Rebel ministers who are material reductionists and to a lesser degree ministerial innovators, and ritualists who are dualists, may be attacked by psychiatry as "lay therapists." Rebel psychiatrists who are spiritual reductionists could be defined by the church as heretics who use religious symbols in unfaithful or illegitimate ways. Practically speaking, however, the latter is a minor problem since there are at present few rebel spiritual reductionist psychiatrists.

Cooperative relations are most probable between ministers and psychiatrists, usually innovators or ritualists, who are specialists. Their debate might concern the exact line of demarcation between their roles. Once it is set, however, they can establish a joint relationship on the basis of complementary competencies. It seems that the individual who is most solidly identified with a single status group, especially if that is his membership group, is most likely to enter this type of cooperative relation. The highly educated among dualists, who truly possess a double competence, may mediate these two specialist roles despite the fact that their dualism may put them in conflict with members of the opposite profession. The mediation of the dualists may consist in providing intellectual and administrative "cross ties" between the two professional specialists.

NOTES

1. The problem of administrative jurisdiction and a selected bibliography on the subject may be found in Robert K. Merton, *et al.*, *Reader in Bureaucracy*. See especially the article by Marshall E. Dimock, "Expanding Jurisdictions: A Case Study in Bureaucratic Conflict," *Ibid.*, pp. 282–291; and the Hoover Commission, "Duplication of Function: A Case Study in Bureaucratic Conflict," *ibid.*, pp. 291–297.

2. The contribution of the division of labor to social relations is delineated by Emile Durkheim, *The Division of Labor in Society*. The problem was presented in its classical form by Aristotle in his *Nichomachean Ethics* and by Plato in *The Republic*. Adam Smith used this particular term.

3. There are a number of ways of classifying the division of labor. For example, Cecil C. North, *Social Differentiation*, proceeds from a biological, functional, and social morphology. Wilbert E. Moore and Arnold S. Feldman, *Labor Commitment and Social Change in Developing Areas*, describe three types of the division of labor according to whether it is division within the work team, between different work positions in the flow of production, or on the basis of authority. Since our interest is in jurisdictions, we will confine ourselves to the simple division according to what is to be done and who is to do it. See also footnote 7.

4. The division of labor according to task or function in a factory, for example, would be based on relatively objective criteria. There would be little disagreement that carpentry is needed in building a wooden rowboat while welding is needed in construction of a steel ship. Counseling functions, however, are influenced by the theoretical perspective of the counselor.

Consequently, our classification is based on the more subjective "conception" of what the nature of the task is.

5. The division of labor according to the "product" or the types of functions is what Max Weber terms "specification of function." See *Theory of Social and Economic Organization*, pp. 218 ff.

6. A division of labor according to the functions performed by a given person is termed by Weber as the "specialization of function." See *Ibid.* Chester I. Barnard says that men specialize but work is functionalized. See *The Functions of the Executive*.

7. This is the simplest typology. More than two roles and two tasks may be involved in effecting healing. A specialized referral service may precede counseling. A psychologist may be called in for psychodiagnostics, an internist for a physical examination, nurses to care for in-patients, an occupational therapist may be either part of therapy or of rehabilitation, and a social worker may help the patient return to the community. These professionals may be considered integral to counseling or as adjuncts to the counselor. On the relations between members of these various mental health professions see Alfred H. Stanton and Morris S. Schwartz, *The Mental Hospital*. We shall be concerned only with differentiation between the ministerial and psychiatric roles in counseling.

8. The proportional excess of ministerial over psychiatric material reductionists does not imply that ministers are more psychologically oriented than psychiatrists but only that the spiritual reductionists do not admit the relevance of psychological considerations. Since the remainder do, in one way or another, it appears that 80 per cent of the ministers and 90 per cent of the psychiatrists are concerned with psychological aspects of counseling. Since only material reductionists do not admit religious factors, it appears that 87 per cent of the ministers and 91 per cent of the psychiatrists are concerned with spiritual elements in counseling. That members of both professions in the sample are concerned with applying both fields is a function of the criteria for admitting an item to this literature. The few who exclude one or the other field tend to be the militant conformists or rebels.

9. Militant conformist reductionist ministers would, of course, seek medical aid for physical illness. The extreme spiritual reductionist, such as the Christian Scientist, who would not do so, does not appear in our sample. Similarly, militant conformist reductionist psychiatrists might attend church, but would not consider ministerial counseling for what they diagnose as psychological disturbance.

10. An illustration of a nonrequited appeal of religious healing for institutional and public support is found in Melvin Tumin and Arnold S. Feldman, "The Miracle at Sabana Grande," *Public Opinion Quarterly*, pp. 125–139.

11. This is the problem in religion of "false" prophets. See Wach, *op. cit.*, p. 334; and Max Weber, *Ancient Judaism*, pp. 287 ff.

12. See H. H. Gerth and C. Wright Mills, *From Max Weber: Essays in Sociology*, pp. 288 ff.

13. Groups of the type mentioned in the text for rebel ministers and psychiatrists are the Association of Psychoanalytically Oriented Pastoral Counselors, the Association for Existential Analysis, and the group around the short-lived *Journal of Psychotherapy as a Religious Process*. Existential analysis need not be religious, as the counseling of Binswanger and the writing of Sartre attest. Existential analysis in the United States, however, seems influenced by religious existentialism.

14. Since "reference group" is correlated with "variant types," it is necessary to test whether this finding might be attributable to the influence of variant subtypes. We do not have enough cases to make this test for psychiatrists, but among ministers who are either militant conformists or ritualists, 66 per cent (38) of those with a religious reference group and 11 per cent (9) of those with a psychiatric reference group choose specialism. Among ministers who are innovators or rebels the comparable proportions are 50 per cent (26) and 38 per cent (52). Thus, the finding holds even with variant subtype held constant. The influence of reference group, however, is greater among the less variant.

15. It is likely that to be a specialist one must be a bit of a dualist as well. One must internalize some aspect of the role of the other to anticipate his behavior in order to interact with him. George H. Mead describes the image of another's role as the complement of the other's actual role. These are two aspects of the same social act. See "The Genesis of the Self and Social Control," *International Journal of Ethics*, pp. 251–277.

16. This is part of what is meant by relating functional differentiation to "system exigencies." See, for example, Morris Zelditch, Jr., "Role Differentiation in the Nuclear Family: A Comparative Study," in Parsons, Bales, and Zelditch, *op. cit.*, pp. 307–351. These system requirements may be latent, that is, not explicitly known to or formulated by the participants. The purposes with which we deal here are those manifestly stated by the authors.

17. This fits the discrepancy in magnitude of difference found in footnote 14. Of the less variant who have a religious reference group (the consistent conforming position), 66 per cent advocate specialism, as opposed to 50 per cent of those who are more variant but have a religious reference group (the inconsistant position). Similarly, of ministers who are more variant and also have a psychiatric reference group (the consistent nonconforming position), 38 per cent are specialists, as compared to 11 per cent of the more variant who have a religious reference group. Though consistency of orientation is more closely associated with specialism

than is ambiguity of orientation, the consistent identifiers with their group are in both cases more likely to be specialists than those consistently not identifying (66 per cent vs. 38 per cent for reference groups and 76 per cent vs. 45 per cent for goals).

18. This conjunction between a consistent self-image and ability to work with others has been noted by students of the "self." See, for example, Prescott Lecky, *Self-Consistency: A Theory of Personality*.

19. Durkheim states in *The Division of Labor in Society*, p. 269, ". . . on the one hand the triumphant segmental organ, as it were, can take care of the vaster task, devolving upon it only by a greater division of labor and, on the other hand, the vanquished can maintain themselves only by concentrating their efforts upon a part of the total function they fulfilled up to then." Durkheim then goes on to discuss the "vanquished" specialists but says little about the "triumphant" specialists, or dualists, and their division of labor. The individual who specializes in organic chemistry or the medical general practitioner who returns to school to specialize in internal medicine broaden rather than narrow the scope of their competence. They are more likely to be given authority over the "generalists" of their profession. Administration becomes a part of the newly specialized function.

20. That Jewish psychiatrists advocate specialism to the same degree as, rather than slightly less than, Catholic psychiatrists may well be a "ceiling effect." The difference may be obscured because the entire distribution is skewed toward the upper limit.

21. The model is limited in that the data refer to group distributions rather than to individual ministers or psychiatrists who have moved through such a process.

22. This is the model of role differentiation described as "binary fission" by Parsons, Bales, and Zelditch, *op. cit.*, esp. pp. 45–54; and by Talcott Parsons and N. J. Smelser, *Economy and Society*, pp. 255 ff.

23. A similar process is involved in what George H. Mead terms assuming the role of the generalized other. See *Mind, Self, and Society*. According to Parsons and Bales, *op. cit.*, pp. 146 ff., this type of new role would be considered a "point of intersection" of "derivatives" of the other roles. This sort of development might be expected as part of "cultural diffusion."

Chapter VIII

Debating the Counselor's Qualifications

HOW DOES A PERSON become a counselor? How are criteria established for allowing one person to assume the responsibility for guiding another person? This is the problem of the criteria upon which a role is allocated to an individual, or the problem of "allocative criteria." The criteria for selecting a counselor would depend on the definition of the jurisdictions of pastoral counselors and religiously oriented psychiatrists. These allocative criteria may refer to other statuses that the counselors occupy. Ministerial spiritual reductionists and dualists would prefer that the role be allocated to ministers. Psychiatric material reductionists and dualists would prefer psychiatric role occupants. Specialists would recruit both ministers and psychiatrists for a cooperative relation. Ministerial material reductionists and psychiatric spiritual reductionists, though they might admit a member of either profession, would prefer that the incumbents be members of their own institutions.

Some nonexplicit allocative criteria are suggested by the characteristics of the writers on the subject of religion and psychiatry. In Chapter I we found that these authors tend to be from the more industrialized societies, from Protestant denominations, and from among the more highly educated, and that they are almost exclusively male.[1] Religio-psychiatric counseling roles probably are occupied by individuals with characteristics similar to those of these authors. This chapter analyzes a few of the considerations which enter in considering a candidate for the counseling role.[2]

INDICATORS FOR ALLOCATIVE CRITERIA

Attributes required to qualify for a role may be classified in terms of the ways an individual comes to possess them. On the one hand, a candidate may acquire his qualifications through training. Role allocation would then be based on criteria of achievement. Achievements required for becoming a counselor may involve religious as well as psychological knowledge or skills and be termed respectively religious and psychological achievement criteria. On the other hand, accession to the role may be contingent upon certain qualities the candidate possesses through no effort of his own, such as birth to a particular family or religious group. These may be termed ascriptive criteria.[3] Ascriptive criteria also may be phrased in terms of either religious or psychological attributes but, because of a paucity of cases, this distinction will not be maintained.

The following are some examples of indicators used in classifying items according to allocative criteria. Though most authors advocate some combination of achievement and ascriptive criteria, the classification is based upon the type of criteria which were predominant in the abstract of the book or article.

Items recommending that counselors be trained in skills and techniques, or learn the theory of psychotherapy, were classified as advocating psychological achievements as criteria for role allocation. Among ministers, Anton T. Boisen, for example, writes of the importance of clinical training for theological students (134). J. S. Cammack discourages priests from engaging in psychotherapy unless they become medically qualified (241). Paul E. Johnson, in a volume on Clinical Pastoral Training, recommends adopting training methods of allied professions (639). Knowledge of a theory of mental disease and its therapy rather than acquiring a skill may be stressed. Oskar Robert Pfister calls upon ministers to familiarize themselves with psychoanalysis (1022). Allen Charles Best points to the special problem areas of marriage, religious beliefs, alcoholism, personal adjustment, sex, and guilt as important for study by the pastor (104).

Among psychiatrists, Robert H. Felix describes counseling as a learned skill (410). James Hurley would train confessors in psychiatry in order to be able to recognize mental pathologies (618). Hjalmar Helweg says the therapist must know the physical constitution of the patient in order to assess its possibilities and limitations (547).

Examples of indicators for religious achievement criteria include Wayne E. Oates' notion of having a counselor prepared to use the Bible diagnostically, explaining that the Bible is a mirror into which a person projects his own concept of himself (973). R. C. Behan believes that psychiatry must be supplemented with study of Catholic theology (76).

Ascriptive criteria for allocating the counseling role may include attributes of personality, considered as given in early childhood, inherited, or as a Divine gift, and attributes possessed by virtue of group membership. For Charles F. Kemp the important method and technique is the personality of the pastor himself (690). Edgar N. Jackson reminds ministers that people come not to hear them but to hear God through them (625). David Rudolph Belgum is concerned with sacraments and symbols and the experience of salvation (88). Rudolph Allers prefers that psychiatrists working with Catholics be Catholics (7).

DETERMINANTS OF ALLOCATIVE CRITERIA

The Influence of Status

"Ideal typically," psychiatric status is allocated to individuals on the basis of their achievements. Medical training, demonstrated by examinations, qualifies one to be a physician and subsequently a psychiatrist.[4] Protestant ministerial status, on the other hand, "ideal typically" is allocated according to ascriptive criteria, by virtue of a "call."[5]

In this group, assumption of ministerial or medical status is a prerequisite for allocation of the counselor role. If these were simply a series of statuses as, for example, being a Catholic is a prerequisite for training as a priest, the allocative criteria of the general status would not necessarily influence the basis of appointment to the counseling role. In this case, however, the counselor role is a specialization within the medical and religious statuses. Therefore, some consistency of allocative criteria between the general status and its specialization might be anticipated. Table 35 shows the dis-

Table 35—Distribution of Ministers and Psychiatrists According to Criteria of Role Allocation

Allocative Criteria	Ministers	Psychiatrists (in Per Cent)
Psychological Achievement	51	74
Religious Achievement	18	17
Ascriptive	31	9
	(383)	(100)

tribution of ministers and psychiatrists according to criteria of role allocation.

Psychiatrists are more likely than ministers to advocate psychological achievements, while ministers are more likely to stress ascriptive criteria for allocating the counseling role. The criteria are, in both cases, consistent with the criteria institutionalized for allocating the medical and ministerial statuses respectively. Before accepting this as evidence for a link between the institutional status of the individual and the allocative criteria he advocates, it is necessary to face several objections. First, much of what was classified as demonstrating achievement criteria involve psychological skills and knowledge. This might exaggerate the importance of achievement criteria among psychiatrists. Were we to assume, however, that achievement criteria are equally distributed among ministers and psychiatrists and that it is the psychological content of the criteria which leads the distribution in the psychiatrists' direction, then religious achievement criteria would be relatively more characteristic of the ministers. Ministers and psychiatrists do not differ, however, in the proportions advocating religious achievement criteria. This suggests that, though the content may be a factor, psychiatrists are still more likely to stress achievement as such in allocating the counseling role.

There is a second objection. In comparing the allocative criteria of ministers and psychiatrists, we are assuming that both have the same type of counseling role in mind. Several conceptions of counseling jurisdictions have been described. Dualists consider counseling the province of a single but doubly competent professional. Specialists think in terms of two roles, one occupied by a minister and the other by a psychiatrist. The qualifications required of a counselor might well be related to the conception of his jurisdiction and whether he must previously have been admitted to the status of minister or psychiatrist.[6] Table 36 shows the criteria for role allocation suggested by ministers and psychiatrists who advocate each of the various forms of structural differentiation.

Table 36—Criteria for Role Allocation Among Ministers and Psychiatrists Who Advocate Various Forms of Structural Differentiation

	STRUCTURAL DIFFERENTIATION (in Per Cent)			
Allocative Criteria	Spiritual Reductionists	Dualists	Specialists	Material Reductionists
Ministers				
Psychological Achievement	15	68	55	66
Religious Achievement	11	9	10	17
Ascriptive	74	23	35	17
	(72)	(134)	(108)	(48)
Psychiatrists				
Psychological Achievement	—	61	81	—
Religious Achievement	—	22	14	—
Ascriptive	—	17	5	—
	(8)ᵃ	(23)	(63)	(5)ᵃ

a. Insufficient cases to show per cent.

By reading Table 36 vertically, we specify Table 35 with form of structural differentiation held constant.[7] Among minister and psychiatrist specialists, the distributions of allocative criteria differ little from those presented in Table 35. Psychiatrists advocate relatively more achievement and ministers relatively more ascriptive criteria. The specialists have in mind two complementary roles each having a limited jurisdiction. One is to be filled by a minister and the other by a psychiatrist. In most cases, the criteria they advocate refer principally to the specialized role occupied by a member of their own profession. Is it, however, the prior statuses of the incumbents which is determinative, or is it the type of activity anticipated for the role which influences the advocacy of the various allocative criteria? A comparison of minister and psychiatrist dualists may help answer the question. Both of these agree that the jurisdiction includes both spiritual and psychological tasks but differ on the prior status, ministerial or psychiatric, required of the candidate. Among dualists, the differences between the ministers and psychiatrists in allocative criteria disappear—except for a slightly greater psychiatric interest in religious achievement, which, given the small number of psychiatrists in the category, is probably artifactual. With the same image of the task in mind, despite differing images of who fulfills the task, ministers and psychiatrists advocate similar allocative criteria. Thus, the image of the task influences the criteria.

A comparison of dualists with specialists within each profession also holds prior status constant and provides a check on the above finding. Both tend to be concerned with a member of their own profession as the incumbent. The tasks differ, however. As a specialist, the incumbent performs the tasks of his own profession in cooperation with a member of the other profession. As a dualist, he is expected to accomplish a double task. Ministers advocating specialism are more likely to stress ascriptive criteria than those advocating dualism. When ministers advocate dualism, that is are concerned with psychological problems, they stress psychological achievements relatively more. Psychiatrists advocating specialism put stress on psychological achievements. Psychiatrists advocating dualism who anticipate concern with religious aspects of the problem are relatively more concerned with ascriptive criteria. With the status of the individual constant but with differing images of the task to be accomplished, different allocative criteria are advocated. The conception of the task rather than the status of the individual influences the allocative criteria advocated.

Only among ministers are there enough reductionists for comment. Material reductionists and dualists advocate similar criteria. Apparently, conception of the task in purely, rather than partly, psychological terms does not increase the tendency to advocate achievement criteria. Spiritual reductionist ministers, who also recommended the counseling be conducted by a minister, and that it be conducted in a traditionally religious way, place considerable stress on ascriptive criteria. The contrast between the criteria advocated by material and spiritual reductionists again suggests that the behavior anticipated in the role is a significant influence on the allocative criteria. Thus, criteria for role allocation, though in part a function of the status of the candidate, are associated with the conception of the task involved in the role.[8] The next section further examines the influence of the conception of the task upon criteria for admission to the role.

The Influence of the Conception of Counseling

The previous section suggested that the criteria for admitting candidates to a role match the behavior expected in that role.[9] This accords with a common observation. For example, in a free market, the role of shoemaker is allocated to candidates showing proficiency in the art of cobbling. The shoemaking task is defined in achievement terms and tends to be allocated on that basis.[10] The task in a social relationship is defined by the norms governing that relationship.

A definition of the counseling role includes a statement of the norms governing the relation of the counselor to his client and of the goals of that relationship. If our reasoning thus far is valid, allocative criteria should be influenced by the conception of appropriate goals and means for counseling. We shall first deal with the goals of counseling. Would the individual whose counseling goal is an instrumental one, such as improving the client's functioning, also advocate achievement criteria for allocating the counseling role? If the goals are conceived in meaning terms, as, for example, involving the resolution of problems of value or purpose, the individual would be less concerned with immediate action upon the world. In this case, would the role tend to be allocated according to ascriptive criteria? The relation between allocative criteria and goals of therapy is examined in Table 37.

Table 37—Ministers and Psychiatrists Who Advocate Meaning and Instrumental Goals for Counseling According to Criteria for Role Allocation[a]

Allocative Criteria	GOALS (in Per Cent)	
	Meaning	Instrumental
Ministers		
Psychological Achievement	23	75
Ascriptive	60	12
	(116)	(139)
Psychiatrists		
Psychological Achievement	39	82
Ascriptive	22	3
	(28)	(39)

a. Items classed as advocating religious achievement criteria account for the difference between the per cent shown and 100 per cent. This category will also be omitted from the succeeding tables.

Among both ministers and psychiatrists, conceiving of the therapeutic goal in instrumental terms is associated with achievement criteria, and conceiving of the goal in meaning terms is associated with advocating ascriptive criteria for role allocation. The differences in proportions are quite striking and further justify the claim that the conception of the counseling goal is a strong influence on the choice of allocative criteria.

There is almost no difference in allocative criteria between ministers and psychiatrists who advocate instrumental goals. Among those advocating meaning goals, however, the psychiatrists are more likely to stress achievement criteria. If allocative criteria are tied to the conception of the counseling goal, in this case the goal of meaning, then why do not the psychiatrists, as well as the ministers, advocate ascriptive criteria? Since ascriptive qualities cannot be attained by effort, and the psychiatrist is reluctant to feel "called," it may be that he settles for religiously formulated criteria which he interprets in achievement terms. This would clarify an otherwise puzzling reversal between the professions. Among those advocating meaning goals for counseling, 17 per cent of the ministers and 39 per cent of the psychiatrists advocate religious achievement criteria. (These percentages are based on the difference between the percentages given in Table 37 and 100 per cent.) This becomes understandable if we assume that under the impact of goals of meaning and a pressure toward ascriptive criteria, the psychiatrist substitutes religious achievement for ascriptive criteria. The counseling goal remains a more potent influence in the choice of allocative criteria than the profession of the individual.

The association between allocative criteria and the conception of the therapeutic task may also be traced in terms of the norms governing counseling means. In pattern variable terms, the significant dimension is that of performance *versus* quality orientation toward the client. The meaning of this orientation in the counselor-client relation is similar to that of achievement *versus* ascription with reference to the allocative problem. This relation between allocative criteria and these counseling norms is shown in Table 38.

For ministers there is a marked correlation between performance orientation and achievement criteria, on the one hand, and between a quality orientation and ascriptive criteria, on the other. The correlation is considerably less marked among psychiatrists. Though

Table 38—Ministers and Psychiatrists Who Are Performance or Quality Oriented Toward Clients According to Criteria of Role Allocation

Allocative Criteria	ORIENTATION TO CLIENTS (in Per Cent)	
	Quality	Performance
Ministers		
Psychological Achievement	25	55
Ascriptive	58	32
	(76)	(235)
Psychiatrists		
Psychological Achievement	64	79
Ascriptive	9	8
	(11)	(72)

the small number of quality oriented psychiatrists makes comment difficult, one would have anticipated that more of them would advocate ascriptive criteria. A mechanism similar to that suggested in the discussion of counseling goals may be at work here. Seventeen per cent of the quality oriented ministers and 27 per cent of the quality oriented psychiatrists advocate religious achievement criteria. Again, psychiatrists may be substituting religious achievement for ascriptive criteria.

In relating the allocative criteria to the conception of counseling, we should not neglect our original finding about the influence of profession on these criteria. Comparing ministers and psychiatrists with the orientational norms held constant, we find that psychiatrists are more likely to advocate achievement and ministers ascriptive criteria. While the conception of the task norms is an important influence upon allocative criteria, it does not account for all of the differences between ministers and psychiatrists in this respect.[11]

There are too few cases of psychiatrists to judge, but it appears that among those advocating a performance orientation, goals do not influence the choice of allocative criteria. Among ministers, means are a more significant influence than goals. Both of these aspects of the counseling task together do not account for all of the differences between ministers and psychiatrists.

We have been treating the allocative criteria and the role orientations as variables to discover the extent to which the occurrence of one implies the occurrence of the other. Empirically, however, all of the combinations exist. The frequency with which each combination occurs would vary from one cultural situation to another.

The coincidence of performance norms with achievement criteria and of quality norms with ascriptive criteria implies a consistency between the allocative relation (the relation of a counselor's prior status to his counseling status) and the counselor-client relation. The criteria for entering the role match the norms to be realized in the role. This is the majority position. There are those, however, who advocate a performance orientation to the client while advocating ascriptive criteria for allocation, and those who recommend a quality orientation to the client but would allocate the role on the basis of achievement. These nonconsistent types are the minority in this sample.[12]

The Influence of Institutional Identification

We began by observing that ministers tend to advocate ascriptive criteria and psychiatrists to advocate achievement ones for selecting a counselor. Part of this difference has been accounted for in terms of their conceptions of the counseling jurisdictions and of the counseling task. We now return to consider the influence upon the choice of allocative criteria of certain aspects of their statuses as such.

Allocative criteria do not seem to be a function of the personal characteristics of the individual, such as his age and education (see footnote 8). Yet they do bear a relation to the characteristics he possesses as a member of an institution. Individuals seem to advocate criteria which will enable people of like mind to gain the positions. The key phrase here is "like mind." Allocative criteria may not be influenced as much by the group with which the individual happens to be affiliated as by the group with which he identifies or to which he is oriented.

Our classification of variant types orders the individuals in terms of their orientation to the religious or psychiatric institutions, in terms of their use of religious or psychiatric language in describing the means and goals of counseling. As ministers adapt to psychiatric language, would they also tend, as psychiatrists do, to advocate achievement criteria for appointment to the role? As psychiatrists become minister-like in their counseling attitudes and adopt religious language, would they also tend, as ministers do, to

advocate ascriptive criteria for role allocation? Table 39 shows the
relation between variant type and criteria of role allocation.[13]

Table 39—Ministers and Psychiatrists of Each Variant Subtype According to the Criteria of Role Allocation Advocated

	VARIANT SUBTYPES (in Per Cent)			
	Militant Conformists	Ritualists	Innovators	Rebels
Allocative Criteria				
Ministers				
Psychological Achievement	15	38	68	75
Ascriptive	80	36	21	8
	(58)	(65)	(213)	(38)
Psychiatrists				
Psychological Achievement	86	82	79	50
Ascriptive	5	2	—	33
	(21)	(37)	(18)	(23)

The more ministers identify with psychiatry the more they advocate achievement criteria. Psychiatrists tend to advocate ascriptive criteria only when they become rebels. Comparing this with
Table 35 we find a near identity between the allocative criteria
advocated by rebel ministers and those advocated by psychiatrists
in general. About three-fourths of the rebel ministers advocate
psychological achievement criteria. There is also a near identity
between the criteria advocated by rebel psychiatrists and those
advocated by ministers in general. About half of the rebel psychiatrists advocate psychological achievement and a third advocate
ascriptive criteria. Thus, allocative criteria seems responsive to the
group whose behavior is emulated rather than being simply a
reflection of affiliation. This is consistent with our finding in
Chapter III that the reference group is a better predictor of attitudes than is the membership group.

The association between allocative criteria and the successive
variant subtypes is not linear. Among ministers, the move from
militant conformist to ritualist is associated with a sharp increase
in the proportion advocating achievement criteria. The move from
ritualism to innovation is associated with another sharp change.
From innovators to rebels, however, the change is small. There is no
reason to expect the relation to be linear, since, although the subtypes are ordered in terms of increasing extent of variation, the
increases between subtypes are not all equal.

There is the possibility that the change in allocative criteria observed here is not the consequence of a shifting orientation to another group, as suggested above, but follows from the new goals introduced by the ritualists and the new means introduced by the innovators. The correlation would then be but further evidence of the influence of the conception of the task upon allocative criteria. To allow for this possibility either the means or the goals, which are highly correlated, should be held constant while comparing allocative criteria associated with each variant subtype. When the content of the goals is held constant, the differences between the variant subtypes in Table 39 persist.[14] Thus, the criteria advocated are influenced by the variant subtype as well as by the conception of the counseling task.

Why, as Table 39 indicates, do ministers abandon ascriptive criteria more readily than psychiatrists abandon achievement criteria as the extent of variation increases? One reason may be that when ministers engage in psychological-type counseling, they have broken more sharply with tradition than have psychiatrists who adopt a religious approach within their counseling practice. The greater change in allocative criteria is just one aspect of the greater depth of ministerial variation. Further, the over-all social context favors achievement criteria. This contextual factor favors ministers moving in an achievement direction and discourages psychiatrists from abandoning these criteria. Ministers and psychiatrists are sensitive to the broader social context because it is within the broader society that they seek the audience for their writings, and it is from these publics that they receive legitimation. The next section deals with the influence of significant publics on allocative criteria.

The Influence of Significant Publics

The group of orientation influences the choices of an individual, in part because he internalizes its standards, which include allocative criteria, and in part because he is prepared to accept its members as role occupants. The viability of a role allocation depends, as well, upon the acceptance of the allocative criteria by others besides the role occupant. A counselor cannot act in his role if his tenure is not considered legitimate by some significant public. The significant publics include not only those with which he identifies, but also groups whose values he may not internalize, because those groups provide clients or support him in the struggle with other groups.[15]

Just as a counselor seeks legitimation from these publics, so an author of a religio-psychiatric book or article expects that the audience to which he addresses his work will consider his contentions legitimate. He would seek their approval of the allocative criteria he advocates. The items have been classified according to whether they are directed to a professional or to a lay audience. The distinction is based on the technical level of the material. Table 40 compares the allocative criteria of individuals writing for a professional and for a lay audience.

Table 40—Ministers and Psychiatrists Writing for Professional and Lay Audiences According to Allocative Criteria

	MINISTERS		PSYCHIATRISTS	
Allocative Criteria	Professional Audiences	Lay Audiences	Professional Audiences	Lay Audiences
Psychological Achievement	62%	31%	74%	69%
Ascriptive	26	55	10	5
	(272)	(97)	(80)	(19)

Ministers writing for a professional audience are more likely to advocate achievement criteria. Those writing for a lay audience are more likely to advocate ascriptive criteria for role allocation. Psychiatrists strongly favor achievement criteria in both instances. It would seem that ministers more than psychiatrists are guided in their formulations by the character of their public. Before drawing this conclusion, however, it is necessary to test for a source of bias in the distribution.

The audience, in addition to being professional or lay, may be concerned with psychological or religious subject matter. A psychologically oriented audience would be more likely to legitimate a counselor on the basis of achievement than would a religiously oriented audience, if only because of the nonempirical status of religion. Further, psychiatrists would be more likely than ministers to write for a psychologically oriented audience. This possible source of bias may be examined by holding the subject matter interest of the audience constant while its professional-lay character is correlated with allocative criteria. Doing this, it appears that the religious or psychological orientation of the audience does not affect the allocative criteria.[16] The differences shown in Table 40 are almost entirely due to the contrast between professional and lay character of the audiences.

How do we know that the associations between a professional audience and achievement criteria, and between a lay audience and ascriptive criteria are not due to the extent of variation on the part of the authors? Ministers, for example, who write for professional audiences are the more variant and so more likely to identify with psychiatry. Perhaps these ministers advocate achievement criteria as a consequence of this identification rather than as a consequence of the character of the audience. Were this the case, the discovered audience influence would simply reflect the previously discovered association between allocative criteria and variant subtype. To test this possibility, Table 41 compares allocative criteria of those who write for a professional and lay audience with variant subtype held constant.

Among ministers within each variant subtype, those who write for a professional audience are more likely than those who write for a lay audience to advocate achievement criteria. Unfortunately, there are too few psychiatrists to make this comparison for them. Among ministers, however, audience influences the choice of allocative criteria independently of the influence of variant subtype.[17] The difference between ministers who write for professional and for lay audiences is greater among the more variant. This is under-

Table 41—Ministers and Psychiatrists of Each Variant Subtype Who Write for Professional and Lay Audiences According to Allocative Criteria

Allocative Criteria	MILITANT CONFORMISTS RITUALISTS (in Per Cent)		INNOVATORS REBELS (in Per Cent)	
	Professional Audiences	Lay Audiences	Professional Audiences	Lay Audiences
Ministers				
Psychological Achievement	21	14	71	49
Ascriptive	65	75	16	34
	(52)	(48)	(199)	(41)
Psychiatrists				
Psychological Achievement	82	—	78	—
Ascriptive	—	—	4	—
	(44)	(8)[a]	(23)	(8)[a]

a. Insufficient cases to show percentages.

standable in terms of the type of legitimation sought by each of the variant subtypes. For less variant ministers, achievement criteria tend to be relatively insignificant. Firmly rooted in the religious institution, they care little about legitimation on the basis of achievements. Consequently, they do not appeal to a professional audience very differently from the way they appeal to a lay audience. They expect primarily ascriptive legitimation from both audiences. When they become more variant, however, and identify more with psychiatry, they tend to seek legitimation on the basis of their achievements. As a consequence, they are more inclined to appeal on this basis to a professional audience, an important source of achievement legitimation, than to a lay audience.

This type of explanation may also help us understand the finding (Tables 40 and 40A) that the psychiatrist is less likely than the minister to consider the audiences in formulating his criteria for admission to the counselor role. Ministerial and psychiatric roles are legitimated in different ways. In an achievement-oriented society where the professions, especially, are defined in achievement terms, both ministers and psychiatrists expect professionals to legitimate the counseling role on the basis of achievement.[18] There is a contrast, however, in the basis upon which ministers and psychiatrists expect legitimation from laymen. Ministers relate to laymen as "charismatics," ascriptively legitimated on the basis of a personal "gift" or on the basis of the aura of their office. Psychiatrists, on the other hand, as professionals, expect laymen to accept them on the basis of their learned skills and knowledge. Consequently, it is not lack of consideration for the audience but rather that the psychiatrist justifies his role occupancy to both professional and lay audiences on the basis of achievement criteria. He is more likely than a minister to display his diploma in his office.

CONCLUSION

Psychiatrists have been found to favor achievement criteria and ministers to favor ascriptive criteria for admitting candidates to the counseling role. This difference between the professions was, in part, accounted for in terms of their conceptions of the counseling task. When counseling is thought of as involving technical operations to aid a client in coping with his environment, the tendency is to demand proof that the potential counselor has achieved the requisite skills and knowledge. When healing is believed to occur through a meeting of "beings" and to be manifest in the discovery of a new value by which to live, the candidate for therapist is expected to demonstrate that he possesses "chrismatic" gifts or a therapeutic personality. The allocative criteria advocated tend to be consistent not so much with attributes the ministers and psychiatrists personally possess but with the criteria institutionalized for allocating the major status of the group with which they identify. Those who advocate psychiatric-type counseling norms and goals, whether they be ministers or psychiatrists, tend to support achievement criteria. Those more closely identified with religion tend to support ascriptive criteria for allocating the counseling role. Allocative criteria also tend to be influenced by what the audiences for the writings accept as legitimate bases for the counselor's authority. Ministers and psychiatrists who direct their work to a professional audience tend to advocate achievement criteria. Psychiatrists are likely to advocate achievement criteria when writing for laymen as well. However, ministers who address themselves to a lay audience tend to advocate ascriptive criteria. In both cases, the criteria match those by which the respective audiences legitimate the author's status.

Ascriptive and achievement criteria have been treated separately and as mutually alternative. This distinction is analytic. In any concrete situation ascriptive and achievement criteria may be combined. Incumbency in a ministerial status may be claimed on the basis of ascriptive criteria while a pastoral specialization is based on subsequent achievement. A psychiatrist who prefers to refer patients to a colleague of his own faith is combining ascriptive with achievement criteria. A requirement that a counselor have a therapeutic personality as well as be skilled in therapeutic techniques combines the two types of criteria.

For ministers in the religio-psychiatric movement, there is increasing emphasis upon an achieved counselor role built upon the prior religious ascriptive characteristics. The achieved elements may eventually dominate the pastoral role. For the psychiatrist, the ascriptive criteria of religious faith may be a partial basis for claiming legitimacy, but the role of the religiously oriented psychiatrist is likely to remain essentially an achieved one. A proclivity for achievement criteria would seem almost inevitable in a movement which is sensitive to its achievement-oriented social context. The impact of the audience upon the criteria attests to this sensitivity. This direction is also suggested by the greater propensity of ministers to accept achievement than for psychiatrists to accept ascriptive requirements as they shift their group identifications.

This could almost have been predicted from the nature of the complaints of ministers and psychiatrists against their institutions presented in the second chapter. Many complaints are phrased in terms of ineffectiveness in accomplishing the healing task, that is, phrased in achievement terms. Yet a big "if" remains. If the conception of the healing task undergoes change, the allocative criteria may change. Achievement norms for the counseling relation are constantly subject to review. As research evidence and popular judgments on the effectiveness of psychotherapy accumulate, traditional procedures are subject to replacement by new procedures considered to be more effective. If, however, the procedures are judged to produce only questionable results, a general discouragment with techniques may set in. This would be an extension of the doubts which some psychiatrists bring to the movement. The consequence could be to force the definition of the task into the area of mystery and increase the salience of ascriptive criteria for role allocation.

NOTES

1. It does not follow from these characteristics of the authors that individuals not possessing them are excluded by a proscriptive norm. Other factors determine these characteristics. Relatively few females, for example, occupy the statuses of clergymen and physician from which counselors and authors are recruited. These are characteristics of role occupants which may or may not be considered in selecting candidates.

2. We are concerned specifically with criteria of eligibility for the counselor role. Allocation of personnel among roles is analyzed by Talcott Parsons in *The Social System*, pp. 114–119. This concern overlaps with, but is not identical with, the question of recruitment to the role and the basis of legitimacy of the authority invested in the role. Recruitment, particularly

as it bears on the sectors of society from which role incumbents are drawn, is treated in Robert K. Merton, *et. al.*, *Reader in Bureaucracy*, pp. 299–352. The means of recruitment are related to the structure of organizations by Amitai Etzioni, *A Comparative Analysis of Complex Organizations*, pp. 151–174. The classic sociological analysis of legitimacy is that of Max Weber, *The Theory of Social and Economic Organization*, pp. 130 ff. and 324 ff.

3. This terminology follows Ralph Linton, *The Study of Man: An Introduction*. It is the role which is achieved by or ascribed to the incumbent. Our terms "achievement" and "ascriptive" criteria are ellipses for role allocation on the basis of attributes which the incumbent comes to possess by dint of his effort, by achievement, or which are ascribed to him regardless of what he does.

4. Sociological factors in the recruitment and training of the physician are described in Merton, Reader, and Kendall, *op. cit.;* and Everett C. Hughes, "The Making of a Physician," *Human Organization*, pp. 2125.

5. The individual endowed with a *sensus numinis* may develop his potentialities through theological training. This training may raise the minister's rank but generally is not the basis of his ordination. Ordination is contingent upon proof of mission. The office of rabbi is, in part, an exception. Since the rabbinate is more a teaching than a priestly status, achievement criteria are significant. At present, in the United States, some Protestant denominations have begun to require training in addition to a "call" to qualify for ordination. The variety of "gifts" and the way they are recognized and developed in various cultures is described by Wach, *op. cit.*, pp. 333 ff.

6. Sometimes role incumbents must satisfy a series of criteria with each succeeding one contingent upon a prior one. For example, if a child must be under five to be admitted to nursery school, the school would not, ordinarily, require ability to read.

7. Only the "form" is held constant since the occupant of the specialist and dualist roles is not identical for ministers and psychiatrists.

8. A person who is himself a candidate for a role might be expected to advocate criteria consistent with attributes he possesses so as to have an advantage in competition for role occupancy. Yet allocative criteria seem independent of purely personal characteristics. Younger people, for example, who are striving to rise in the system might be expected to favor achievement criteria, while older established individuals, more secure in an already attained position, might be expected to rely upon ascriptive criteria. Nevertheless, we find that 65 per cent (112) of ministers who were 45 years of age or less when they wrote their item and 67 per cent (48) of those over 45 advocate psychological achievement criteria. Age does not

seem to influence ministers in their choice of allocative criteria. There are not enough cases to compare psychiatrists of different ages.

People who have undergone more training might be expected to be more likely to recommend that training be considered as relevant in role allocation. All psychiatrists, of course, have a doctorate. Among ministers, however, who have not attained a doctorate 60 per cent (49) advocate psychological achievement criteria while 61 per cent (179) of those holding a doctorate do so. Apparently the level of educational achievement does not influence the allocative criteria advocated.

9. The question might be why they should not approach perfect consistency since it would seem logical to select people for a task in terms of their ability to execute that task. Departure from this model is due, in part, to the exigencies of the social network in which the role is embedded. For example, the distribution of power in the society may be considered in the appointment of a government official in addition to questions of his suitability for the task.

10. There may, of course, be additional requirements unrelated to cobbling. The shoemaker may have to be a male or belong to a particular age or ethnic group.

11. Table 38A shows the distribution of allocative criteria with both goals and means held constant.

Table 38A—Ministers and Psychiatrists with Each Type of Goal and Means of Counseling According to Allocative Criteria

	GOALS OF COUNSELING			
	Meaning		Instrumental	
	ORIENTATION TO CLIENTS			
Allocative Criteria	Quality	Performance	Quality	Performance
Ministers				
Psychological Achievement	20%	54%	16%	69%
Ascriptive	67	41	48	16
	(67)	(39)	(19)	(81)
Psychiatrists				
Psychological Achievement	—	77%	—	77%
Ascriptive	—	15	—	6
	a	(13)	a	(35)

a. Insufficient cases.

12. Each of the two consistent and two nonconsistent types has a social meaning. The conjunction of achievement criteria for role allocation and performance orientation to the client is characteristic of the professional relationship. The professional earns his right by effort, is expected to exert effort, and may expect effort on the part of the client. When either refuses

to abide by these obligations, the other has the right to terminate the relationship. In our sample, this is characteristic of militant conformist and ritualist psychiatrists and rebel and innovator ministers.

The conjunction of ascriptive criteria and quality norms typifies the religious relationship. Obligations are dictated by a "substantial" tie existing between the role partners. Neither has the right to surrender these obligations nor to terminate the relationship at will. When the counselor terminates the relationship it is an act of excommunication or disowning. When the client severs his tie, it is apostasy or desertion. The break is traumatic and surrounded by ceremonies. This is characteristic of militant conformist ministers and some rebel psychiatrists.

When allocative criteria and the norms of orientation are nonconsistent, the obligations of counselor and client tend to be asymmetrical. One who is ascribed a role but expected to perform is one who is obligated to provide services without reciprocity in that situation. This type of relation is characteristic of the faith healer. He does not choose his "charismatic" qualities but, having them, he is obligated to use them for the good of the community. The healer's client has the right to terminate the relationship on the basis of poor performance. The healer cannot legitimately escape his obligation.

Those who gain access to the role on account of performance but once having the role are not obligated to continue in their performance comprise the fourth type. Their situation is similar to that of a war veteran. The community is obligated to render respect or provide facilities to the role incumbent. The incumbent is not required to reciprocate in that situation. This relationship may be terminated by the role incumbent but the community may not unilaterally renege on its obligations. The psychiatrist works to pass his "boards" but then may be considered by some patients to hold authority by virtue of the diploma on the wall or the pastoral counselor may claim status by virtue of clinical training and then conduct healing services or rely on the "charisma" of office. Some innovating psychiatrists and ritualist ministers would fall in this category.

13. The ensuing argument could have used the reference group classification as an indicator of identification. The indicator for identification would then be the locus of standards they accept rather than the linguistic membership of the means and goals they advocate for therapy. The results of the argument are essentially the same in either case.

14. To specify Table 39, holding goals constant, the four variant subtypes will be compared in two groups. We should have some indicator of goals which is independent of the variant subtype. We shall use our classification of the content of the goals though it does not fully meet this condition.

Table 39A—Ministers and Psychiatrists of Each Variant Subtype who Advocate Meaning or Instrumental Goals for Counseling According to Allocative Criteria

	GOALS OF COUNSELING			
	Meaning		Instrumental	
	VARIANT SUBTYPES			
Allocative Criteria	Militant Conformists Ritualists	Innovators Rebels	Militant Conformists Ritualists	Innovators Rebels
Ministers				
Psychological Achievement	8%	67%	29%	75%
Ascriptive	87	24	51	9
	(40)	(75)	(35)	(80)
Psychiatrists				
Psychological Achievement	—	—	87%	53%
Ascriptive	—	—	—	12
	(10)ᵃ	(7)ᵃ	(23)	(17)

a. Insufficient cases to show percentages.

With the goal of couseling held constant, the more variant ministers tend to advocate achievement criteria and, at least among those with instrumental goals, the more variant psychiatrists to advocate religious achievement or ascriptive criteria.

15. There must be some measure of empathy with the group from which one seeks legitimacy but this does not imply that one would like to be a member of or even be like that group.

16.

Table 40A—Ministers and Psychiatrists Writing for Religiously and Psychologically Oriented Professional and Lay Audiences According to Allocative Criteria

	RELIGIOUS		PSYCHOLOGICAL	
	(in Per Cent)			
Allocative Criteria	Professional Audiences	Lay Audiences	Professional Audiences	Lay Audiences
Ministers				
Psychological Achievement	61	32	67	25
Ascriptive	27	56	20	50
	(242)	(81)	(30)	(16)
Psychiatrists				
Psychological Achievement	76	67	72	—
Ascriptive	12	16	8	—
	(41)	(18)	(39)	(1)

17. Comparing the two groups of variants with audience held constant, it is apparent that variant type is a more significant influence than is the audience on allocative criteria.

18. This does not contradict the argument that the ministerial status is ascribed. Achievement criteria may become relevant for the minister after his "call." Within the clerical system he may assume some specific ministry on the basis of demonstrated competence. A priesthood may be hereditary but a novitiate would be instructed in how to perform a sacrificial ritual.

PART TWO

A Case Study: The Religio-Psychiatric Clinic

This study of pastors and psychiatrists began in the spring of 1956 with a case study of the Religio-Psychiatric Clinic in New York. The results of this case study provided the hypotheses which guided the study of the literature of the religio-psychiatric movement. Now that the broader study has been completed, this case study provides a concrete illustration of some of the principles described in the earlier chapters. The reader will find in it a microcosmic view of minister-psychiatrist norms in the process of formation and change in an organization which has reached an advanced stage in the process.

Chapter IX

How the Clinic Came to Be

THE CLINIC'S BEGINNINGS

"COULD YOU INTRODUCE ME to a Christian psychiatrist?" The question remained suspended. Despite his heavy patient load, Iago Galdston had time to discuss Western civilization or the place of values in psychoanalysis. He was equally at home in the synagogue and in the Catholic church. He took neither too seriously. Quotations from Latin and Greek classics mingled with precise references to Dr. Freud and assertions on the state of man. His eyes would twinkle as he drew himself up behind the lectern and prepared to section his opponent's logic with impeccably correct and clipped English phrases. Dr. Norman Vincent Peale's question, however, caught him off guard.

When the Marble Collegiate Church (Dutch Reformed) had been built on the corner of Fifth Avenue and Twenty-ninth Street, New York, the spire towered above the surrounding residences of its well-to-do parishioners. When Dr. Peale arrived he found the church boxed in among New York's garment lofts. People standing in knots on the corner spoke Yiddish and Italian as well as English. On Sunday morning the sewing machines and quick lunch counters were quiet. A well-dressed congregation arrived by cab and car from uptown. Some paused near the church to watch the Empire State Building growing toward the clouds. Worshipers heard the dynamic new minister say that they too could reach up and possess the future. Some not so well dressed parishioners also discovered Dr. Peale's church. The deepening depression dumped these despondent souls on his steps. He offered charity to those who had abandoned hope and preached faith to those whose world was devoid of charity. These desperate souls might fall prey to demogogues. The air was full of cries of false prophets preaching illusory salvation by uprooting a devilish social order. These poor could be saved by faith in God and works in this world. The abstract theological doctrines of seminary professors seemed impotent to Dr. Peale. They could not change lives. He was called to preach to the times, to bring a personal message and a practical guidance. The forlorn man must dispel his despondent thoughts. The defeated man must believe in his ability to win and, unflinchingly, turn his efforts toward success.

Dr. Peale sensed that the hopelessness of these people was precipitated by, but not rooted in, the blows of the depression. Histories of torn homes and subtly vicious parents lurked behind erratic behavior. Dr. Peale sought guidance from Dr. Clarence W. Lieb, his personal physician. Help, however, would come from a psychiatrist. Not every psychiatrist could help. Psychiatrists Dr. Peale had known were not value committed in their own lives. What enfranchised them to guide these souls? Their flaunted secularism and ethical relativism precluded his turning to them. Dr. Lieb arranged a meeting with Dr. Galdston. Dr. Galdston perhaps had not understood the question. Dr. Peale again leaned across the table and asked him, "Could you introduce me to a Christian psychiatrist?"

Was it fortuitous that a Protestant minister put this question to a Freudian analyst? Perhaps Freudians outnumbered Jungians and Adelerians in New York or were more likely than their somatically-oriented colleagues to share a dais with a minister. Whatever the reason, the meeting was portentous. Dr. Iago Galdston scribbled a note: "Dr. Smiley Blanton, Assistant Professor of Clinical Psychiatry at Cornell."

Dr. Blanton engaged Dr. Peale with intimate vignettes of General Lee and President Davis. Soliloquies from Shakespeare and quotations from Carlyle illustrated the war narrative. When Smiley Blanton was born in Unionville Tennessee in 1882, the smoke of the War Between the States had hardly cleared. Strict morality at home supported a code of chivalry without. To face the neighboring boys with stomach strength was to gain honor. Dr. Peale saw an energetic popular philosopher who taught character-weak men moral strength and treated women with Southern courtesy.

Dr. Smiley Blanton had known the inside of Dr. Freud's study in Vienna as well as the inside of a church. He complained against religious orthodoxies. "Evolutionism is an established scientific fact," he said, "but man needs to find order and meaning in the evolved world." Healing miracles at Lourdes could be understood as a transference to the symbol of the Virgin. Liberal Protestantism was spared his barbed critique. Dr. Peale was charmed by a folk exegesis of technical psychiatric concepts. He listened intently to Dr. Blanton's illustrative cases of confused people he had helped in daily practice, and to his apt citations from Herbert Spencer.[1]

Dr. Peale devoted himself to counseling. Dr. Blanton received referrals of obviously pathological parishioners. Professional cooperation became friendship while mounting applications drove informality toward organization. In 1937 they established the Religio-Psychiatric Clinic as a free service of the Marble Collegiate Church. Their joint authorship of *Faith is the Answer* in 1940 publicized the partnership more and more. Troubled people found their way to the church clinic. Letters arrived from across the country. Some correspondents received a pastoral letter. Others were referred to a psychiatrist or to a minister in their locale. A few jouneyed uninvited from the South and the Midwest to meet this minister-psychiatrist team.

Dr. Peale's *Power of Postive Thinking* eventually sold over two million copies. Now applicants stormed the clinic doors and deluged him with mail. The demands of national popularity were imperious. As radio programs, lectures, and magazine articles absorbed his day, his connection with the Religio-Psychiatric Clinic narrowed to a formal presidency. New ministerial specialists, combining the cloth and psychoanalysis in one person, arrived to help with counseling. R. Ridgely Lytle, M.A., Oxon., joined the clinic in 1948. Mr. Lytle was slight of build but bore himself with Anglican dignity. He wore blue serge with vest and tie more often than the clerical collar. Mr. Lytle could hold a sobbing girl's hand and then offer a Freudian interpretation of her behavior. Love was central to both religion and psychoanalysis. It did not matter which religion as long as the personal loving relationship was there.[2]

Following the publication of *The Art of Real Happiness* in 1950, Dr. Blanton had less time for clinic patients and Dr. Fred U. Tate was invited to share the burden of the psychiatric director. Though not intensely attached to his Judaism, Dr. Tate bore religion no animus. He rather enjoyed the association with ministers. Those working with him in intake conferences saw a diagnostician who after the first few sentences of the case report could hypothesize the syndrome.[3]

By 1953 the clinical services expanded beyond the ability of the Marble Collegiate Church budget. The Religio-Psychiatric Clinic severed its affiliation with the Church, and the newly created American Foundation of Religion and Psychiatry assumed the responsibility. Dr. Peale became president of the Foundation, and a group of business leaders friendly with Dr. Peale formed the executive committee.

An administrative staff was appointed to devote full time to development of the Clinic and to raise funds for its maintenance. The Foundation declared the Clinic nonsectarian and so recognized the existing state of affairs. The staff included Jews as well as Protestants. Clients were Jewish, Catholic, and Protestant. Official nonsectarianism also permitted individuals, foundations, and municipal authorities who would be reluctant to support a church to contribute to the clinic. A license was granted the Foundation to operate a psychiatric clinic.

Administrative and clinical expansion opened the door to another venture. Rev. Frederick Kuether (Evangelical and Reformed) arrived in 1951 after chaplaincies in prisons and mental hospitals. He did not admonish clients spewing out tales of inhuman deeds but rejoined with a "now-where-do-we-go-from-here" attitude.[4]

As director of the Council for Clinical Training, Mr. Kuether had accumulated experience in the clinical psychological training of ministers and seminarians. In 1953 he established a Department of Training at the Foundation which, by 1955, was well under way. Weekly case conferences were pivotal. Minister trainees presented their current cases to other ministers, psychiatrists, psychologists, and social workers. Personal analyses of trainees were conducted by psychiatrists and Mr. Kuether himself. A weekly seminar in analytic literature introduced the trainees to systematic theory. Staff psychologists explained intelligence and personality tests. A ministers-only seminar related their psychological training to religious ideas. Trainees worked with Mr. Kuether instructing visiting clergy during summer seminars. Over drinks in the evening they discussed their own reactions to the strains of the day.[5]

Research at the Clinic

The Foundation plan called for a research department. What function research would serve was not clear. The secretarial staff thought research might record the number of patients treated and their disposition for a report to the city's Department of Welfare. The business manager imagined a researcher would write public relations brochures and magazine articles about the work of the clinic. The development department saw a relation between research and fund raising. Staff members variously expected a researcher to produce a new psychological test for assessing progress in psychotherapy, to condition pupillary reflexes, and to record patient reactions to chemotherapy. A few wondered whether the researcher would be reporting their behavior to Drs. Blanton and Peale. Ministers and psychiatrists hoped a researcher would help them verbalize what they were doing. Questions were posed. Could research evaluate cooperation between ministers and psychiatrists? Were people cured through church healing services? Could the power of prayer be measured?

Dr. Galdston, now head of the Executive Committee on Medical Information of the New York Academy of Medicine, chaired the research committee. His committee members were business and social leaders from the metropolitan area. The years had sustained his interest in psychiatry and religion. He had penned several articles and edited a book in the field. Yet he felt uneasy about the Foundation. The Academy of Medicine was concerned about non-medical people invading the sphere reserved for the licensed physician. Rumors had reached Dr. Galdston that ministers at the Religio-Psychiatric Clinic dealt not only with the moral issues, but also practiced psychotherapy. Dr. Galdston insisted that an outside agency be called in to do the research. He recommended the Bureau of Applied Social Research at Columbia University.

Following a period of participant observation by the author of this book at the Religio-Psychiatric Clinic, the Bureau presented a draft proposal in the summer of 1956. It recommended a broad program of research to aid the Clinic in crystallizing its thinking about the relation of religion and psychiatry, to improve clinical services, and to guide other cooperative ventures in the field.

By late fall, tension was mounting between Dr. Blanton and Dr. Galdston. Partly related to Dr. Blanton's interest in the work on extra-sensory perception of Professor Rhine of Duke University. Dr. Blanton combined findings from the extra-sensory field and the power of "transference" to explain faith healing.[6]

The Bureau submitted nominations at the Foundation's request for a new professional research committee. The following January the committee mentioned in the Acknowledgements was formed, with Dr. John Cotton as chairman.

Routine at the Clinic

An office suite adjoining the Marble Collegiate Church bore the sign "Religio-Psychiatric Clinic." Chairs upholstered in orange plastic blended with pale blue walls and deep green carpeting. A secretary was scheduling appointments while a girl sobbed answers —name, place of birth. . . . The secretary's eyes met the girl's, but her hand continued filling the blanks on the intake questionnaire. A man in the reception room fingered *Look* magazine. Alongside, a young Negress controlled her child. An attractive brunette, Mrs. Elizabeth Ehling, B.D., stood at the reception room door, smiled, and gently motioned the woman and child down the corridor. On the bookshelf in the seminar room Burton's *Anatomy of Melancholy* stood alongside Sullivan's *Interpersonal Theory of Psychiatry,* Fromm's *Escape from Freedom,* Boisens' *Religion in Crisis and Custom,* and David Roberts' *Psychotherapy and the Christian View of Man.*

Elizabeth Lyons was trying to boil water for instant coffee and gulp it down in the ten minutes between patients. Miss Lyons, a tall carrot-topped psychiatric social worker, complained about the mistreatment of patients in other clinics. Schizoid performing artists were her specialty. One cried on the other end of her telephone and she replied like a stern parent to an unruly child. Her patients were encouraged to organize a self-employment agency and to come to an evening reading circle and Saturday teas. Dr. Galdson called her over-enthusiastic.

Hourly breaks brought three or four staff members to the kitchen. I chatted with them about therapeutic practice, experiences bringing them to the clinic, or religious problems arising in therapy. Sometimes we gossiped about absent staff members. Lunch hour found six or eight staff members heating a can of stew or opening sandwiches. Movies and plays around New York started a conversation. Only art theaters existed. Analysis of the coming presidential election continued to flow. Few Republicans spoke up.

Each Thursday morning staff members gathered for a case conference. Outside psychologists, psychiatrists, or ministers attending were hard put to distinguish this from a case conference at any other psychiatric clinic. Ministerial trainees analyzed therapeutic sessions in terms of the patient's family relations. Renée Fodor, a stocky woman with a ready smile and a concentration camp number on her arm, gave the "psychologicals"—results of the Rorschach, TAT, Sentence Completion, and Wechsler Adult Intelligence Scale. Dr. Tate commented on oral symbolism in the case. Dr. Holt explained his I-Me approach and discussed the maturity of the patient's self-image. Mr. Lytle lamented that the patient had not known love and asked that he receive it at the Clinic. Dr. Blanton's analogies with some ethic of the South or with patients of his own were eagerly awaited. Lunch together and general conviviality closed the conference. The case, comments, and commensality were ritually renewed each Thursday. I could not help but wonder if things would be different were I not observing.

The instant the researcher steps into a social situation, it is no longer what it was the moment before. Awareness of being observed will at least increase rationality and lessen erraticism. Behaviors may be tailored to gain the observer's approval. Questions themselves crystallize thoughts about subjects that might otherwise have remained nascent. Plying members of the staff about differences between ministers and psychiatrists, or the theological implications of certain ministerial practices certainly brought these issues to their attention.

Discussion Groups at the Clinic: a Source of Data

We turn now to one aspect of the clinic, the relations between ministers and psychiatrists. We are particularly interested in the norms and values regulating those relations. The information gleaned from participant observation was supplemented by an analysis of a series of specially organized planned discussions involving six ministers and six psychiatrists. They included Dr. Smiley Blanton (footnote 1), Dr. Fred Tate (footnote 3), Rev. Fred Kuether (footnote 4), Rev. Frank West (footnote 5), Rev. Hugh Hostetler (footnote 5), and Rev. Ridgley Lytle (footnote 2). The other discussants were Rev. Clinton Kew,[7] Rev. Herman Barbery,[8] Dr. Eugene Braun,[9] Dr. Herbert Holt,[10] Dr. Maria Fleischel,[11] and Dr. Preston McLean.[12]

The 12 were divided into three discussion groups. Each group consisting of two ministers and two psychiatrists, discussed the same question for a period of 40 minutes. The discussions were tape recorded. At the conclusion of the period, the membership of the groups was rotated and each of the three new groups was given another question for discussion. This process was repeated five times. This produced three independent discussions on each of five questions or fifteen discussions in all. Each of the 12 ministers and psychiatrists participated once in a discussion on each question. The rotation of group membership was such as to maximize interactions.

The questions were formulated on the basis of hypotheses established during the participant-observation period. They concerned

potential minister and psychiatrist role conflicts. The first question
was as follows:

1. It has been suggested that ministers and psychiatrists who
   associate themselves with a religio-psychiatric clinic are, in
   a manner of speaking, "rebels" against their respective professional groups.
   A. Is this so?
   B. If so, does being a rebel imply that they differ in person-
      ality and values from their colleagues?
   C. If so, how would these differences in personality and
      values impinge upon their counseling relationships?

The intent of this query was to elicit information on the professional self-images of ministers and psychiatrists. It asked that
they define their professional roles, relate their role definition to the
one institutionalized in their profession, and reveal some of the factors which led them to the clinic.

The second question concerned their relationship to clients:

2. Given was the case of a patient—male, age 25, married, no
   children, senior year student in a Protestant theological seminary, who came in overwrought because of his inability to
   control his active homosexuality. The diagnosis reveals the
   beginning of schizoid process and paranoid delusions of
   power. How would his treatment in a religio-psychiatric clinic
   differ from that in a hospital mental hygiene clinic?
   A. Regarding the objectives of treatment.
   B. Regarding the process of treatment.
   C. Regarding the results of treatment.
   D. If there is a difference, what factors may account for it?
   (Discuss the same case assuming that the patient is a senior
   year student in a medical school.)

The problem of homosexuality was introduced to instigate discussion on the relation of the therapist to the moral values of the
patient. Ministerial and medical students were mentioned to tease
out contrasting attitudes toward them and expected role behaviors
in each profession. It was also hoped that the responses might reveal
ideas about characteristics which qualify or disqualify individuals
for these professional statuses.

The third question regards the relationship of ministers and psychiatrists to their own institutions.

3. Assuming that a minister in this clinic was criticized by the traditional church authorities as an ethical relativist and one who perverts or dilutes real religious teaching, and
Assuming that a psychiatrist associated with this clinic was criticized by other psychiatrists as a party to "lay therapy" and as an opportunist,

   A. What position do the *psychiatrists expect the minister* to take *vis-à-vis* the *traditional church?*
   B. What position do the *ministers expect the psychiatrist* to take *vis-à-vis* the *medical profession?*
   C. What reactions have the ministers and psychiatrists to the expectations of the other?

It was hoped that the discussions around this theme would show points of strain between ministers and psychiatrists and mechanisms by which they reduce tensions between themselves and those attendant upon their estrangement from their own institutions.

The role relationship between ministers and psychiatrists in the Religio-Psychiatric Clinic was the target of the next question.

4. In the process of working with clients of a church-related clinic, at what points does the minister and at what points does the psychiatrist become a "layman"?

   A. Which activities are the exclusive province of the minister?
   B. Which activities are the exclusive province of the psychiatrist?
   C. What advice might the psychiatrist seek from the minister? (Assume that the minister has had clinical training and experience.)

In responding to this question, discussants were expected to do two things: to define the functions of the new institution, and then to decide which to allocate to ministers and which to psychiatrists. This question was also designed to reveal what happens within the clinic when both groups claim the same functions.

The final question was aimed at specifying the scope of the relations of ministers and psychiatrists to clients.

5. Should the counselor extend his relationship with the clients beyond the counseling situation?
   A. If so, under what conditions?
   B. If so, to which relationships?
   C. If there are limiting conditions, how is the counselor to know when they are met?

Why was it necessary to arrange discussion groups to answer these questions? Could the information not have been gleaned from interviews of each of the six ministers and six psychiatrists? From interviews alone it would have been possible to delineate some of the norms and values relating ministers and psychiatrists to one another, to their institutions, and to their clients. The discussion, it was hoped, would provide insight into the way norms and values change or emerge. The minister-psychiatrist interaction is in itself a factor in the change of norms. These discussions could repeat in microcosm the development of norms which occurs through the more macrocosmic interaction of ministers and psychiatrists at the clinic.

The verbatim protocols were analyzed thematically. Since a purpose of this case study was to discover hypotheses for a larger work, importance was not attached to the frequency of occurrence of categories. A category rarely found in this particular group could be significant in the study of other types of ministers and psychiatrists. A ministerial or psychiatric position was considered important if it fit into a logically consistent picture.[13]

Moving from an actual statement to an implied norm requires principles of interpretation.[14] The method of interpretation followed was similar to what Max Weber intended by his concept of *verstehen*. As applied in this case study, the method resembles the interpretation of protocols of the Thematic Apperception Test. Instead of debating the substantive validity of the statements, the TAT interpreter infers personality patterns from them. Personality interpretations may, of course, be related to the correctness of the statements. Logicality of opinion, however, is not the primary referent. In the present instance, the analysis is more often sociological than psychological. The interpreter asks what the statement implies about the relationship of the speaker to some other individuals. For example, a minister may say to a psychiatrist that he opposes Freud's "image of man" as animal-like but that Freud's therapeutic techniques are good. The interpreter would not ask whether Freud's "image of man" is really animal-like. In one context he might understand the minister as saying to the psychiatrist, "We have things in common which enable us to work together." In another context the minister might be saying, "It is possible for me to work with you without suffering condemnation by the church." With this brief introduction, we move to an analysis of tensions within religion and psychiatry which led the participants to the Religio-Psychiatric Clinic.

Why Ministers and Pyschiatrists Join the Clinic

Why do these six ministers work in a new institution partly outside the church? What estranges them from the parish ministry? Why are they willing to endure attacks by certain elements in the church which say they are diluting and perverting religious teachings? Why do these six psychiatrists vary? Why do they endure aspersions by the medical profession that they are betraying the profession by associating with "lay therapists"? Why do they associate with ministers despite accusations about their integrity and charges that they are opportunists?

The following are a few excerpts from the discussion protocols which suggest some of the motives leading these ministers and psychiatrists to affiliate with the Religio-Psychiatric Clinic. In this first interchange strain is perceived as due to a lack of self-fulfillment in the "home" institution.[15]

MR. TODD: The church attracts many sick people because it avowedly expresses love. I am impressed by the amount of illness in church youth groups.

MR. ROBERTSON: A tragedy in the organized church is the lack of opportunity it provides for self-understanding. I want to be part of something where we gain the ability to help others through work with self.

DR. NORTON: Both the ministry and psychiatry attract a great many sick people. In psychiatry there is an attempt to correct one's illness. In the ministry you have to fight upstream to do so.

The ministers at the Clinic have faced emotional difficulties of their own and have seen the emotional problems of their parishioners. Mr. Todd suggests that the church cannot meet emotional problems because its love is merely "avowed." Mr. Robertson confirms this feeling. Since they have found relief through psychotherapy, others might also be helped in a psychologically-oriented situation. No sooner is this motive expressed than the psychiatrist, by drawing an analogy, signals its legitimacy in terms of psychiatric values. There is a missionary element in this desire to share the benefits of psychotherapy with fellow-sufferers.

Strain may be blamed on a perceived conflict between personal and institutional values.

MR. TODD: The Protestant church is very moralistic. I wanted to have dancing in the back of my country church. The elders rose up and said, "No, you can't have it here. This is the place of God, and it exists for His glories."

DR. NIELSON: If a minister accepts such a rigid doctrine, we cannot work with him. There are certain situations in which we must be permissive.

DR. NORTON: The duty of the psychiatrist is to help sick people. The minister may feel a conflict between helping a person and helping God.

MR. RIEDELL: Some things have troubled me about the church. My family goes to the Presbyterian church in our community. I went a couple of times on Sunday morning when I was free. In one of the sermons the minister came right out and said that the Presbyterian church stands for voluntary, complete abstinence from alcohol.

MR. TODD: Orthodox Christians try to live either by literal scriptural doctrines or by rigid intellectualism.

DR. LINDQUIST: Intellectualism cuts out the emotional. That is why it is sterile.

DR. NIELSON: No religious formulation has the right to violate scientific facts. You have no right to argue, as Bishop Usher did, that man was created 5,000 years ago. Evolution has been proved. Depth psychologists have proved that man is governed by unconscious impulses. The ordinary morality of the orthodox church violates this fundamental teaching of science.

The minister supporting liberal social values and scientific norms may encounter opposition in a conservative parish. Dr. Norton refers to the desire of the ministers to provide counseling services and says that the demand that the minister be the moral leader of the community and committed to support its values may be incompatible with individual pastoral services. Dr. Norton's statement encourages Mr. Riedell to express his conflict with the values of the Presbyterian church and Mr. Todd to criticize literalism. Neither attacks his own denomination. Mr. Riedell is ordained as an Evangelical and Reformed minister and Mr. Todd as a Presbyterian. Dr. Lindquist provides support and Dr. Nielson sanctions the priority of scientific norms. This type of normative and emotional support originally encouraged Mr. Todd to reveal dissatisfaction with his parish situation.

The previous excerpt illustrated the problem of identifying with scientific counseling values while in a religious institution. The following excerpt reflects a conflict among religious values.

MR. ROBERTSON: I have tried to deal with people within the structure of the church and could not get close enough. The sacraments and the ordered public worship can be helpful, but they set barriers I could not overcome between the people and me.

MR. TODD: My need to maintain the structure of the institution was getting in the way of my personal relationships with people. I find freedom in this situation.

DR. TUFF: You do not want to play a role with the patient but want a direct human relationship.

DR. NIELSON: A strong current is bringing the disciplines of religion and psychiatry together. In a book called *What Man May Be*, Harrison of the Massachusetts Institute of Technology said that 96 per cent of the people believe in a God. I spoke to a Jewish patient who said the Jewish God is rather silly and the Christian God doesn't amount to anything. I said, "Well, I don't insist that you accept the God that the Jews developed in their orthodox religion, nor the concept that any particular Christian church developed." People are willing to accept something in the universe above themselves which is the source of life and which gives order, meaning, and value to life, but they resent an orthodox formulation of it. Ministers who work here should be able to modify their church and their formulations.

Protestantism, relative to Catholicism, emphasizes personal relationships. These men selected the ministry partly out of their need for a personal relationship. Mr. Robertson and Mr. Todd report that their parish experiences do not reflect the church's ideal and conflict with their need. Drs. Tuff and Nielson support them in their rebellion against impersonality.

We turn from the motives of ministers to those of psychiatrists. Ministers at the Religio-Psychiatric Clinic devote full-time to counseling. They generally do not retain a parish position. Psychiatric membership, on the other hand, does not imply abandonment of traditional psychiatric practice. Psychiatrists' association with the Religio-Psychiatric Clinic is in lieu of attendance at a secular clinic or hospital. Their break with the traditional role is considerably less radical.

Psychiatrists may smart under their "second-class medical citizenship."

DR. NYMAN: Psychiatry is looked down upon by all other fields of medicine. Only after hospital patients have gone through all the tests and treatments are they sent to psychiatry.

When working with ministers, psychiatrists enjoy relatively high status. This suggests that one motive for associating with the Clinic may be the relative prestige it offers.

Psychiatrists may encounter a conflict between the norm of objectivity institutionalized in medicine and the psychotherapeutic pressure toward a more personal relationship.

DR. TUFF: I'm a rebel; I am rebelling against not seeing people treated as individuals. My co-professionals think I am educating competitors. With them it is a question of economics and prestige. I want to restore the intimate doctor-patient relationship necessary for healing.

The psychiatrist generalizes this norm from his broad medical status to his psychotherapeutic role. Dr. Tuff finds the medical norm of affective neutrality incompatible with therapeutic requirements and is caught in a conflict within the psychiatric status.

The psychiatric status is lonely.

> DR. EDEN: I cannot sit in my office and practice on an isolated island with four to six patients and feel satisfied with myself. The minister and the psychiatrist should work together in a team.

The psychiatrists' work isolates them from the direct intellectual and emotional support of colleagues. There is a further temptation to restrict professional contact because their income directly reflects therapy hours. The need for professional companionship is partly responsible for sending doctors into nonremunerative clinic and hospital work as well as to the Religio-Psychiatric Clinic.

Ministers expressing strain find immediate support and response from the psychiatrists. Psychiatrists receive no echo from ministers. This may be because the psychiatrists can readily identify with ministers in conflict with moralistic and structural demands of the church since they may face a similar religious problem. The problem of isolation, however, finds no counterpart in the life of ministers trying to escape the intense social demands of the parish. Paradoxically, however, the minister may feel alone in these intense, yet superficial, relations.

Further, the minister finds it difficult to identify with the psychiatrist's prestige problem. Though he is also troubled by being on a lower economic level than the elders of his church, and by the ebbing of religious authority, he looks upon the psychiatrist as a culture hero, a representative of science. The psychiatrist does little to destroy this image, so, for the relative prestige he gains, he must forego sympathy.

The general order of steps leading these ministers to vary from the traditional church seems roughly to follow the one which emerges from the analysis of literature. Variation begins with a feeling of personal estrangement from the church which may be related to a conflict between their personal values and those of the institution or to their feelings that they cannot help people within the institution. Contact with psychotherapy focuses their attention on a particular sociocultural context which is legitimate in terms of the broader social values and still legitimate in terms of basic church values of "helping people." This enables them to vary without breaking with the church. In this sense, the new variant movement takes on the character of a "reformation" rather than a complete "conversion" or "apostatization."

The psychiatrists' motivation to variation is related to their feeling of helplessness in the face of mental illness, and is compounded by their isolation in private practice. A clinic affiliation is a chance to "compare notes," and the fellowship of the church offers support. Though they suffer low status among their medical colleagues, they gain status as the experts, the men with the "know-how" among the "lay therapists."

The motivations to variation of ministers and psychiatrists in this church-clinic setting converge. The ministers believe the psychiatrists will teach them new "techniques" which will increase the effectiveness of their ministry. The psychiatrists seek to become more effective through unveiling the mysteries of religious fellowship. The Religio-Psychiatric Clinic emerges as a double-variant institution. By being simultaneously peripheral to religion and medicine, it enables both ministers and psychiatrists to vary from their "home" professions without relinquishing membership.

How They Meet Institutional Reprisals

Variation is an adaptation to a strain. Yet it brings new strains. As we observed through analysis of the literature, the institutions exert pressure upon variant members. Direct physical coercion is not available either to the church or to medicine in our society. Defrocking a clergyman or canceling a physician's license are penalties imposed in the most serious cases. The physician, however, who receives no referrals and the minister not acceptable to a Board of Elders are in trying straits. Further, variants carry their own internal controls, since they still consider themselves ministers and psychiatrists and have not consciously withdrawn fealty from their groups.

Had the break been complete, the overt pressures would be less effective. In that case, the ministers and psychiatrists would transfer their allegiance and emotional dependence to the new institution and develop a negative image of the old. The Religio-Psychiatric

Clinic, however, partakes of both the ministry and psychiatry. The participants in it must come to terms with the pressures in and upon them. This section will show some ways that ministers and psychiatrists at the Religio-Psychiatric Clinic adapt to the pressures from their respective groups. Another section could be written on the adaptations of the institutions as a consequence of the variation.

Much of the pressure exerted upon the variants is attitudinal. Its effectiveness is contingent upon its being perceived. The following excerpts reveal attempts to deal with the perception.

MR. RIEDELL: I think there is some acceptance now of psychiatry within religious bodies.

DR. NIELSON: I don't think there is as much criticism of psychiatry working with religion as people think.

Pressure is met by denying its existence. Denial, ordinarily considered a psychological mechanism, can, as we see above, become established through social consensus. Each supports the other in the denial until it becomes a norm.

This norm is strengthened by citing leaders who approve of the new venture.

DR. NIELSON: A good indication of doctors' attitudes is that the American Medical Association has asked me to write an editorial on religion and psychiatry. The head of the A.M.A. said the doctor must bring God into the sickroom. He told of a woman with cancer. She said, "Can't you do something for me? Can't you pray for me?" He said, "Yes, I'll pray for you," and he knelt down by her bed and he prayed. She was ill several months longer, but pain was reduced by this prayer so that she was able to endure it.

In view of the pressures upon this group, denial is too unrealistic a mechanism to be fully effective. Some variation must be admitted. When it is, a new set of mechanisms for reducing the strain comes into play.

MR. TODD: Were I really pressed by the Presbyterian church, I would stand up for the principles I believe we express here in the Clinic. If I were to be kicked out, I would still stand on them because I believe in them.

DR. NIELSON: I don't believe that any church would go so far as to turn you out.

Mr. Todd, recognizing the possibility of conflict, appeals to the value of standing for the right. The stance is heroic. The identification of the personal with the clinic values is a request for support from the new solidarity. Dr. Nielson's reply, minimizing the danger, undercuts the anxiety and limits the responsibility of the new institution. He questions the validity of the appeal on a heroic basis.

The following excerpt illustrates a less aggressive stance *vis-à-vis* institutional pressures:

MR. ELLIS: I would welcome the opportunity to go to my bishop and tell him exactly how I operate as a counselor in this religio-psychiatric setting.

Explaining increases visibility. The assumption is that if they are more clearly seen they will be better understood and pressure will not be applied.

MR. TODD: I would expect the psychiatrist to strengthen his ties with other doctors. It is important that we do not get cut off on a limb. I want to strengthen my ties with my church to maintain communication.

Explaining not only increases visibility but minimizes estrangement. When conciliation is ineffective, other forms of strain reduction appear.

DR. LINQUIST: Mr. Todd, you solved the problem in the parish by getting out.

MR. TODD: I solved it by packing the board until I was able to control the situation.

Actual withdrawal from the situation is an extreme solution. The use of a political power technique to reduce the pressure may be a way of averting the withdrawal. Mr. Todd's combination of a militant stance with fear of being cut off suggests that attack is engagement, a way of retaining a relationship.

MR. TODD: If we go along and do not broadcast what we do, no one will bother us. I am not begging for a knock on the bean.

DR. LINDQUIST: This is all right as long as it doesn't affect your attitude to the patients.

DR. NIELSON: Doctors feel that no one but an M.D. can do psychotherapy. You should not talk about doing psychotherapy because they would crack us on the head. It is off the record so to speak. But there has been so much quackery and mistreatment of the sick by people who meant well that I think it is good insurance to have a sick person examined by a doctor.

Strain may be reduced by decreasing visibility through a redefinition of the situation. Dr. Nielson also proposes avoiding situations which might lead to strain by retaining medical diagnosis.

Appeal to basic values in defense of their work also functions to enable them to resolve internal conflicts. The following statements have less to do with external pressures than with internal problems.

Ministers and psychiatrists justify their variation to themselves by an appeal to basic values of their institutions.

MR. YOUNGS: We are thought to be ethical relativists. I have come up against this as a pastoral counselor here. I take this criticism as an opportunity to go back to the New Testament, to the spirit, teaching, and practice of Christ. What is going on here is the dynamic ground of the faith in which we believe.

MR. ROBERTSON: I see in my present work a return to the heart of a healing ministry.

DR. NIELSON: Ministers here are as much in the framework of religious training and teaching as a regular minister in a church. Carlyle says that "Religion is constantly weaving for itself new vestiges."

DR. NORTON: I think of myself more as a person than as a psychiatrist. The first patient I had asked me if I were a Freudian. I was baffled by the whole thing. The criticism of the psychiatrist for associating with people of different disciplines presents a problem in knowledge. In *Science and the Modern World*, Whitehead proposed to end the divorce not only between science and theology, but also between all areas of our knowledge. The analyst attacks the religious thinking of 50 years ago. By joining hands it is possible to bring knowledge up to date.

Strain was met above by denying that the parent institutions considered them variant. Here, regardless of the charge, the self justification is in terms of precedent. Mr. Youngs and Mr. Robertson claim consistency with the basic values of the church, with the spirit of Christ, and with the essence of religion. Dr. Nielson supports their view. Dr. Norton indicates that his behavior demonstrates respect for scientific knowledge and progress. He also suggests that the psychiatric critique is not directed at modern religion, but at a primitive form which no longer exists.

Sometimes the appeal is oriented to people rather than principles.

MR. TODD: I look at the prophets and see men who did not like conformity. I look at the life of our Lord and see a man who was a rebel. He broke new ground and the institutions could not stand it. This is the same kind of thing.

MR. ROBERTSON: The dean of one of the most famous seminaries in this country advocated reaching for a new kind of relationship as a rebellion against the organized church. The question is being asked in every seminary.

Strain is reduced by identifying with present or former heroic variants. Dr. Norton's reference to Whitehead has a similar function. Identification with early leaders or founders parallels the appeal to basic values.

The variant may conceptually minimize the forces opposing him in his own institution.

DR. NYMAN: The greater part of the church is against psychiatry. If Mr. Ellis dares to go to his bishop, he will have to select carefully which bishop to go to. I know Episcopalian bishops who have condemned people to hell for daring to go to a psychiatrist. There is less objection on the part of psychiatrists to religion.

DR. NIELSON: A psychiatrist would not have to defend himself for working with a minister before most psychiatrists. The crank fringe, the conflicted, neurotic sort, might think that there can be no relationship between religion and psychiatry. They are few and far between. As for the Roman Catholic church, the Pope said that psychiatry and psychoanalysis have their place in the church. A prominent Catholic divine gets up and berates psychiatry. But what one man says doesn't represent the fundamental attitude of the church.

DR. NYMAN: Those who oppose us have to examine their own conscience to discover what is behind their feeling. Many psychiatrists do not like the magical type of religion.

The barb of criticism is softened my minimizing its source. Dr. Nyman argues that opposition does not exist among psychiatrists but only among ministers. Dr. Nielson recognizes the existence in psychiatry but limits it to a crank fringe. The opposing Catholic divine is not representative. Dr. Nyman considers psychiatric opponents either poorly analyzed or opposed to something else such as magical religion. With the opposition delimited and negatively stereotyped, it may be discounted. In fact, the demand for change becomes justified.

The process of drawing the fangs of the opposition through negative stereotyping continues.

MR. RIEDELL: The word religion means to wind together. It can get you all tied up or it can be a relatedness.

DR. LINDQUIST: Religion may be stagnation and sickness or something lively.

MR. RIEDELL: I have been phantasizing on the accusation that we dilute and pervert religion. In working intensively with individuals in trouble, I have developed a really alive religion. It isn't my religion that is ethically relative and perverted. The fixed religious doctrine in the church is limited to those who cannot face reality.

The stereotyping may be personal as well.

MR. YOUNGS: Some of these bishops who oppose us are getting along in years. They do not represent the dynamic trends within Christianity today. Among men under 45 in the Episcopal,

Methodist, and Presbyterian churches, you find a remarkable receptivity to psychiatric practice.

MR. ELLIS: The church has officially recognized the field of psychiatry. Every candidate for the ministry in the Episcopal church must see a psychiatrist and go through psychological tests. Unfortunately a lot of our church members over 40 have not quite caught up.

DR. NIELSON: Humanism is a vague, washed-out, pitiful sort of a fiddle-faddle in which everybody believes in sort of a vague goodness. I am irritated by it because I think it is a lot of nonsense. A few fine intellectual people can get along with vague humanism. But most people have to feel that when they have done their level best, they can depend on orderliness and meaning.

DR. TUFF: Psychiatrists are interested in perpetuating their legal, economic, and social status. Any relationship which can endanger their preferred position is seen as a danger. You can call it paranoid. I might be called a rebel by my colleagues but I think I am in the Hippocratic tradition of medicine.

Negative stereotypes characterize the religion of the opposition as stagnated and sick. The opponents themselves are old and old-fashioned. Opposing psychiatrists propose a vague humanism or are only interested in protecting their legal and economic status.

A few hypotheses suggest themselves. The first attempt to meet the pressures is to deny that they exist. When these pressures must be admitted, the ministers and psychiatrists try to face the agents of control directly, to communicate, explain, and, in general, reduce their estrangement from their institutions. Some withdraw from the conflict-producing situation. The existence of a break, however, is denied. Differences between old and new values are minimized by being called "semantic." Moving from ministerial to psychiatric terminology is a matter of "translation."

A residual pressure is met by deflecting it to something other than what these ministers and psychiatrists are doing. Psychiatry is said to be opposed only to the religion of 50 years ago or to the magical type of religion. Religion only conflicts with old forms of psychiatry such as early Freudian thinking. They attempt to isolate the opposition. Only a small minority is opposed to them—most ministers and psychiatrists are becoming more tolerant of the new movement. Having isolated this minority opposition, negative stereotypes are attached to it. Opposition exists only among "old" churchmen or is characteristic of the "crank fringe," of "neurotic" psychiatrists and ministers.

Reality requires that these ministers and psychiatrists recognize a modicum of their own variation. In so doing they identify with other value-positive or honored variants. Ministers admit rebellion against the traditional church and class themselves with prophets of yore who rebelled against conformity. Just as the prophets were persecuted in their own times only to be appreciated in later days, so it will be with this group. Strain is also met by emphasizing the positive values of the Religio-Psychiatric Clinic and stressing solidarity with it. This represents a partial transfer of the security system to the new institution and also contributes to managing internal strains arising in the new institution. Identification is mediated by the development of a basic rationale for the new institution. The next chapter considers this institutional rationale, its development and its functions.

NOTES

1. Dr. Blanton's 1904 B.S. from Vanderbilt entitled him to teach speech at Cornell. Poetic and literary interests found expression in a short stage career. Later, with an M.D. from Cornell University Medical College, he taught mental hygiene at the University of Wisconsin and clinical medicine at the University of Minnesota and became Professor of child study at Vassar. By 1927, he held the diploma in Psychological Medicine from the Royal College of Physicians and Surgeons in London.

2. Ridgely Lytle's excellent record in philosophy and history at Princeton sent him as a Rhodes Scholar to Merton College at Oxford. By the time he received his M.A. in theology from Oxford in 1922, he had been a Captain of Field Artillery and an ordained deacon in the Episcopal church. He was successively chaplain at Princeton and Rochester and rector of St. Andrew's Church in Wilmington, Delaware. For six years he pursued academic studies in psychoanalysis and underwent a personal

analysis. His first three years of work at the clinic were guided by a control analyst.

3. A 1943 M.D. from Middlesex College preceded Dr. Tate's service as a medical officer with the Public Health Service and a residency in neuropsychiatry at the Marine Hospital on Ellis Island. Turning from electroencephalography to psychotherapy, he studied at the Post Graduate Center for Psychotherapy in New York from 1948 to 1951.

4. Mr. Kuether received his B.D. in 1934 at Eden Theological Seminary. His clinical training began over midnight pots of tea in Anton Boisen's kitchen at Elgin State Hospital. A decade before, Mr. Boisen emerged from an attack of schizophrenia convinced that dementia praecox was a disorganization of the inner world, a way of resolving an inner crisis, and related to religious experience. Mr. Boisen's dedication to the chaplaincy was evangelical, and Mr. Kuether was a rapt disciple. Mr. Kuether was a chaplain in a midwest federal reformatory and was teaching at Garrett Biblical Seminary during the early '40's. Chaplaincy and seminary remained his life-pattern until he assumed the directorship of the Council for Clinical Training.

5. Hugh Hostetler, the Clinic's first full-time trainee, arrived early in 1956. The word "love" came easily and naturally to his lips. Born in Sugarcreek, Ohio, in 1922, he had wandered as far as Bethel College in Northnewton, Kansas, to earn his A.B. in the natural sciences. After a ministry at the First Mennonite Church in Ransom, Kansas, he entered New York's Union Theological Seminary and was sent to an East Harlem parish. He and his wife remained in this parish on the periphery of violence for five years beyond his 1950 B.D. Through the Council for Clinical Training, he experienced the closed wards at Bellevue. Mr. Hostetler accumulated 750 hours of personal and 350 hours of supervised analysis.

Within a few months, the second full-time trainee arrived. Frank West, A.B. Summa Cum Laude and Phi Beta Kappa from Lehigh, was ordained in the Presbyterian church U.S.A. After graduation from Union Theological Seminary in 1953, he was called to three rural mission churches in Ohio. Though chaffing under the moralistic restrictions of a rural parish, he earned the Ohio Presbytery's citation of "Rural Pastor of the Year" in 1955. At St. Elizabeth's Hospital in Washington he was introduced to clinical training. His training eventually included 400 hours of personal analysis and 250 hours of psychoanalytic supervision.

6. Dr. Blanton invited Dr. Ash, a member of the Royal Medical Society who had relinquished his medical practice to devote himself to faith healing, to lecture at the Clinic. Dr. Ash described a force coming out of his finger tips which when held over a patient's infected leg caused the infection to recede. From California Dr. Blanton brought Dr. William

R. Parker, who subsequently wrote *Prayer Can Change Your Life—The Scientific Proof that Prayer Can Bring You What You Want*. When Dr. Parker, a Professor of Speech at Redlands University, found himself on the verge of a nervous breakdown, he began to pray and in a few months was entirely well. Dr. Parker set up counseling groups. One group received traditional group psychotherapy. A second group prayed generally for therapy. A third group used prayers specifically related to their difficulties. Dr. Parker reported that members of the third group showed most improvement.

7. Rev. Clinton Kew, a Harvard-trained Episcopalian, has together with his psychologist twin brother Clifton Kew written on cooperation between religion and psychology. He counsels, conducts healing services, and answers pastoral letters from correspondents throughout the country.

8. Rev. Herman L. Barbery came from England to earn a B.D. at Garrett Biblical Institute in 1936. After serving as a Methodist pastor, he became an army chaplain in 1944. In 1951, he was elected to the Synod of the Reformed Church in America and appointed associate minister of the Marble Collegiate Church. He has been associate director of the Religio-Psychiatric Clinic since 1946 and has had 150 hours of personal analysis and 50 hours of supervision.

9. Dr. Eugene J. Braun received his M.D. from Charles University in Prague in 1931. He served as a medical officer with the Czechoslovak division of the French Army and then the British Transport Navy before coming to the United States in 1947. After a residency in psychiatry and neurology, he became senior psychiatrist at Brooklyn State Hospital in 1953. He was a staff psychiatrist at the Religio-Psychiatric Clinic from 1952 until his death in 1959. Dr. Braun was affiliated with the Dutch Reformed church.

10. Dr. Herbert Holt earned his M.D. at Lausanne in 1938 and came to the United States from his native Vienna immediately thereafter. He has practiced pediatrics and neuropsychiatry and was associate attending physician at Vanderbilt Clinic until joining the staff of the Religio-Psychiatric Clinic in 1955. His religious affiliation was Jewish at the time of the discussions.

11. Dr. Maria F. Fleischel came to the United States after receiving her M.D. from the University of Vienna Medical School in 1937. A psychiatric residence at Bellevue Hospital was succeeded by a lectureship at the Post-Graduate Center for Psychotherapy. She joined the Religio-Psychiatric Clinic in 1956. Her religious affiliation is Jewish.

12. Dr. Preston G. McLean received his M.D. from Louisiana State University School of Medicine in 1947. He took a psychiatric residency at a Veterans Administration hospital in 1953 and joined the Religio-Psychiatric Clinic in 1956. His religious affiliation is Baptist.

13. On logical consistency as a mode of interpretation in social science, see Max Weber's *Methodology of the Social Sciences.*

14. The problem of the inferences between concepts and indicators is discussed by the author in "A Typology of Concept-Indicator Relations," and *Some Differences in Modes of Research Between Psychologists and Sociologists.*

15. The excerpts have been edited so as to remove the redundancies and elliptical forms of the spoken language. An effort was made not to distort the meaning of the statements. Some of the statements are responses to the exigencies of the immediate discussion situation and some were tentative notions held by the individual at that time. The participants would not necessarily express themselves in the same way under different circumstances or at a later time. In view of this, the following edited quotations will be flagged by pseudonyms.

Chapter X

Staff Relations and Patient Relations

NEGOTIATING AN ALLIANCE BETWEEN PASTORS AND PSYCHIATRISTS

The Institutional Slogan: An Expression of Mechanical Solidarity

EMILE DURKHEIM[1] identifies two types of social solidarity. In one people are bound together through the interdependence of the social tasks they fulfill. The physician is bound to the soldier because he depends upon him for defense. The soldier needs the physician to tend his wounds. Durkheim calls this "organic solidarity." People are also bound to one another because of their likenesses, because of their subjection to a common destiny, or by ties of affection. This relation he terms "mechanical solidarity." These two forms of solidarity are only analytically distinct. In any concrete situation, individuals are bound together both organically and mechanically.

Mechanical solidarity at the Religio-Psychiatric Clinic attenuates strains due to variation. External pressure on the institution and its members could lead to their defection from the new group and its consequent disintegration. Organic solidarity at the Clinic emerges as the participants evolve norms defining ministerial and psychiatric jurisdictions and qualifications for admission to the counseling role. Ministers and psychiatrists arrive at the Religio-Psychiatric Clinic with a stock of general American culture norms and specialized professional norms defining their relationships to patients, clients, or parishioners. They even bring some preformed norms to guide their relation to one another. The new institution presents a new problem. Through redefining their relationships they define the nature and function of the new institution.

We have discussed pressures of the religious institution on variant ministers and of the medical institution upon variant psychiatrists. The attainment of organic solidarity within the Religio-Psychiatric Clinic may also entail conflict. A context of mechanical solidarity is necessary to support the relations through these tense moments.

The mechanical solidarity of the Religio-Psychiatric Clinic is expressed by a slogan justifying its existence. We will term it the "basic institutional rationale." This basic institutional rationale is established early and underlies the subsequent evolution of more specific and substantively oriented norms.

The following excerpts illustrate the achievement of solidarity and its link to the basic institutional rationale.

MR. ELLIS: I have rebelled only against certain trends in the church such as the tendency to emphasize the letter of the law at the expense of the spiritual and moral. I am not a rebel against the authority of my bishop nor of the general convention, nor against the ordered service in the Episcopal church and the wearing of the vestments.

DR. EDEN: I don't feel that I am a rebel. I am only more openminded than some of my colleagues.

MR. ELLIS: You are taking the word "rebel" as indicating hostility. I'm not a rebel against the Episcopal church but protest against rigidity in our outlook.

DR. EDEN: We are going along the same fairway.

MR. WYN: About fourteen years ago, I wandered out of the path of the average clergyman because I became interested in mental health. In that sense I am a rebel.

DR. EDEN: When doctors say I'm a rebel to medicine because I live with theology, I try to engage in conversation. There is more to medicine than applying an antibiotic.

Each admits his rebellion. When Dr. Eden hesitates, the ministers press him until he concedes that he is a variant. Before solidarity is achieved in the new variant institution, each relinquishes part of his allegiance to his membership group. Each sacrifices a part of himself to demonstrate his devotion to the new institution.

MR. RIEDELL: Most ministers associated with clinical training in a mental hospital are not accepted by their institutions. My seminary practically wrote me out for associating with a psychiatric group.

DR. LINDQUIST: This is true. Many analysts oblige themselves not to teach a lay person on pain of losing their membership in the A.M.A.

MR. RIEDELL: At William Alanson White all nonmedical people sign a statement that they will not practice psychoanalysis.

MR. ELLIS: Clergymen on the staff have had years of study in counseling. Though I am not a psychiatrist, I am not in the same category as ministers who have had no training.

Dr. Lindquist and Mr. Riedell claim support from the new institution on the basis of sacrifices they have made in joining. Mr. Ellis's claim is founded upon the time he devoted to study.

MR. TODD: I was never aware of the privilege of being with this Clinic until I talked with a clinically trained minister in Washington. He went all around Washington to find a doctor who would provide medical supervision. They all told him they would jeopardize their positions in the A.M.A. if they did. The psychiatrists and ministers here feel more strongly about their convictions than about complying with their institutions. We support each other and try to convince our critics.

Mr. Todd offers support in return for the psychiatrists' sacrifice. He asks that the support be mutual. It cannot, however, be demanded and given simply for past acts, but must be related to future promise. This leads to the discussion of the institutional rationale.

DR. EDEN: Generally my patients are hostile toward their religion and toward themselves.

MR. WYN: Religion is in the psychiatrist's personality. He has love and patience. He will accept hostility. Many psychiatrists are more religious than clergymen. Most clergymen ram theology down your throat. This is not love.

DR. NORTON: Clergymen in this clinic can offer the resources of religion for alleviating anxiety. A psychiatrist too can impress a patient by feeling no difficulty about having a religious interest.

MR. WYN: People who come here are not interested in which religious communion or faith the psychiatrist professes. The fact that he is connected with religion is enough.

The rationale is expressed through Mr. Wyn's assertion of the religious contribution of the psychiatrist. Dr. Norton rejoins citing the psychological contribution of the minister. Mr. Wyn's allusion to the nonsectarian character of this contribution expresses solidarity with the Jewish psychiatrists and shows a trend toward nondenominationalism among the ministers.

DR. NIELSON: Whenever you do anything different, you meet with resistance and resentment. For a long time, ministers have felt that psychiatry threatens their work. Psychiatrists have thought of religion as accusing people of wrongdoing. In the last twenty years, there has been a complete change. The church and psychiatry realize that they need to work together.

DR. NYMAN: Psychiatrists and ministers should work closely together. They can contribute to each other and to their patients. Yesterday Rev. Ellis asked me to see a patient. I examined the patient and found some organic difficulties besides the psychological. I dealt with the medical problem and the psychological problem related to it. Rev. Ellis dealt with the pastoral counseling part. It worked out very well.

DR. NIELSON: It does not pay and is not right and does not work and does not help to pour out moral observations on a person because he has acted upon some unconscious impulse.

No one wants to see a person be a thief, or a liar, or completely promiscuous. They want him to be honest and kind. But how are you going to get them that way? This combination of religion and psychiatry opens up a way that is better, more powerful, and more effective.

MR. ELLIS: The goal of both ministers and psychiatrists is the diminution of fear, anxiety, and resentment, so as to enable a client to fulfill himself as a person. The psychoanalytic process and the spiritual process are basically the same.

The following exchange illustrates another way of making the point.

DR. EDEN: We have no differences between us.

DR. LINDQUIST: We are all talking about personality growth and development. This is a reaching out of the various disciplines toward each other.

MR. TODD: Using personal relatedness as its common ground.

The basic rationale for the institution has been established. It is expressed in assertions that it is good for ministers and psychiatrists to work together. This slogan expresses the value that cooperation is good, and its academic specification that interdisciplinary teamwork is good. More specific justifications follow. Dr. Nyman refers to complementary skills. Cooperative effort is linked to the common goal. Both strive to help man be honest, kind, and without anxiety or resentment. The newly achieved solidarity is signalled in assertions of near identity.

The establishment of the basic rationale and the subsequent achievement of solidarity follows a pattern. At first, each denies that he varies from his membership group or its norms. Each is pressed by the other to admit to some variation as a basis for establishing the new solidarity. Each attacks certain norms of his own institution, elements in psychiatry and religion that have been "distorted." Then each identifies acceptable elements in the other group. These tend to be aspects neither has rejected from his own institution. This done, the ministers have established a "toe-hold" in psychiatry and the psychiatrists have laid claim to a small bit of ministerial territory.

With this mutual straddling of religion and psychiatry, the new institution is shown to evolve naturally from the old ones. The Religio-Psychiatric Clinic is a common ground for the two "parent" institutions. The process proceeds in an oscillatory fashion with each tentatively making a strong statement only to backtrack on it in terms of the reactions of the other until the consensus is reached. Similar exchanges recur a number of times. Each time the participants ritualistically repeat this pattern of establishing or reaffirming the basic rationale. In the face of strains set up in the evolution of subsidiary norms, each reaffirmation of the slogan reassures that the underlying integrity of the institution remains.

The need to establish mechanical solidarity is so great that the substantive content of the discussions may become secondary. In parts of the discussions, individuals contradict their positions within a few sentences in order to agree with the others. Conflicts seeming to defy resolution are ignored or passed over. Time and again the theme recurs that there are no differences, and time and again the chorus resounds to the utopian advantages of cooperation.

Establishing Professional Jurisdictions:
The Foundation of Organic Solidarity

The principal norms of the Religio-Psychiatric Clinic are those regulating relationships between ministers and psychiatrists and those relating each of them to patients. This section will examine the development of some interprofessional norms. The next section focuses on norms involved in the therapeutic role.

Where is the line to be drawn between the religious and psychiatric functions? This is the problem of structural differentiation. Following the delineation of functions, criteria are established for admitting individuals to each of the roles. This is role allocation. In a concrete situation, the processes of differentiation and allocation become intertwined. Organic solidarity is attained through consensus regarding these norms.

The following excerpt shows the attempt to locate areas of exclusively ministerial and exclusively psychiatric activity:

DR. NORTON: The exclusive province of the psychiatrist is one of diagnostics, particularly the discrimination of organic components of a problem and the use of drugs and somatic therapy.

MR. ROBERTSON: I agree that the area of organic damage is the exclusive province of the psychiatrist.

DR. TUFF: In addition to a biological training, we are also better trained psychologically. I just know more than you do. When you will know more than I know, you won't have to come to me.

The psychiatrists select treatment of the organic as an exclusive function. This is accepted by the ministers. When, however, the psychiatrists claim priority in psychodiagnosis, the ministers resist. Instead of directly claiming psychodiagnostic rights, the ministers propose that their definition of the new institution does not exclude the psychiatrists from any function except the sacramental.

MR. ROBERTSON: The only thing which Protestant churches feel to be the exclusive province of the minister is the administration of the sacraments of the Lord's Supper and of baptism. Beyond that, the minister has no exclusive province. If a psychiatrist would feel that prayer would help, fine. This is a real Protestant view. Every person is his own priest and a priest to others before God.

DR. EDEN: I wouldn't think of attempting anything like this. If a patient discusses his religion, I analyze the thought process. If he is using religion in a way detrimental to his best interests, I may point it out. If a delusional system is brought up within the religious framework, I may try to break it down but I would call in my friends in the ministry to help me. I am not an authority on religion.

MR. ROBERTSON: If it is therapeutic and sound to pray, why should psychiatrists not pray as well as ministers? If it is not therapeutically sound, a minister has no business praying.

DR. EDEN objects to the lack of differentiation of functions. Mr. Robertson, in trying to carry the point, moves from an appeal to the basic "Protestant view" to justification in terms of the psychiatric value of the "therapeutically sound."

DR. TUFF: The minister has a dual role. In church he functions as a priest. Here, he functions as a pastor. In this clinic the minister and the doctor both try to help the patient overcome his psychosis. They might differ in technique. The Protestant minister is obligated to treat in terms of the teaching of Jesus Christ.

MR. YOUNGS: As a Protestant minister I am not confined to a limited historical Christian view. I draw upon the insight of the race as revealed in other traditions.

DR. EDEN: I do not agree with you, Dr. Tuff. I'm Jewish but not a Jewish psychiatrist.

DR. TUFF: I do not treat people as a Jewish psychiatrist. A minister, though, has certain religious assumptions. He is a minister doing pastoral counseling. People address him not as Joe Blow but as a minister.

MR. ROBERTSON: Let me speak for myself. One is first a human being. The fact that I am ordained a Protestant minister may enter in. There is a potential within Protestantism for an almost complete lack of earthly or institutional framework. The essence of Protestantism is spiritual power . . . standing over and above or against all institutions and judging constantly all human institutions including the church.

DR. TUFF: You feel that but I still don't see the exclusive provinces of the minister.

MR. ROBERTSON: I have none. If a person would come and ask for the sacraments, you could administer them.

DR. TUFF: I do not feel that I should.

MR. YOUNGS: This is the essence of Protestantism. Spirit is primary. Church, forms, regulations are secondary. The Holy Spirit speaks directly to each and every individual, whether he be a minister or a layman. There is the divine in each.

Dr. Tuff cites evidence of functional specificity in the ministerial role. He suggests denominational obligations limiting a minister but not restricting a psychiatrist. Mr. Robertson characterizes the relationship in terms of the "human being" but Dr. Tuff says this begs the question. Mr. Robertson minimizes the significance of the church affiliation by appeal to the "Protestant principle."

MR. YOUNGS: Since the minister is organically related to a church, he is in a position to integrate the sick individual into a dynamic, creative, loving fellowship of the church.

DR. TUFF: This is an additional resource that I don't have, except in my therapeutic group. However, my group is not a fellowship having permanent character.

DR. EDEN: We define psychotherapy differently. Psychotherapy is a relationship between a trained person and someone who comes to him. The aim is to remove symptoms, modify behavior, prevent behavior from becoming destructive. This is all within the pastoral role as well as the psychiatric role. A minister can be trained, if he has the capacity and the desire.

DR. TUFF: I got everything I know in the ten years after I left medical school.

MR. YOUNGS: That applies to us. We are still taking courses.

DR. TUFF: Fine! You are doing it.

When Mr. Youngs refers to the role of church fellowship in therapy, Dr. Tuff redefines this as an "additional resource." The fact that each may have "additional resources" is accepted. Dr. Eden then relates his "additional resource" to training. Achievement norms have already been accepted by the ministers. An achievement orientation led them into clinical pastoral training. This provides a basis for ministerial capitulation to a more restricted role definition on the basis of training.

DR. TUFF: You and I together treat the patient. That is the ideal with which we started.

DR. EDEN: We are a team.

DR. TUFF: A new modality will be created here. Eight or ten people with our intellectual, moral, financial, and community resources can achieve much more.

The ministers having conceded, the psychiatrists move to crystallize the new norm. Roles will be differentiated on a functionally specific basis and allocated according to achievement criteria. The psychiatrists reward the ministers' agreement with approval and the offer of solidarity. Affirmations of solidarity reduce strain consequent upon the abandonment of the prior ministerial position.

Criteria for Choosing Counselors

With the possibility of functional specificity established, the discussion centers upon the specific ministerial contributions to therapy. Functions may be allocated to ministers in terms of special features of the minister-counsellee relationship.

MR. RIEDELL: In another church-related clinic, I worked with a woman of 28 who had one child by a marriage which had ended in divorce. She fell in love with a young fellow who was being discharged from the service. I saw them continuously, married them, and then saw them until they left the city. A psychiatrist could not function in this situation. I would not dare to interfere in a medical process. You psychiatrists would not want to interfere in any strictly religious process.

Mr. Riedell indicates that a minister was helpful precisely because he could meet the counsellee in several roles.

DR. NORTON: A clergyman can be of tremendous help in motivating and giving permission for a patient to be ill and to seek help.

MR. WYN: Letters we receive ask if we think they need to see a psychiatrist, and where can they find one who will understand their problem.

DR. NORTON: The minister becomes not the harsh but the good permissive father. This helps the patient come to grips with his problems.

MR. RIEDELL: Some people are not in a position to undertake psychotherapy. The minister has a special function which is a kind of magic. By using symbols, the minister gives a temporary relief.

They agree that a minister is most useful in the early phases of therapy. He can break the resistance of some patients to psychiatric help. The ministers relate this ability to specific religious symbols which they know how to employ.

MR. RIEDELL:　I have been working with a homosexual who had a strict religious background. As he arrived at certain insights, he put them into religious as well as into psychiatric terms. This is an intangible consequence of his knowing that I am a minister.

MR. WYN:　A lady came in who had been in a mental institution, received shock therapy, and had a little psychoanalysis. She said, "As a last resort, I want some religion." She used religious phraseology and I did too. It's important to be able to speak the language of the patient.

The minister can communicate with religiously-oriented patients where the psychiatrist might fail. He can speak the language of his patient.

DR. NIELSON:　The minister helps assuage the morbid sense of guilt of the patient. In the patient's mind he speaks with authority about matters of right and wrong. I have a patient who married although she was very strongly masculine. She had a child and then did not want sex. Her husband was passive enough to accept it. They lived together for twenty-five years without sex relations. Then he died and she feels that she's committed a great and unforgiveable sin for getting married. She holds on to that sense of guilt with the rigidity of a snapping turtle. I sent her to Rev. Ellis who softens her sense of guilt. No psychiatrist could help that woman until she was assured by a minister that she has not committed a sinful act.

One function of the psychiatrist is to remove unconscious barriers to a normal religious life. I have a man whose father is a devout orthodox Jew. This boy thinks religion is bunk. I can help him to realize that his attitude toward religion is a reaction to his resentment toward his father. I remember a case of a wife of a minister. She was about 50 years old and had three children. Her husband was a dull fellow without much charm. This girl had had sex relations when she was sixteen one summer night under the flowers and the blossoms and the honeysuckle of the South. It was only once, but she kept wanting it all the time. She had an obsessive feeling that she was a very sinful woman. She talked with a minister who made her see that she had this impulse in the unconscious and could not be punished for something that didn't eventuate in behavior.

DR. NORTON: I have a Catholic girl who used to masturbate when she was thirteen. Priests told her to confess this and to tell her mother. In Catholic theology the thought is the same as the deed. It is hard for the clergyman to alleviate the guilt.

MR. ELLIS: In a choice between guilt because of a violation of church discipline and the health of the person, the emphasis should be on health, or, to use a theological term, the salvation of the person.

MR. TODD: Many Protestants have an intense need to strive after morality. When Mr. Ellis talks about the flower growing in the fields and not having to produce, just growing, this eases the person. I have used this Biblical illustration.

DR. NORTON: I have used the story of the widow's mite with a minister's wife in treatment. She was perfectionistic.

In meeting problems of guilt the minister is not restricted to the early phases of therapy. This is a basis for his participation in therapy beyond the early sessions. The ministers suggest that they relieve guilt feelings because of their theological training. This would exclude psychiatrists. The psychiatrists react.

DR. LINDQUIST: A person is able to work out guilt feelings with a well-trained psychotherapist regardless of whether he is a minister, social worker, or psychiatrist.

DR. NYMAN: There are certain guilt feelings over which a psychiatrist has no influence because he does not have the authority.

DR. LINDQUIST: Guilt feeling is not relieved by authority but by being recognized by the patient.

DR. NYMAN: Many Roman Catholics who go to confession are relieved of guilt.

DR. LINDQUIST: The following week they have a guilt feeling about something else because of underlying guilt. You deny the effectiveness of psychotherapy.

DR. NYMAN: In a hospital a resident does not do as good therapy as an assistant director. Authority has great influence on some patients.

DR. LINDQUIST: To get the patient's personality to grow and develop, he has to be led, not overawed by authority.

DR. NYMAN: We have to be practical. In mental hospitals, it makes a difference when an authority comes to the patient.

DR. LINDQUIST: You were dealing with the insane. Part of their illness is overevaluation of authority.

Dr. Nyman appeals to the minister's "charisma" but Dr. Nielson emphasizes moral leadership.

DR. NIELSON: The minister can interpret the ways of God to man, as Milton said. In the minds of people, he is a moral authority. Since we deal so much with a morbid sense of guilt it's almost inevitable that we require the help of the minister. The moral issue has to be raised. A man who is going to leave his wife and marry another woman just because he thinks he wants another woman is doing something which would be regarded as unwise or immoral. It is not going to work out or bring him happiness.

After a brief exchange, and some resistance, the psychiatrists agree that the ministers' ability to deal with guilt is related to his being accepted as a moral authority. This defines an area of specific ministerial competence.

Ministers speak of the "quality of the relationship" and of the "Protestant principle," and of the importance of spiritual power. The emphasis is upon general, rather than specifically differentiated, roles. The psychiatrists, on the other hand, try to delineate counseling functions requiring training and competence.

On matters essentially external to the clinic there is no difficulty in reaching agreement. Sacraments are the exclusive province of the minister and organic treatment is reserved to the medical psychiatrist. A clash arises, however, in reference to the psychotherapeutic relationship.

The resistance of the ministers to the psychiatric position is not solely ideological. Role differentiation is simultaneously rank differentiation. For ministers to accept the psychiatric norm of differentiation and allocation would be to acquiesce in a lower rank within the Religio-Psychiatric Clinic. Nevertheless, by accepting training and competence as a criterion, the ministers perforce assign to themselves a lower rank as the less trained.

The psychiatric position on achievement criteria was destined to win out. The ministers as well as the psychiatrists are embedded in the over-all achievement-oriented culture. Since both accept an instrumental theory of therapy, training becomes the logical criterion. The psychiatrists can state that the distinction will hold only until the ministers know as much as they do.

It is agreed that ministers provide an entrée into therapy for religiously oriented people. Their theological training and knowledge of religious symbols and scriptures qualify them here. It is also agreed that they should specialize in problems dealing with a sense of guilt. They are able to do this because of their position as moral authorities. The basis for organic solidarity in the Religio-Psychiatric Clinic has been established.

Both ministers and psychiatrists counsel clients at the clinic. What is the difference between the minister-client and the psychiatrist-patient therapeutic relation? The next section turns to this question.

A NEW RAPPORT BETWEEN THERAPIST AND PATIENTS

Our attention shifts from the minister-psychiatrist to the therapist-patient relationship. The cooperation of ministers and psychiatrists in the Religio-Psychiatric Clinic is contingent upon a consensus about their relation to the patient. We will analyze their orientations to the patient. Ministers and psychiatrists enter the clinic with a predisposition to relate to the patient in ways influenced by their traditional status norms. As they interact and achieve a consensus, each varies from his traditional role definition.

Norms of Inclusiveness and Exclusiveness of Concern

Typically, the psychiatrist's is a specialized relationship. Contact with the patient is limited to the specific therapy situation. The nature of the minister-parishioner role tends to be more diffuse, as the minister meets his parishioners in many roles. Consequently, when ministers and psychiatrists cooperate, the scope of interest problem tends to arise.

The role of affectivity in the therapeutic relationship is a closely associated question. In medicine, the doctor-patient relationship has traditionally been affectively-neutral, and this orientation has carried over into medical psychotherapy. Traditionally, the ministerial relationship has been expressive. This has also carried over into pastoral care, as the imperative to be loving.

Both the psychiatrists and the ministers involved in this new institution are ambivalent about these problems. The psychiatrists are not completely certain that the therapeutic role should be clearly segregated. The ministers are not sure that it should be as diffuse as traditionally defined for them. The following excerpts reflect the crystallization of a new norm.

MR. ROBERTSON: A woman in therapy here had never had a birthday party in the fifty-three years of her life. The therapist arranged a small party for her. Several of us were present. This is an extension of the relationship beyond the counseling session.

MR. ELLIS: This has therapeutic value. My analytical training was that the therapeutic relation was one thing and the social or personal another thing. For many years I bent backwards by not seeing the client socially.

DR. NIELSON: I am considered a sad fish and a maverick by New York analysts because I do not follow a rigid, formalistic attitude by saying good-bye and good-day. That is about all they will say for weeks on end. Dr. Freud did not follow this therapy. He was quite free to see people outside of the analytic hour. I've played golf with a man when I felt that only in that way could I break through his resistance. On the other hand, there are dangers. I saw a girl who was an only child of a dominating mother who had broken up four engagements. The old lady was a cannibal and a tyrant. She reached the point in her analysis where she had to decide to stay around with mama the rest of her life or to get married. That night, we went down the elevator together and we came out the door together. I didn't want to act as though she had the smallpox or the plague and turn off and walk away. We had a casual conversation. We talked of the weather, how nice the Virginia mountains were. The next day she said, "Dr., I'm through, I'm not coming back anymore." I said, "That's quite all right, if that's what you want. Would you mind telling me why?" She said, "Because you're such a fool. Walking up the street and having this conversation I realized that you were a very stupid fellow and I don't think you can help me anymore." You do find situations in which going beyond the counseling relationship destroys any possibility of helping the patient.

The ministers justify a relationship beyond the therapeutic hour. Dr. Nielson presents an example in which the extension of the relationship destroyed it. Situational factors pressing ministers toward diffuseness are revealed in the following excerpts:

MR. ROBERTSON: A minister in a church is constantly faced with the demand that he meet the parishioner-counsellee in other relationships. There is a need for ministers set apart from the social and ecclesiastical life of the church. If they are seeing a parishioner, they are not forced to relate to him in other situations.

DR. NIELSON: When counseling in a small church with one minister, this is difficult.

. . . . .

DR. EDEN: I say no, categorically, to the problem of extending relationships. That is the end of it.

MR. RIEDELL: I am ambivalent. There are situations where you cannot confine yourself to the counseling relationship. At the coffee hour after church, I meet my clients socially. In the office, they know they are in a specialized relationship for fifty minutes. I invited a man I see at the church to a party at our house. He was single and an interesting guy. This has not interfered with counseling.

. . . . .

DR. EDEN: Cannot the psychiatrist be warm and friendly without mixing intimately with patients?

DR. NYMAN: He should be friendly but not mix socially. That interferes with the transference and might jeopardize therapy. I do not mind going to a psychotic patient's for dinner.

DR. EDEN: I try not to.

DR. NYMAN: I go if I am forced. I do not want to offend but I go reluctantly. I would rather go to a psychotic whose transference is poor than to a neurotic.

. . . . .

MR. TODD: The majority of analysts are in large metropolitan areas. They do not bump into their patients.

DR. LINDQUIST: I talked to an analyst in a "hick" town. If he meets a patient in a grocery store, he does not like it. Students in a psychoanalytic training school have social, medical, and psychiatric meetings where they meet their analysts. This is not detrimental to the relationship.

MR. YOUNGS: I frequently meet individuals at church services. I do not avoid it. Three of my clients are always there when I preach.

DR. LINDQUIST: When I was in analysis, I would not miss any lecture my analyst gave.

Mr. Robertson points out that it is in the nature of the minister's status to have multiple relations with his parishioners, but feels it limits therapeutic effectiveness. For Dr. Nielson, the problem is not the diffuseness, but the inability of the therapist to control it. The assumption is that the effectiveness of a therapeutic relationship depends upon the therapist's ability to manage it. Dr. Nyman is concerned with the effect of loss of control on the transference. For Dr. Lindquist, this problem is less acute for analytic candidates. The consensus is that the therapist should be free to restrict the relationship. This raises the question of accidental meetings with patients.

DR. EDEN: I walked into the drugstore for lunch and saw a new woman patient eating blueberry pie. I was not sure I recognized her. Since she didn't give me encouragement, I did not do anything. I just sat down and felt badly. When she came to the clinic, she said, "Why didn't you say hello to me?" I said, "I wasn't sure with all the people I meet." She never came back.

MR. RIEDELL: I have been a chaplain in a federal prison for twenty years. This was a clearly defined relationship. They were in jail and I was the chaplain. A number of times, while traveling, I recognized boys who had been there. I leave the initiative in their hands. Some do not want to remember prison.

DR. NYMAN: Many prominent psychiatrists mix socially.

DR. EDEN: Rosen lives with his patients.

DR. NYMAN: Many patients seek opportunities to meet with the psychiatrist.

DR. EDEN: This is acting out dependency needs.

MR. WYN: I met a patient on a TV show who blotted out the fact that I had met him in any other relationship. Patients step over the boundary as part of growing in therapy.

DR. EDEN: They are testing their adolescence.

MR. RIEDELL: If the client wants to know what kind of a human being you are outside of the structured setting, we cannot deny him this.

Dr. Eden's inability to reciprocate the diffuse expectation of the client damaged the relationship. Mr. Riedell is prepared to leave the initiative to the client.

The above excerpts concerned having several role relationships with a patient. What of symbolically extending the relationship within the therapeutic hour? When this occurs, the specific orientation takes the form of a quasi-diffuse orientation.

MR. WYN: A psychotic girl who had stolen cookies at the age of four and was embarrassed by being forced to return them brought in two little packages. What was I going to do? She ate half and I ate the other half.

DR. EDEN: I had someone in the theater who gave me a pair of diamond studded cufflinks at Christmas. I interpreted that I did not want to wear her heart on my sleeve. She brought me a book which I accepted. A psychotic patient brought me a tie clasp with the head of a terrifying god on it. It isn't necessary for them to buy us with a gift. We accept them as they are. When they pay us our fee, that's all we expect.

Gifts are legitimate for a minister but not for a psychiatrist. Dr. Eden analyzed the psychodynamic aspects of this norm.

MR. RIEDELL: My students in clinical training came for three, six, or nine months. In the early years, we played ball, sat around and drank beer and talked. This loused up the professional relationship, because I was using them to meet my needs for social life. When I realized what was going on, I refused to have my students come to the house. This also did not work.

DR. EDEN: You were dealing with your countertransference.

MR. TODD: The doctor or the minister should not involve his own needs in extending the relationship. The minister in the parish may be lonely. He needs relatedness with people. This was my experience.

DR. LINDQUIST: If it becomes exploitation of the parishioner or the patient, it is destructive.

Agreement on limited extension of the relationship is implied in the above. Extension, however, must not be a function of the therapist's needs, of his countertransferences.

DR. TUFF: If I am a father symbol to a patient who has a need to comply, he will feel good if I come to his birthday. Therapeutically, I might be fortifying something I am trying to get him to give up.

DR. NORTON: If you are aiming at dissection of the transference neurosis, you will be impersonal though not unfriendly. If you are trying, in brief therapy, to give a patient correctional emotional experience, you may be friendly. There are even occasions for exchanging life experiences. If your goal is characterological reconstruction, you do not engage in this kind of thing.

DR. TUFF: A therapeutic situation exists even when eating lunch with a patient. I have to find the symbolic meaning of whatever I do.

Limiting the relationship is less important in brief therapy than in analytic therapy. Since brief therapy is more common among pastors, this allows a solution consistent with their diffuse status norms. The analysts retain flexibility. The decision rests on the meaning of the relationship to the patient. The extension must be consistent with therapeutic goals.

Consistent with the norms of their primary statuses, initially the ministers bring their diffuse and the psychiatrists their specific orientation to the psychotherapeutic role. The agreed conditions for extending the relationship, in terms of the type of therapy and its meaning to the patient, signifies a move in the diffuse direction for the psychiatrists and in the specific direction for the ministers. Consensus is reached by subdividing the basic therapist-patient relationship into phases. This solution does not require either to abandon his position. A more refined definition of psychotherapy is developed, allowing for specific and diffuse relationships at different times and under different conditions.

Norms of Impulse and Restraint

Ideal typically, religion prescribes affectivity for the minister-parishioner relationship. The psychiatrist, generalizing from the physician's orientation, tends toward affective neutrality. This difference underlies conflict on the problem of countertransference. The psychiatrist would terminate the relationship if unable to control his affection for the patient. If he could not control negative countertransference, he would look into the completeness of his own analysis. The minister tends to feel that an affective element is always present and always positive. It is an expression of "transcendental" love. In religious tradition, the minister is but a mediator or a channel for the love of God. Ministers in this clinic assume an "immanent" orientation. The psychiatrists press them to control this "immanent" feeling.

DR. NORTON: A difference between the psychiatrist and the minister is apparent from the tradition of saintly behavior. St. Francis of Assisi lies abed with leperous sores. The physician is someone who gives understanding not love. Many psychiatrists use their wish to be loving to deny their hatred and contempt for the patient. The minister can gratify his wish to love in a professional relationship without feeling incongruity.

DR. LINDQUIST: I'm a human being first and then a doctor. When I feel it would help the patient for me to lie down and play on the floor, I do it.

MR. TODD: You cannot isolate the minister as the one who gives love from the doctor as the one who gives understanding. When you give understanding, it is love. When you give love, understanding follows.

DR. NORTON: The love the psychiatrist shows comes in doing his job. He is there to do a good job and to make a living out of it. A psychiatrist, by definition, is not loving. Otherwise he would not be a psychiatrist. He would be off loving somebody.

MR. TODD: God's love means caring for people, an ultimate concern for people in which your own needs are not involved.

DR. LINDQUIST: The patient's purpose is not to get love but to allow himself to grow. We can substitute anything that facilitates growth in therapy for the word love.

DR. NORTON: Many psychiatrists try to make up for lack of technical knowledge and good hard brutal work in their own analysis by loving the patient.

DR. LINDQUIST: The patient often has more sense than the psychiatrist and understands the meaning of it as a rationalization of an exploitative attitude.

DR. NORTON: We feel that if we could work without hostility, we would be full of love. Actually, loving is tough business.

MR. YOUNGS: Love is proved by a steady, consistent procedure, week after week, month after month.

MR. TODD: Ministers have a need to jump right in and love everybody.

DR. LINDQUIST: This impulse is not therapeutic. It has to be analyzed and controlled.

Dr. Norton attributes the ministers' appeal for an affective norm to a psychological need of the therapist—a reaction formation. The affective norm is defended by enlarging the definition of love. First it includes being human and playing on the floor, then it gathers under its wing understanding, doing a job, and ultimate concern. With both sides relatively unmoved, the discussion proceeds to the therapeutic consequences of an affective orientation.

DR. NORTON: The tragedy is that there is not that much love to go around among psychiatrists. This is particularly so with psychotic patients. There is nothing more devastating than to be the St. Francis of the locked ward. You know damn well that you are to be shifted to the open ward in two months.

DR. LINDQUIST: I visited a ward for six months and became friendly with the nurse. One time I told her something with which I was terribly emotionally involved. A deteriorated patient who hadn't talked for years suddenly slipped out of the psychosis and began to talk about my personal problem.

DR. NORTON: In treating psychotic patients the therapist can legitimately act out his own neuroses and give them a type of love they never experience. With a neurotic, one's neurotic countertransference is an obstacle to treatment.

MR. TODD: Why is neurosis valuable for work with a psychotic and not with a neurotic?

DR. NORTON: Madam Sechechaye was acting out a neurotic wish when she took in a psychotic girl.

MR. TODD: I understand you now. Many ministers feel a need to love but with a paranoid patient this may be destructive.

Dr. Norton shows the disastrous consequences of an affective orientation in a segmented role relationship. Interpreting affectivity as acting out a neurotic drive leads to agreement that it may be destructive. Affectivity is called a substitute for knowledge and work. Worse than this, affective therapists may be exploiting the patient. These are sanctions which the psychiatrists impose upon the ministers as an effort to get them to relinquish the affective norm. The differentiation of the psychotic from the neurotic situation gives the ministers an out. Assured that affectivity has a place with psychotics they can concede the psychiatric position with reference to neurotics. In effect, this is a major concession, since almost all the patients they see are neurotics.

DR. NORTON: Were a homosexual psychiatrist to ask me for treatment, I would try to get out of the case. I take one role as a person's physician and another as the psychiatric director of a hospital who must decide whether to hire or fire him. I must deal with my own countertransference.

DR. TUFF: I would be appalled and angry with him, but I am his physician. He did not come to me for judgment. I would ask myself to what degree I am angry about what he had done to little boys. If I can be objective, I might undertake the treatment.

DR. NORTON: These feelings are grounded in one's autobiography. I recall a patient who had a hobby, during the war, of throwing Japanese prisoners out of an airplane at 30,000 feet without a parachute. I would not accept him for treatment. This would be too horrible. Other physicians regard this as a fascinating case and would do good work.

DR. TUFF: If you are part of a treatment team, you might have to do the therapy.

DR. NORTON: A schizophrenic is fantastically perceptive. He may know more about your unconscious than you know at the end of your own analysis. He immediately fathoms your revulsion.

There is consensus that negative countertransference be controlled. Dr. Norton suggests that the therapist should not take a case where he cannot control his feelings. He does not believe feelings may be concealed from a psychotic. Previously, the ministers were enabled to accept an affectively neutral norm by differentiating treatment of the psychotic from that of the neurotic. The psychiatrist accepts affectivity by distinguishing the relation to the person as such from judgments about his behavior. Affectivity may enter under a universalistic norm. The next section turns to the problem of universalism and particularism in psychotherapy.

Norms of Lawful and Personal Relations

The traditional psychiatric orientation defines the therapeutic relationship universalistically. The therapist classifies the patient according to his syndrome and prescribes treatment in view of it. The patient expects not a personal relationship but treatment of his malady according to the canons of psychiatric practice. The ministerial position, on the other hand, is primarily particularistic. The immediate personal relationship is crucial.

The following excerpts concern the universalistic and the particularistic norms in psychotherapy.

MR. TODD: A schizophrenic boy told me that he had had an affair with a girl. When she went away, he was anxious and had some drinks. I said, "Drinking is all right, but you are not getting at the cause." Some preachers say I was a relativist. Drinking is evil and I encouraged this boy to drink.

DR. NIELSON: The modern minister realizes there are forces in people's minds making them do things against their conscious will. To tell these people they are evil and sinful does not help them.

MR. ELLIS: This touches on the matter of value. The value for me is the fulfillment of an individual. Love recognizes freedom of choice.

DR. NIELSON: A man with three children is getting a divorce. He has no complaints but thinks he is in love with someone else. He has as much chance of making a go of the second marriage as I have of growing hair on my bald head. He picked out an impossible woman, with a paranoid mother and who has been a playgirl. How would the minister bring this man to realize the values he is flouting without saying he is sinful?

MR. ELLIS: I would stress his fulfillment as an individual.

DR. NIELSON: He thinks marrying this girl will fulfill him.

MR. ELLIS: It will be necessary to point out the factors in his unconscious leading him to pick a destructive woman.

DR. EDEN: If, after he explores it, he still wishes to go ahead, that is up to him.

MR. ELLIS: The Good Lord Himself cannot do anything about it.

Mr. Todd argues that it is therapeutically necessary to hold some church values in abeyance. Dr. Nielson cites the patient's immunity from judgment because of the force of the unconscious. Mr. Ellis introduces an overarching value of "self-fulfillment" taking precedence over traditional church values. The discussion is shifted from the choice of patient goals, which may not be influenced, to an examination of motivation, which the therapist can clarify. Exploration of motivation may be subject to the universalistic norms of psychiatry.

DR. EDEN: This man has confused his genital feelings with his affection. He could never really love.

MR. WYN: There is love where there is transference. Religionists may call it the "laying on of hands," or the cross around your neck.

DR. NIELSON: Everybody is alone in this world sitting on the threshold of his personality calling for the world to come and love him. We come in alone and we go out alone. Betwixt and between we are frightened children. In the Protestant church a man's conscience and his God face one another without interposition.

Dr. Eden interprets motivation according to the universalistic norms of psychiatry. Mr. Wyn and Dr. Nielson stress the particularistic elements of the transference relationship and of man's conscience facing God.

The psychiatrist advocates particularistic elements in discussing the question of relating in a "role"[2] or as a "person."

DR. TUFF: You cure him because of the humanness of your relating to him. Most psychiatrists see the individual as a role, a patient, not as John or Mary.

DR. LINDQUIST: A therapist should first be human and then a minister or a psychiatrist.

Dr. Tuff feels that therapy includes particularistic aspects but wonders how a psychiatrist bound to his "role" can accomplish it.

DR. TUFF: Rev. Youngs, if a fellow minister comes to you who is seducing little boys, he comes because he suffers. He administers the sacrament of his church while doing this and is in conflict.

MR. YOUNGS: A minister came to me who fulfills this description. My attitude toward him was one of understanding and not rejection.

DR. TUFF: As a human being you can understand him, but you are a minister. I assume that this is against the tenets of your religion.

MR. YOUNGS: Homosexuality is against the tenets of religion. It is one of the sicknesses of the human race. If a minister looks at a homosexual colleague from the standpoint of morals, he must realize that we are all sinners. My first question is how can I help him? How shall I relate to him? Second, what resources can I draw upon to help this man?

A place has been found for both the psychiatrists' universalistic and the ministers' particularistic orientation. The initial phases of therapy would stress particularism while the ensuing analytic process would follow universalistically defined procedures. The principal motif of therapy would be universalistic. In this, the ministers have moved further from their "ideal typical" position than have the psychiatrists.

Norms of Doing and Being

The medical status is defined by its performances. This performance orientation is generalized to the psychiatrist-patient relationship. A minister, particularly as a healer, does not acquire his office by virtue of performances but consequent to evidence of charismatic qualities. In the following excerpts, ministers and psychiatrists are divided on the performance-quality dimension. The immediate question is whether a homosexual must assume an obligation to cooperate and change.

DR. LYMAN: The Lord will not accept a sinner who does not intend to correct his sin. You have to impress on a patient, "You are a sinner and the Lord accepts you, provided that you try to help yourself and cooperate with your therapist."

MR. ROBERTSON: That is your feeling. God will accept him regardless of that.

DR. NYMAN: You mean the Lord accepts the sinner even if he remains a sinner?

MR. ROBERTSON: Unconditionally.

DR. NIELSON: You are still a child of God no matter what you do.

DR. NYMAN: What about the judgment?

DR. NIELSON: We leave that to God. If the person does not change his ways, he suffers anxiety, unhappiness, confusion, and puzzlement.

DR. NYMAN: A large number of homosexuals do not feel guilt.

DR. NIELSON: The most vital thing in all healing, whether it is physical or mental, is a dynamic transference. If you want to use theological terms, a fellowship with God, a healing power in the Grace of God.

MR. ROBERTSON: We must be willing to accept the man, regardless of whether he wants to change.

For Dr. Nyman, the patient performances are essential to therapy. Dr. Nielson bridges the two approaches by relating transference to Grace. Transference is an initial aspect of the therapeutic relationship which cannot be intentionally achieved. Therapeutic performances become the key after transference is established. Mr. Robertson closes with a sharp demand for quality orientation. Acceptance by the therapist is not a function even of the patient's desire to change. Mr. Robertson, however, would terminate the relationship if he chooses not to change. In this he departs from the image of the minister ever calling to the penitent.

DR. NIELSON: If a homosexual is happy, he will not come for treatment. Sometimes you analyze his problem and show him why he is a homosexual and he still says, "That's the only kind of life I've been leading." Who are we to say he is a sinner?

DR. NYMAN: Almost every homosexual says, "I'm a homosexual; I don't want to discuss it but I don't sleep, I don't eat
well, I am depressed, etc." You cannot treat his insomnia or his
anger alone. They are manifestations of anxiety and guilt. Those
without anxiety will not come unless forced by their wives or by
the authorities. The patient can relieve guilt only by being
punished. Either the Lord will punish him or the police or the
F.B.I. If everybody fears to punish him, he punishes himself.

Dr. Nielson suggests that there is a self-selection. Those who do
not want to change will not come. Dr. Nyman argues that since
homosexuality may be a defense, the patient does not know the
proper goal for himself.

The discussions do not reveal change in either the ministers' or
the psychiatrists' position. Other observations, however, suggest
that the trend at the Religio-Psychiatric Clinic is toward an instrumental conception of therapy. Eventually, the ministers accept the
psychiatrists' norm of obligatory performance. As ministers accept
the training criteria for the allocation of their role, they tend to
accept a performance orientation toward the client.

Norms of Responsibility and the Collectivity

Both the minister and the psychiatrist are expected to be collectivity oriented, to place the interest of the community before their
own. A common refrain of the discussion groups is "Is it good for
the patient?" Both the minister and psychiatrist, however, conceive
of a responsibility transcending that to the patient. The psychiatrist
feels obligated to the "immanent" collectivity, to the society that has
licensed him to practice. The minister, on the other hand, accepts
his ultimate responsibility to God and, through Him, to society.

This difference in the collectivity orientations emerges in the
discussion on the limits of "privileged communication." "Privileged
communication" is an imperative for both the physician-patient and
the minister-parishioner relationship. Both medical and religious
circles, however, debate the extent to which information about a
threat to society should be retained in secret. The physician tends
to feel constrained to act upon the information and restrain the
patient. The church, with its transcendental reference, allows a
somewhat broader conception of the privilege. For Catholics, the

seal of the confession tends toward the absolute. Protestant ministers are more ambivalent about its limits.

DR. NORTON: I have had experience with a senior medical student whose initial episode of homosexuality lasted over a year. Hospitalization was the final resort of his doctor. If such a person intends to become a psychiatrist, he should be discouraged. If he wants to work in hematology, he could be encouraged.

MR. YOUNGS: The clinical pastor can help the homosexual ministerial student discover whether he would like to continue in the ministry.

DR. TUFF: I have four ministers in private practice who are homosexual as a defense against paranoid-schizophrenia. Their motivations are mixed. They seek love, dedication to others, pride, prestige, power, and social status as well. One is an Episcopal priest who has seduced many of his acolyte boys. He is trying to work in youth groups where he could use his authority to enter homes. His coming for treatment is unusual.

Primary responsibility is to the patient. The problem of the homosexual about to enter the ministry or medicine is turned to an analysis of his motivation. Will he be personally fulfilled in his intended occupation? When the seduction of acolyte boys and work in youth groups is introduced, the social implication becomes obvious. External restraint of these patients is avoided by classifying them as special. That they come for treatment shows their interest in changing.

DR. EDEN: A man may make a wonderful physician or clergyman while functioning homosexually.

DR. LINQUIST: I doubt whether a person on the genital level of a homosexual can make a good minister or a good physician. If he cannot relate in a relaxed way to the opposite sex, how can he be a good minister to the women in his parish?

Dr. Eden avoids the social issue by segregating sexual and occupational behavior. Dr. Linquist rejects the distinction and the way is open for drawing the social implication.

DR. LINDQUIST: It would pose a problem if a minister of a community were to have uncontrollable homosexual impulses. The seminarian would have to be over them before entering the ministry.

DR. EDEN: I would not lock him away.

MR. ELLIS: He need not feel responsibility for his homosexuality. Anxiety engendered in his childhood happens to find this expression. Our work would be to illuminate his anxiety. God accepts everyone with His infinite love and patience, no matter what he does.

DR. LINDQUIST: Why is he not responsible for his homosexuality?

MR. ELLIS: To the extent that he is unaware of what impels him, he cannot be morally or religiously responsible.

DR. EDEN: According to the law, he is responsible.

MR. ELLIS: Yes, before the law and society he must take the consequences.

Dr. Lindquist feels responsibility to protect the community. Mr. Ellis shifts to the question of the patient's own responsibility for his actions. He argues that he need not suffer religious responsibility, since he is unaware of what impels him. He must, however, accept the social consequences of his acts.

MR. RIEDELL: In several situations where somebody notified the authorities, the man had to leave the ministry whether he recovered from homosexuality or not. The social stigma is so great that there is a risk in notifying church authorities.

DR. NYMAN: I have two kids sent by seminaries. They asked me to take care of them and report when they are well. I gave a green light to one. He is back teaching.

DR. NIELSON: It depends upon the degree of homosexuality. If this man were seducing little boys, there would be a serious question about allowing him to become a minister. If the man were merely an average homosexual and found some mature adult with whom he could express his homosexuality, it would be another matter.

Mr. Riedell dissociates his responsibility from that of the church authorities. Dr. Nyman cites an instance in which even the church as a social institution looked to him as a responsible and legitimate authority. Dr. Nielson feels that when there is a threat to others, the therapist would be constrained to act. Observation at the Clinic suggests that the psychiatric position will prevail. Despite their suspicion of institutional structures, the ministers are not sufficiently transcendentally oriented to ignore a threat to society.

THE TREND IN COUNSELING NORMS AT THE CLINIC

The outcome of these discussions is not definitive. It is possible, however, to speculate on the direction in which the therapeutic norms are evolving in this Clinic. Doubtless, both ministers and psychiatrists will continue to offer nearly comparable types of counseling services. The discussion suggests that ministers will accept restrictions on the scope of the therapeutic relationship. Given this trend, along with the fact that the Religio-Psychiatric Clinic is separated from parish life and its ministers devote full time to pastoral counseling, it might be anticipated that the norms finally institutionalized will be characterized by specificity rather than diffuseness. Clients will be seen at the office. These ministers will not meet them in other roles.

The relationship will tend more to be characterized by affective neutrality than by affectivity. Feeling will remain as interest and concern rather than as an expression of countertransferences.

The reaction of the psychiatrists against the "impersonal" elements in the physician-patient relationship would tend to attract them toward the ministerial particularistic rather than their traditional universalistic orientation. With the clinic's stress on training in the techniques of psychotherapy, the particularistic orientation may be only transitional and is likely to be relegated to the initial phases of therapy. The ministers' support of a quality orientation is merely a token stand. The pressure of their broader cultural orientation, the influence of their psychological training in general and of the psychiatrists in particular assures an eventual performance orientation.

Both the ministers and psychiatrists agree upon a collectivity orientation with primary responsibility to the patient limited by social responsibility. In sum, then, the counseling provided by the clinic will tend to be guided by norms of specificity, affective neutrality, universalism, and performance. Thus, on this level the pastoral counselors accept something similar to a traditional psychiatric orientation. These are the rebels described in the study of the literature.[3]

NOTES

1. Emile Durkheim, *The Division of Labor in Society*.

2. "Role" has been defined sociologically in terms of social expectations of behavior and as a position in a social system. As used by psychologists, it often refers to "role playing" or pretending to be what one consciously is not. Dr. Tuff uses the term in the pejorative sense of masking the self.

3. Six years have passed between the discussions and this publication. In the meantime, the Clinic's training program has expanded under Mr. Kuether's direction. He is now assisted in the venture by some of his former trainees. Mr. Kuether, himself, has reduced his participation to half time while developing a private counseling practice outside the Clinic. The early trainees, Mr. West and Mr. Hostetler, are now almost entirely engaged in private practice, though both also serve as pastoral counselors of suburban churches. Mr. Barbery continues as the counseling specialist at Marble Collegiate church, and Mr. Lytle maintains his counseling responsibilities at the Clinic. Mr. Kew has been giving increasing effort to healing services at the church. Drs. Blanton and Tate serve as psychiatric directors of the Clinic, though some of their original responsibility has been assumed by a minister administrator, Mr. Arthur Tingue. Dr. Fleischel has since withdrawn from active participation, while Dr. McLean has become increasingly active in the training program. Dr. Holt, who, in the interim, has been appointed a bishop of the Old Catholic Church, continues to provide analytic supervision for ministerial candidates. Dr. Braun passed away a few years ago.

PART THREE

Conclusion

Chapter XI

A Pathway Between Religion and Science

THE HEALING SITUATION provides the occasion for an inter-change between two major social institutions: religion and science. Science is brought to religion through pastoral counseling and religion is carried to science through religiously oriented psychiatry. Pastors and psychiatrists who occupy statuses in, or are oriented to, both institutions act as mediators of culture. Some of these mediators of culture identify with the core of their institutions. Others belong only peripherally. Those simultaneously peripheral to both institutions are ensnared by competing concepts of healing and chafe over their inability to realize the values and ideas of both. Pastors and psychiatrists firmly identified with their own institutions are troubled by their inability to bring healing and look to the other institution for aid. These transmitters of culture include ministers who seek to effect relatedness and psychiatrists who seek related-ness to be effective. Across the religio-psychiatric boundary, these ministers and psychiatrists exchange ideas about man's mental and spiritual afflictions and evolve norms for proceeding against these afflictions. They examine one another's standards for judging procedures, selecting goals, and assessing outcomes.

What draws a minister or a psychiatrist to the periphery of his own group in search of help for healing? The character of the sectors of society from which the movement recruits participants suggests some of the factors. Ministers tend to come to the movement from social positions where their traditional religious ethos is exposed to the impact of the ethos of science. Protestant ministers, who seem more vulnerable to the scientific ethos, are more likely than Catholic priests to be recruited to this movement. Catholic priests who live as a minority in a Protestant environment are more likely to become interested. Ministering to a congregation of the higher socioeconomic strata or acquiring a higher education further increases exposure and the probability of recruitment. Under the influence of the scientific ethos, the minister is concerned to wreak change and is distressed if progress is imperceptible. He is encouraged to look to the instrumental techniques of science in general, and of psychiatry in particular, to effect that change. The influence of this ethos upon ministers may be attenuated by institutional control. Because hierarchical authority permits greater behavioral and attitudinal surveillance, ministers of an episcopally organized, in contrast to a congregationally organized, church are less likely to stray from tradition.

Psychiatrists tend toward the periphery of their group when, in the face of failure to effect cure, they are exposed to the ethos of religion. This exposure becomes of consequence for psychiatrists whose professional behavior is in some way subject to religious authority. This may come about either because of the psychiatrist's personal religious commitment or because the church has some control over recruitment of patients. Episcopal church polities facilitate the inculcation of a religious ethos among psychiatrists partly because of their greater control of clerical behavior and partly because they are more likely to formulate a doctrinal position on pastoral questions. These conditions are more likely to obtain among Catholic than among Protestant psychiatrists. Within Protestantism, psychiatrists associated with Anglicanism are most affected.

While these nonconformist ministers and psychiatrists exchange ideas and attitudes at the peripheries of their institutions, other ministers, similarly exposed to the scientific ethos, and other psychiatrists, similarly exposed to the religious ethos, are angered by their own tendencies to abandon tradition. Responding to this ambivalence, they assume a firm stand as militant conformists at the institutional center. Psychiatric militant conformists attack psychiatrists at the periphery as opportunists flirting with lay therapists. Ministerial militant conformists charge that clergymen who introduce psychological attitudes are perverting religion. Militant conformists are participants in the movement along with the nonconformists. This distinguishes them from the mass of ministers and psychiatrists who simply conform to their institutions and are apathetic to this movement. In the very process of stemming strange influences, they acquaint themselves with and deal with the new ideas and, as a result, contribute to the interchange.

Ministers and psychiatrists who participate in the religio-psychiatric movement are but a small proportion of those exposed to the scientific ethos and to the religious ethos respectively. What determines that these, of all the exposed ministers and psychiatrists, seek out one another? Further, what determines whether these individuals participate as militant conformists or as nonconformists? Nonconformist participants, as distinguished from their indifferent colleagues, tend to look to a nonmembership group as a source of behavioral standards or as their reference group. Militant conformists among the participants tend to be those who retain their own group as their reference group but apparently do so with some ambivalence. The minister's orientation to psychiatric standards and the psychiatrist's orientation to religious standards is one mechanism through which religion and science influence one another. Through this shift in reference groups, ministers come to judge their work according to standards of efficiency and psychiatrists become critical of the sufficiency of their own instrumental approach. From judging one's behavior according to the standards of another group, it is but a short step to adopting the goals of that other group. Ministers with a psychiatric reference group follow psychiatric preference and view counseling as a way of helping clients "function" better. Psychiatrists who take a religious reference group feel, like ministers, that their task is to help the individual in his search for purpose and values.

A psychiatric reference group may lead ministers to incorporate psychological ideas into their traditional pastoral activities, to use psychological themes for sermons, and to refer hapless parishioners to psychiatrists. Ministers who, in addition, establish psychological-type counseling services tend to feel that the psychiatric services with which they sympathize are in some way closed to them or their parishioners. This ambivalent attitude toward psychiatric services, especially the psychoanalytic, is apparent in the case of ministers who accept the procedures of psychoanalysis but are uneasy about its philosophy and who fear the influence upon parishioners of non-religious analysts. Through psychological pastoral counseling services they adapt the method of psychiatry to their own ends. While ministers with a psychiatric reference group introduce scientific attitudes into religion, those who provide counseling services introduce scientific procedures as well.

Why should ministers or psychiatrists select a nonmembership group as a reference group? Shift in reference group may be a response to the individual's ambiguous situation in his own group. Ministers selecting a psychiatric reference group tend to be those who, despite their high educational rank, belong to low status denominations and, by virtue of this membership, are relegated to low community rank. Their orientation to psychiatry is one way of trying to meet this lack of consistency in their ranks by raising their religious rank through associating it with a new expertise. A shift in reference group may also be a consequence of a widening of the individual's horizon through a broader, though not necessarily more advanced, educational background. Further conditions predisposing ministers to select a psychiatric reference group include approval of psychiatry by their denominational groups or by the audience for whom they write and an opportunity to interact with psychiatrists.

These ministers and psychiatrists migrate toward the periphery of their groups and explore one another's counseling culture in an effort to improve their own counseling. What happens to this counseling relationship under the influence of institutional estrangement? Change in this relationship may be examined by taking the militant conformists as a base line. Militant conformist ministers tend to orient toward parishioners in counseling according to norms of affectivity, quality, particularism, and diffuseness; militant conformist psychiatrists orient to their patients according to norms of affective neutrality, performance, universalism, and specificity. The

resulting relationships have been termed integrative and instrumental counseling respectively. As they become institutional nonconformists, alienated from the cultures of their own groups, they
tend to adopt norms for counseling similar to those characteristic
of the other group. Three institutionally nonconformist types have
been identified. Ritualists retain their group's language to describe
what they do but express their goals in the language of the other
group. Innovators express their goals in the language of their own
group but describe their means in the language of the other group.
Rebels describe both their means and their goals in the language
of the other group. Innovators are more institutionally dissident
than ritualists, and rebels are the most dissident of all. As they
move toward the periphery of their groups, they import counseling
norms from the opposite institution. Innovating ministers tend
toward a performance orientation and rebel ministers add affective
neutrality and universalism. Innovating psychiatrists become particularistic and rebel psychiatrists add affectivity, quality, and
diffuse orientations. This realizes their original objective of gaining new approaches, and, hopefully, more effective ones for counseling. At the same time, the counseling role appears as another
part of the mechanism by which religion and science influence one
another.

These ministers and psychiatrists adopt changed institutional
and role relations in an effort to alleviate their sense of ineffectiveness or to resolve their sense of value conflict. In changing, however, they become subject to new criticisms and new pressures
through attacks upon them by militant conformists. Since even institutionally estranged individuals carry seeds of militant conformism
within themselves, these ministers and psychiatrists admonish themselves in conscience. To allay the attacks of others and to relieve
their own consciences, they proffer rationales for their new behavior and attitudes. If they are but slightly dissident, they may
justify themselves by pointing to other members of the group who
have behaved in a similar way. If they have broken sharply with
the ways of their institution, they are more likely to justify their
actions by reinterpreting the norms or concepts which define the
situation. Some rationales reinterpret the situation by denying that
dissidence exists since religion and psychiatry are essentially the
same. These types of rationales tend to be offered by individuals

whose sharp break involves advocating affective and diffuse norms for counseling, that is, norms which blur the distinctions between the counseling partners. They also tend to be offered by individuals with a divided sense of identity for whom they function to deny the split. On the other hand, those who sectionalize their world, who, by an affectively neutral counseling orientation objectify it, and, by a specific counseling orientation, restrict the scope of the relation, are more likely to argue that religion and psychiatry are indeed different but that they are complementary in their application to healing. Individuals with a clear sense of identity are also apt to offer this type of argument as a way of defending their position within their own group and their cooperation with members of the other group. Rationales contribute to the interchange between religion and science because besides dealing with already existing situations, they advocate a form for future exchange. They buttress the legitimacy either of blurring distinctions between the fields or encouraging a separate but complementary relation between them. The concrete problem of the relation between the fields comes to the surface as a jurisdictional issue.

Jurisdictional issues arise when ministers and psychiatrists do not simply seek behavioral and attitudinal guides from one another, but confront one another as counselors. They concern the division of responsibility for counseling. Those at the periphery and those at the center of their groups tend to assume reductionist positions. Individuals who are peripheral to religion but oriented to the center of psychiatry reduce counseling to a purely psychological task for a single psychologically trained counselor. Individuals peripheral to psychiatry but oriented to the center of religion reduce counseling to a purely spiritual task requiring but a single charismatic or "gifted" counselor. Those who take the other institution as a reference group, while remaining rooted in their own institution, tend to be dualists who, though recognizing both psychological and spiritual aspects of personal misery, allocate responsibility to a single counselor competent in both areas. Those taking their own group as a reference group and also firmly rooted in it but sympathetic to the role of the other profession advocate jurisdictional specialism. Both the task and the role are differentiated on a religious and psychological basis. Specialism tends to be advocated by ministers whose attitudes are internally consistent. They tend either to be but slightly institutionally dissident and pursue counseling as a way to meaning and purpose, or they are very dissident and see in counseling the psychiatric-type goal of improving functioning. Conceivably the former consider themselves religious specialists cooperating with psychiatrists and the latter consider themselves psychological specialists within the ministry who may receive referrals from other ministers. A specialist jurisdictional position rather than a dualist one is associated with conditions similar to those which inhibit rather than promote participation in the movement. A Catholic, for example, or one who belongs to a "maximum type" religious organization, is more likely to be a specialist than a dualist. The more educated, the professionally elite, are apt to be dualists rather than specialists.

The type of jurisdictional settlement determines whether the exchange between religion and psychiatry takes place conflictually or cooperatively. Reductionists and dualists may exclude members of the other profession as either incompetent or unnecessary for counseling and so put the relationship on a competitive basis. The reductionist positions block any exchange but the radical shift from one reductionism to the other. Dualism, on the other hand, encourages the assimilation of religious elements into psychiatry and psychiatric elements into religion through the competition between members of each profession who consider themselves fully adequate to a religio-psychiatric task. Were dualism a frequent position, it would become increasingly difficult to distinguish a counseling pastor from a counseling psychiatrist. The specialist position promotes a cooperative interdependence through encouraging each institution toward increasingly differentiating its function with respect to that of the other institution. The tendency to specialism is strongest among innovating ministers and ritualist psychiatrists, both of whom advocate psychological means to attain religious-type goals. This commonality seems to be a basis for consensus. Since innovation and ritualism are also the most popular forms of adaptation in the respective groups, counseling in the religio-psychiatric movement might well tend toward concern with moral and spiritual values inculcated by the techniques of psychiatry.

Ministers and psychiatrists do not always agree upon who should be a counselor. The criteria they advocate for admission to the role are a function of their conception of the counseling task.

On the one hand, admission may be based on ascriptive criteria such as personality, religiousness, or group affiliation. Ascriptive criteria tend to be advocated by those who see a minister as the role occupant and who define the relationship in terms of helping a client find meaning and purpose. On the other hand, counselors who satisfy achievement criteria, who possess training or skills, are sought by those who conceive of the counselor as a psychiatrist and of, counseling as a technical procedure intended to improve the client's functioning. Ministers and psychiatrists tend to apply the criteria for admission to their own broad statuses to the selection of candidates for the counseling role. The group of orientation is an even more profound determinant of the allocative criteria advocated than is the membership group. An individual who identifies with psychiatry, irrespective of whether he is a minister or a psychiatrist, tends to advocate achievement criteria. One who identifies with religion tends to advocate ascriptive criteria. An individual writing for a professional audience tends toward achievement criteria and one writing for a lay audience tends toward ascriptive criteria. The dominant trend seems to be toward selecting counselors on the basis of training in psychological skills and knowledge. Psychologically trained individuals recruited to the counseling role become an avenue of scientific influence on religion.

What may we say in general about the role of the religio-psychiatric movement in this process of institutional exchange? The part of the exchange described here involves members of one institution seeking a solution to counseling problems from members of another institution. In pursuit of this solution, they are drawn away from their own institutional culture, accept new norms guiding their counseling relationships, and eventually evolve new types of relations with the members of the other institution. From the point of view of the broad social system, the religio-psychiatric movement, through its ministers and psychiatrists, acts as a bridge between religion and science writ large. Why has an intentionally created movement arisen to link these two institutions? Other institutions, such as the economy and the family, do not require an intentionally constructed mechanism to integrate them. They are joined "naturally" because the same individuals participate in both. In Western society, it is common for scientists to be part of religious culture. They acquire a religious status by birth. Ministers, however, are not likely to be active contributors to scientific culture. Those who establish such a link tend to do so through advanced education. Catholic priests, especially the religious, are almost the only clergymen to be found frequently in scientific statuses. For example, Tielhard de Chardin was a paleontologist, and the monks at the Benedictine Monasteries of Monte Cassino and Montserrat write on archaeology and social science. Protestant ministers, rabbis, and secular Catholic priests who do pursue doctoral degrees tend toward philosophy if their interests are theological, education if their interests are missionary, and psychology if their interests are pastoral. Psychiatrists and psychologists are their bridge to the scientific world.

Conversely, the pastoral ministry is the bridge upon which the psychiatrist meets religion, not as a worshiper, but in a way relevant to his endeavor. Through this relationship between the psychiatrist and the pastoral counselor religious influence reaches science. Religious and scientific exchange is also mediated by philosophy. The philosophical and the "practical" encounters are not entirely separate. It will be recalled that a good proportion of the literature on psychiatry and pastoral work is concerned with philosophic questions.

There is another peculiar feature of the religio-psychiatric exchange. Individuals who mediate the relation between the family and the economy, for example, enjoy compatible memberships in both institutions. These institutions may compete for their time or energy but only infrequently present conflicting norms for the same situation. The religio-psychiatric interchange is riven with incompatible norms. Further, we have found that the relationship is engineered by the dissidents in each group. Consequently, rather atypical institutional images may be communicated. At the extreme, these dissidents may be so estranged from their own groups that their movement could remain in limbo between the groups. Rebel ministers may establish counseling services outside the church which are also unacceptable to psychiatry. Rebel psychiatrists may consider the "existential" counseling relation as a full religious experience with no need of official religion. Under these conditions, the bridging function of the religio-psychiatric movement could be stillborn. This fails to be a serious possibility at present because the extreme dissidents play only a small part in the exchange. The exchange tends to be mediated by moderately variant innovators and ritualists. Jurisdictionally, they tend to be specialists who are able to develop a complementary relation. The extremists may serve an exemplary function in presenting an image of a limiting case. They are likely to be the most thoroughly educated in the opposite field and so best able to introduce religious ideas into psychiatry and psychiatric ideas into religion. These ideas then become available to the innovators and ritualists. A practical moral of this study is that the yeomen of cooperative exchange are those who view the other field sympathetically while retaining firm roots in their own field.[1]

NOTE

1. A follow-up to this study which includes books and articles published between 1958–1962 may be found in Klausner, Samuel Z., "The Mellowing of the Religio-Psychiatric Movement."

Appendix

THIS APPENDIX expands the introductory description of research procedure. Detail is added about the selection of items for the bibliography and the way they were abstracted. Since not all items were abstracted and a good part of the study is based on those that were, the representativeness of the abstracted items will be examined by comparing certain of their characteristics with the characteristics of the nonabstracted items. This is followed by a description of the procedure for collecting personal data about the authors, an examination of the implications of having used the item rather than the individual author as the unit of analysis, and the implications of equating books and articles in the analysis.

DATA GATHERING

Developing the Bibliography

It will be recalled that items selected for analysis were, by and large, writings of ministers about mental health and of psychiatrists about the role of religion in psychotherapy. The focus was on professional materials. The search for appropriate items began with the library catalogs, periodical indices, and professional abstracts under such headings as "mental health," "healing," "psychology," and "psychiatry." With the aid of a professional librarian, a list was assembled of 109 subject headings under which relevant material might be found. When an article was found in a journal, the tables of contents or the indices of other volumes of that journal were skimmed for additional items. As each book came to hand, its footnotes and bibliography were searched. The libraries searched included those of Columbia University, Columbia's Teachers College, Union Theological Seminary, Jewish Theological Seminary of America, the New York Academy of Medicine, Fordham University, and New York Public Library. This procedure, supplemented by additional items obtained through the author questionnaire (see below), produced a bibliography of 1,364 items. Seventeen of these were authored anonymously. Only the 1,347 for whom authors were identified were retained for analysis. Judging from the declining rate of discovery of new items at the time this search was halted, we had the impression that the universe of material, as defined, published through 1957, would consist of about 1,600 items. Though the bibliographic sources in any language which produced an item were pursued, the fact that only the above libraries and reference works were used may mean that foreign language items are underrepresented.

Abstracting the Items

Abstractors were instructed to write précis using the writer's own words. No evaluative statements were to be included in the précis. The abstractors presented their abstracts for discussion at weekly seminars. This helped to develop abstracting techniques and to maintain procedural uniformity among the abstractors. Abstracts were typed on McBee cards. They varied from 20 to 7,000 words, with the modal abstract about 300 words in length. The length of an abstract was less a function of the length of the item than of the density of ideas.

Representativeness of the Abstracted Items

An attempt was made to procure and read all of these items. The 608 items which were not abstracted tended to be those which were more difficult to secure from the libraries during the period of study. To the extent that these differ from the more accessible items, a bias is introduced into the study. We have some information about the nonabstracted items from the bibliographic references which may be used to examine the nature of the bias. Table A-1 compares the abstracted with the nonabstracted works with respect to their form, date, and place of publication.

Table A-1—Form, Date and Place of Publication of Abstracted and Nonabstracted Writings in the Field of Religion and Psychiatry

	Abstracted (739)	Nonabstracted (608)
Form of Publication		
Book	31%	31%
Article	65	58
Dissertation, Pamphlet	4	11
Total	100%	100%
Date of Publication		
through 1932	10%	19%
1933–1947	21	21
1948–1957	69	60
Total	100%	100%
Location of Publisher		
United States, Canada	82%	59%
England, Ireland	8	8
Germany (German Swiss)	3	15
France (French Swiss)	5	7
Italy, Spain, Greece	1	8
Scandinavia	—	1
Other	1	2
Total	100%	100%

The abstracted items slightly overrepresent articles and under-represent dissertations and pamphlets. This may be due to the relative accessibility of professional journals in bound volumes in libraries and the delays involved in interlibrary loans of dissertations. The abstracted items also include relatively fewer early and relatively more later publications. This may be due to recently liberalized acquisition policies of libraries and the greater chance of a library's losing an item over the years.

The difference in geographic distribution is the only one of the three parameters large enough to influence the study findings. The excess of American, relative to German and southern European, publications among the abstracted may, be due to the relatively greater availability of the former in New York City libraries and to the relatively smaller number of abstractor hours given to foreign language as opposed to English reading during the period of the study. This should be kept in mind especially in interpreting cross-national findings. In general, the meaning of this bias is that the characteristics of American items, insofar as they differ from the characteristics of European items, may be exaggerated.

Personal Data

The attempt to obtain personal information about the authors of these items began with a search for their addresses in biographical sources such as the directories of the *American Psychological Association, American Medical Association,* etc., as well as denominational directories of clergymen, *Who's Who,* and *Psychological Abstracts.* When we could not locate an author and his affiliation was not available from the dust jackets of his books, we inquired of his publisher or of the editors of journals in which his articles had appeared. A list of those whom we could not identify was sent to 30 prominent scholars in the fields of religion and psychiatry with a request for information. Ultimately we were able to identify all but 146 of the authors. These latter tended to be persons not in the field who, though they had written an article on a subject falling within our purview, had major interests elsewhere. Each author located received a short questionnaire requesting information about education, occupation, experience, religious affiliations, and other publications. An original mailing and two follow-ups brought a 70 per cent return. If the nonrespondents were listed in a professional directory, the information available there was used. In some cases, their occupations and religions could be inferred by inspection of their writings, from the nature of the publication, and from titles given along with their names. These inferences are not given in the bibliography in Volume II but were used in our analysis.

DATA ANALYSIS

The Problem of the Unit of Analysis

Selection of the unit of analysis was a difficult problem. Should books be treated differently from articles? Should the writings rather than the individual be the unit? On the first question it seemed that according to any criterion of "significance," such as importance in the development of the field or impact on an audience, some articles were more "significant" than some books. Having no simple way of assessing this, all writings were equated as "items" for analysis. The second problem concerns the classification of authors who had contributed more than one item. By using individuals as the unit it would be possible, for example, to select a single item at random for each author and use these for analysis, or to analyze separately authors of one, two, or more items, or to construct an index combining the characteristics of the several writings of each author. It was decided that since most of the analysis concerns abstract dimensions of a "social system" rather than of attitudes of concrete individuals, each item would be treated as if authored by a separate "actor" rather than by an individual. Thus, if a single minister wrote an article in 1930 and another in 1940 this was considered as two "ministerial" inputs to the field. The "actor" was classified according to his attributes at the time he wrote. Thus, the same concrete individual might appear once as an innovating minister and another time as a ritualist minister.[1]

By comparing the characteristics of the population defined according to these criteria with the characteristics of the population defined by other possible criteria, it is possible to assess the impact of these decisions on the study.

Authors Versus Items as the Unit of Analysis

What difference would it have made in our results had authors instead of items been the units of analysis? To answer the question, a single item was selected at random for each author. This provides a population of authors, regardless of the number of items each contributes, for comparison on some salient parameters with the population of items actually used in the study. Since the study is concerned only with ministers and psychiatrists, the comparisons are made within these two groups. Of the 780 different authors, information is available on the professions of 582 (authors of 1,132 items) of whom 372 are ministers, 120 are psychiatrists, and 90 members of other professions. Table A-2 compares the two author

Table A-2—Comparison of Population of Authors and of Items on Several Characteristics

Item	Authors	All Items
Profession		
Ministers	64%	67%
Psychiatrists	21	21
Psychologists	10	8
Others	5	4
Total	100%	100%
	(582)	(1132)

Item	MINISTERS		PSYCHIATRISTS	
	Authors	All Items	Authors	All Items
Education				
Hold Doctorate	73%	77%	—	—
Less than Doctorate	27	23	—	—
Total	100%	100%	—	—
	(168)	(466)	—	—
Religion				
Roman Catholics	30%	28%	34%	40%
Protestants	65	67	44	41
Jews	5	5	22	19
Total	100%	100%	100%	100%
	(369)	(746)	(108)	(226)
Form of Publication				
Book	34%	30%	23%	22%
Article	54	63	75	73
Dissertations, Pamphlet	12	7	2	5
Total	100%	100%	100%	100%
	(372)	(751)	(120)	(237)
Location of Publisher				
United States, Canada	78%	76%	75%	73%
England, Ireland	8	8	7	8
Germany (German Swiss)	4	5	13	16
France (French Swiss)	5	6	5	3
Southern Europe	2	4	—	—
Other	3	1	—	—
Total	100%	100%	100%	100%
	(372)	(745)	(119)	(235)
Variant Subtype				
Militant Conformists	24%	20%	18%	16%
Ritualists	16	12	46	39
Innovators	44	49	16	13
Rebels	16	19	20	32
Total	100%	100%	100%	100%
	(234)	(445)	(79)	(139)
Reference Group				
Psychiatric	26%	24%	51%	40%
Double	39	44	40	49
Religious	35	32	9	11
Total	100%	100%	100%	100%
	(242)	(474)	(80)	(139)

groups with the portions of the total sample known to have been authored by members of the same profession.

Assuming that the author would be the "correct" unit, then by using the item as the unit, articles are slightly overrepresented and dissertations and pamphlets underrepresented among ministers. This is to be expected since an individual writes but one dissertation and many articles. Militant conformists and ritualists among ministers are underrepresented as opposed to innovators and rebels. Among psychiatrists, ritualists are underrepresented and rebels overrepresented. Among psychiatrists, our tabulation would show too few with a psychiatric reference group and too many with a double reference group. In the other cases, there are no differences between the populations. Even where differences exist, they are not of such a magnitude as to have affected the conclusions of the study. Differences of this magnitude in the study were generally not regarded as having interpretive significance.

The Differentiation of Books from Articles among the Writings

The other decision was to treat books and articles equally as items. What difference would it have made had each been analyzed separately? To check this, Table A-3 compares the population of books with the population of articles on several classificatory characteristics.

Looking at the reference-group figures first, it appears that among ministers and psychiatrists book authors are more oriented toward religion than are authors of articles. Among the authors, ministers are more likely than psychiatrists to write books instead of articles. Had books, for example, been given twice the weight of articles, the results of the study would have shown a smaller degree of variation among ministers and a greater degree of variation among psychiatrists. Separate analyses, holding books and articles constant, would show that ministers are less religious than we found them to be. Their greater propensity to be among the authors of books tends to exaggerate the picture of their religiousness. Similarly, psychiatrists would be found to be more religious than they have been painted. We find that Catholics publish more articles and Protestants more books. This would have little influence on the minister-psychiatrist comparisons since the finding is in the same direction in both cases. In Protestant-Catholic comparisons, however, the Protestant book authors would carry relatively more weight than the Catholic book authors, and so, had we held form of publication constant, we would have found Protestants slightly more and Catholics slightly less religious than they were described as being in the text. Similar interpretations might be placed on the

Table A-3—Characteristics of Authors of Books and Articles

Item	FORM OF PUBLICATION		Total	
	Books	Articles	(in Per Cent)	
	(in Per Cent)			
Profession				
Ministers	33	67	100	(700)
Psychiatrists	24	76	100	(225)

Item	MINISTERS (in Per Cent)		PSYCHIATRISTS (in Per Cent)	
	Books	Articles	Books	Articls
Reference Group				
Psychiatric	23	24	32	45
Double	40	47	49	46
Religious	37	29	19	9
Total	100	100	100	100
	(159)	(296)	(31)	(102)
Variant Subtype				
Militant Conformists	24	18	12	18
Ritualists	19	9	41	37
Innovators	40	52	6	16
Rebels	17	21	41	29
Total	100	100	100	100
	(150)	(288)	(32)	(101)
Education				
Hold Doctorate	80	77	—	—
Less than Doctorate	20	23	—	—
Total	100	100	—	—
	(122)	(309)	—	—
Religion				
Roman Catholics	18	36	34	44
Protestants	77	59	55	34
Jews	5	5	11	22
Total	100	100	100	100
	(222)	(471)	(53)	(162)
Location of Publisher				
United States, Canada	74	76	65	78
England, Ireland	15	5	8	8
Germany (German Swiss)	6	5	21	10
France (French Swiss)	4	7	6	3
Other	1	7	—	1
Total	100	100	100	100
	(222)	(464)	(52)	(171)

following facts. Among ministers in England there is a greater tendency to publish books than articles. Specification of the above table by religion shows that this is especially true of Protestant clergymen. Among psychiatrists in the United States there is a greater tendency to publish articles than books. Specification by religion shows this to be true of Protestant psychiatrists. Catholic psychiatrists, especially in the United States, are more likely to publish in book form. Among German psychiatrists there is a greater tendency to publish books. This last difference disappears with religion held constant, showing that this merely reflects the greater proportion of Protestant psychiatrists among German authors. These differences should be kept in mind when interpreting the study. Since we still have no criterion of the relative "significance" of books and articles, we cannot speak of these differences as having "distorted" the conclusions of the study. Certain information, however, is lost which might have appeared had we allowed the additional complexity of analyzing these two forms of publication separately.

A NOTE ON THE BELIEF INDICES

The Religious Belief Index follows a format developed in studies carried out by the Survey Research Center at Michigan and the Bureau of Applied Social Research at Columbia. The Psychiatric Belief Index was constructed for use in the present research. In the former case, individuals have been asked to read the statements and check the one which seemed closest to their opinion. Here, the statements were used as guides for coding. The coding instruction was to classify the book or article as a whole according to the statement which seemed best to characterize the content of the book or article with reference to these questions. These categories would not necessarily be those the authors would choose were they asked. A few examples follow. Rudolf Dreikurs wrote an article entitled "The Religion of Democracy" which appeared in *The Humanist* in 1955. He argued that the advent of democracy coincided with the revolt against the supernatural, and he described science as engaged in a struggle against revelation. This writing was classed in category seven of the Religious Belief Index. William A. Cameron in his 1931 book on *The Clinic of a Cleric* described man as a spiritual being who needs spiritual forces to overcome fear, and contended that this is best accomplished through a confessional centered in the love of Christ. This book was placed in category one of the Religious Belief Index. William Sargant in his

1957 book *The Battle for the Mind* said that religious and political beliefs are fixed and destroyed through the manipulation of physiological mechanisms by the scientific practitioner. This item was placed in category one of the Psychiatric Belief Index. James Gillis' writing on "Psychiatry of Prayer" in the *Catholic World* in 1953 said that there is much dangerous nonsense in psychoanalysis and that many psychoanalysts are opportunists. This article was placed in category seven of the Psychiatric Belief Index.

HINDSIGHT

Were the study to be repeated, the investigator would follow the same decisions regarding the unit of analysis. Items rather than authors would be the units and books would be combined with articles. The first because, technically, we are interested in "actors" rather than individuals and, practically, it would make no difference. The second decision would be retained for reasons of parsimony in view of the goals of this study. With respect to the latter decision, a study in a restricted area to analyze the differences between book and article writing would be a worthwhile contribution to the sociology of communication. One could not, however, generalize these decisions to another substantive area.

Some procedural changes could be made were the study to be done again. The abstracting step could be dispensed with. Assistants could be trained to code from the book or article directly while retaining some significant statements for qualitative treatment. This would also allow a test of intercoder agreement which would provide more assurance of "construct validation." Further, though there happened in this case to be little difference between the abstracted and the nonabstracted items, a more systematic sampling procedure, planned in view of the time available for the study, would have been preferable as a basis for selecting items.

NOTE

1. On this use of the abstraction "actor" as that aspect of a concrete individual participating in a particular "social system" see Talcott Parsons and Edward A. Shils, *Toward a General Theory of Action*, pp. 9ff.

Glossary of Technical Terms

THE CORE TECHNICAL TERMS of the study—role, status, institution, and variation have been defined in the appendix to Chapter I. These terms and many others in this report are used in the sense commonly understood among social scientists. This glossary is intended to provide a quick reference for some terms used in a special sense or which are neologisms of this study. Full definitions and a number of examples of the indicators used in classifying the items according to the following concepts are to be found in the pages listed in the right-hand column.

Name and Category of Concept	Capsule Definition	Pages on which Concept is First Defined and Indicators are Given
Global Classifications		
Religious Belief Index	Adherence to religious doctrines	32
Psychiatric Belief Index	Adherence to doctrines regarding the scope of scientific legitimacy	33
Reference Group	That group from which individual takes evaluative standards	61f.
Therapeutic Goals		
Meaning Goals	Advocate therapy to provide a life orientation or a sense of purpose	68f.
Instrumental Goals	Advocate therapy to help individual adapt to his surroundings or to function better	68f.

Counseling Norms

Quality-Performance	Whether to orient to client in terms of his inherent attributes or in terms of what he does	96f.
Affectivity-Affective Neutrality	Whether or not to become emotionally involved with client	98f.
Universalism-Particularism	Whether to orient to client as an instance of a general law or in view of special relation he has to therapist	100f.
Diffuseness-Specificity	Whether to consider a broad or narrow range of relationships of or with the client	102f.

Variant Subtypes

Militant conformists	Advocate means and goals of therapy appropriate to own institution	25f., 30f.
Ritualists	Advocate means of therapy appropriate to own institution and goals appropriate to other institutions	113, 115
Innovators	Advocate goals appropriate to own and means appropriate to other institutions	114, 116
Rebels	Advocate means and goals appropriate to other institutions	114, 116f.

Rationales

Rule oriented	Justify self with reference to ideas or values	138ff.
Socially oriented	Justify self with reference to behavior of other individuals	138ff.
Consolidating	Justify self by arguing for the identity of religion and psychiatry	140ff.
Complementing	Justify self with reference to complementary relation of religion and psychiatry	141
Harbinger	Justify self with argument that religion leads to psychiatric goals or vice versa	141f.

Jurisdictional Differentiation

Material Reductionists	Counseling task considered purely psychological and may be handled by single psychological-type role	155ff.
Spiritual Reductionists	Counseling task purely spiritual and may be handled by single religious-type role occupant	155ff.
Alternativists	Counseling task either psychological or spiritual, and either ministers or psychiatrists can do counseling	155ff.
Dualists	Counseling has both psychological and spiritual aspects but a single counselor may be competent in both	155ff.
Specialists	Counseling has both psychological and spiritual aspects and a psychiatrist (psychologist) is required for former and a minister for latter	155ff.

Allocative Criteria

Psychological Achievement	Counseling role to be allocated to individual trained in psychological methods	175ff.
Religious Achievement	Counseling role to be allocated to individual possessing certain inherent "gifts"	175ff.
Ascriptive	Counseling role to be allocated to individual possessing certain inherent "gifts"	175ff.

Bibliography of Cited Religio-Psychiatric Works

7. Allers, Rudolph, "Confessor and Alienist," *American Ecclesiastical Review*, XCIX (1938), 401–13.

11. ———, *The Successful Error*, New York: Sheed and Ward, 1940.

25. Anderson, Camilia M., *Beyond Freud*, New York: Harper & Row, 1957.

55. Barbour, Clifford E., *Sin and the New Psychology*, New York: The Abingdon Press, 1930.

61. Baudouin, Charles, "Sublimation et synthèse" ("Sublimation and Synthesis") *Revue de Theologie et de Philosophie*, (January, 1953), 46–56.

76. Behan, R. C., "Christian Approach to Psychiatry," *Hospital Progress*, (February 29, 1948), 49.

79. Beirnaert, Louis, "Sin and the Christian Sense of Guilt," *Conflict and Light*, Bruno de Jesus-Marie (ed.), London: Sheed and Ward, 1952.

80. ———, "L'eglise et la psychoanalyse" ("The Church and Psychoanalysis"), *Études*, CCLXXV (November, 1952), 229–37.

81. ———, "L'attitude chretienne en psychotherapie" ("The Christian Attitude in Psychotherapy"), *Études*, CCLXXVII (June, 1953), 356–64.

82. ———, "La Question du merveilleux" ("The Question of the Miraculous"), *Études*, CCLXXIX (November, 1953), 214–24.

88. Belgum, David Rudolph, *Clinical Training for Pastoral Care*, Philadelphia: Westminster Press, 1956.

90. Bennett, F. S. M., *A Soul in the Making or Psycho-Synthesis*, Chester,

England: Phillipson and Golder, Ltd.; London: Marshall and Company, Ltd., 1924.

102. Bernet, W., *Inhalt und Grenze der religiösen Erfahrung* (Content and Limits of Religious Experience), Bern: P. Haupt, 1955.

104. Best, Allen Charles, "Pastoral Work with Adjustment Problems," Unpublished Ph.D. thesis, Boston University, 1950.

115. Bitter, Wilhelm, *Psychotherapie und Seelsorge* (Psychotherapy and Pastoral Work), Eine Einfuhrung in die Tiefenpsychologie (Introduction to Depth Psychology), Gesammeite Vortrage der Arbeitstagung (Collected Lectures of the Work Sessions), Bern: H. Huber, 1951.

122. Blake, John A., "The Fourth Category of Personality Needs: A Critical Analysis of a Psycho-Theological Problem," *Mental Hygiene*, XXXVII (1953), 337–83.

123. Blanton, Smiley, and Ross, M. H., "Sin or Symptoms?" *Survey*, LXIII (1929), 265–68.

124. ———, and Peale, Norman Vincent, *Faith Is the Answer*, New York: Carmel, 1955.

133. Boisen, Anton T., "The Sense of Isolation in Mental Disorder: Its Religious Significance," *American Journal of Sociology*, XXXIII (1928), 555–68.

134. ———, "Theological Education via the Clinic," *Religious Education*, XXV (1930), 235–39.

136. ———, *The Exploration of the Inner World: A Study of Mental Disorder and Religious Experience*, Chicago: Willet Clark, 1936.

142. ———, "The Minister as Counselor," *Journal of Pastoral Care*, 11, No. 1 (1948), 13–22.

154. Bonnell, John Sutherland, *Pastoral Psychiatry*, New York: Harper & Row, 1938.

156. ———, "Is Faith Healing Valid Today?" *Religion and Human Behavior*, Simon Doniger (ed.), New York: Associated Press, 1954, 125–33.

161. Booth, Gotthard, "Conditions of Medical Responsibility," *The Review of Religion*, XIII (March, 1949), 241–58.

173. Boyd, Richard White, "The Use of Group Psychotherapy in the Professional Training of Ministers," Unpublished Ph.D. thesis, Boston University, 1952.

174. Braceland, F. J., "Clinical Psychiatry Today and Tomorrow: An Introduction," *Faith, Reason, and Modern Psychiatry, Sources for a Synthesis*, F. J. Braceland (ed.), New York: P. J. Kenedy & Sons, 1955, 5–28.

186. Brinkman, Robert E., "Standards for a Full-Time Program in the

Light of the Experience of the Council for Clinical Training," in *Clinical Pastoral Training*, Seward Hiltner (ed.), Commission on Religion and Health, Federal Council of the Churches of Christ in America, 1945.

197. Bruder, Ernest E., "A Clinical Trained Religious Ministry in the Mental Hospital," *Quarterly Review Psychiatry, Neurology*, 11 (October, 1947), 543–52.

239. Cammeron, William A., *The Clinic of a Cleric*, New York: R. Long, R. R. Smith, Inc., 1931.

241. Cammack, J. S., "Confessor and/or Psychotherapist?" *Clergy Review* (April 18, 1940), 290–303.

242. Campbell, Charles Macfie, *Delusion and Belief*, Cambridge, Mass.: Harvard University Press, 1926.

256. Cavanagh, J. R., and McGoldrick, J. B., "Psychiatry, Philosophy, and Religion," *Fundamental Psychiatry*, Milwaukee: The Bruce Pub. Co., 1958, 533–48.

260. Choisy, Maryse, *Psychoanalyse et Catholicisme* (Psychoanalysis and Catholicism), Paris: L'Arche, 1950.

265. Chrichton-Miller, Hugh, *The New Psychology and the Preacher*, New York: T. Seltzer, 1924.

268. Clark, Glenn, *How to Find Health Through Prayer*, New York: Harper & Row, 1940.

273. Cleator, Kenneth Irving, "A Comparison of Theology with Respect to the Concepts of Salvation and Integration," Unpublished Master's essay, Union Theological Seminary, New York.

282. Coe, George Albert, *The Religion of a Mature Mind*, Chicago: F. H. Revell Company, 1902.

293. Corcoran, C. J. O., "Thomistic Analysis and Cure of Scrupulosity," *American Ecclesiastical Review*, CXXXVII (November, 1957), 313–29.

313. Dalbiez, Roland, *Psychoanalytical Method and the Doctrine of Freud*, New York: Longmans, Green & Co. (11 Volumes), 1941.

340. Dicks, Russell L., *Pastoral Work and Personal Counseling*, New York: The Macmillan Co., 1944.

349. Dodd, Aleck D., "Relationship Therapy as Religious," *Journal of Psychotherapy as a Religious Process*, I (1954), 41–61.

368. Dunbar, H. Flanders, "Medicine, Religion and the Infirmities of Mankind," *Mental Hygiene* (January 18, 1934), 16–25.

369. ———, "Mental Hygiene and Religious Teaching," *Mental Hygiene*, XIX (1935), 353–372.

383. Eissler, Kurt Robert, *The Psychiatrist and the Dying Patient*, New York: International Universities Press, 1955.

384. Eliasberg, Wladimir G., "Moral Values and the Psychiatrist," *The Psychiatric Quarterly Supplement*, XXIV (1950), 278–85.

385. Elkisch, F. B., "Some Practical Points of Jung's Analytic Psychology," *Blackfriars*, XXVII (December, 1946), 461–66.

390. Ellard, G. A., "Sanity and Sanctity: Recommendations for Religious," *Review for Religious*, III (September 15, 1944), 307–25.

400. Fairbanks, Rollin J., "Standards for Full-Time Clinical Training in the Light of the New England Experience," *Clinical Pastoral Training*, Seward Hiltner (ed.), Commission on Religion and Health, Federal Council of the Churches of Christ in America, 1945.

410. Felix, Robert H., "The Hard Core of Counseling," *Pastoral Psychology*, I, No. 3 (1950), 34–7.

413. Fletcher, Joseph, "Standards for a Full-Time Program in the Light of the Graduate School of Applied Religion, *"Clinical Pastoral Training*, Seward Hiltner (ed.), Commission on Religion and Health, Federal Council of the Churches of Christ in America, 1945.

415. ——, "Concepts of Moral Responsibility," *Journal of Pastoral Care*, VI, No. 1 (Spring, 1952).

421. Ford, John C., "Depth Psychology, Morality, and Religion." *Proceedings of Fifth Annual Meeting: Catholic Theological Society of America*. Washington, D.C., 1950, 64–149.

425. Forsyth, David, *Psychology and Religion* (2nd ed), London: Watts, 1936.

437. Frankl, Viktor E., *The Doctor and the Soul*, Trans. R. and C. Winston, New York: Alfred A. Knopf, 1955.

441. Franzblau, Abraham N., "Rabbi or Psychiatrist," *Central Conference of American Rabbis Journal*, (October, 1953), 46–50.

447. Friedman, Maurice S., "Healing Through Meeting: Martin Buber and Psychotherapy," *Cross Currents*, V (Autumn, 1955), 297–310.

453. Gasson, John A., "Religion and Personality Integration," *The Human Person*, M. B. Arnold and J. A. Gasson (eds.), New York: The Ronald Press, 1954.

469. Gemelli, Agostino, *Psychoanalysis Today*, Trans. J. S. Chapin and S. Attanasio, New York: P. J. Kenedy & Sons, 1955.

474. Gerber, Israel J., "Pastoral Clinical Training in Operation," *The Reconstructionist*, XIV, No. 3 (1948), 14–19.

482. Ginsberg, Sol W., "Concerning Religion and Psychiatry," *Child Study*, XXX, No. 4 (1953), 12–21.

500. Goldbrunner, Josef, *Holiness Is Wholeness*, New York: Pantheon, 1955.

505. Gordon, J. Berkley, "The Relation of the Church to Mental Hospitals," *Psychiatric Quarterly Supplement*, XX (1946), 23–9.

509. Grant, Pryor, "The Moral and Religious Life of the Individual in the Light of the New Psychology," *Mental Hygiene*, XII (1928), 449–89.

516. Gregory, Marcus, *Psychotherapy: Scientific and Religious*, London: The Macmillan Co., 1939.

520. Gross, George A., "The Function of a Chaplain in Psychotherapy," *Bulletin Menninger Clinic*, XVI, No. 4 (1952), 136–41.

529. Haas, Alfred B., "The Therapeutic Value of Hymns," *Pastoral Psychology*, I, No. 9 (1950), 39–42.

532. Hadfield, J. A., "The Psychology of Spiritual Healing," *Psychology and the Church*, O. Hardman (ed.), London: The Macmillan Co., 1925.

547. Helweg, Hjalmar, *Soul Sorrow: The Psychiatrist Speaks to the Minister*, Trans. Jens Grano, New York: Pageant Press, 1955.

551. Herrick, Everett C., "The Place of Clinical Training in the Theological Curriculum," *Clinical Pastoral Training*, Seward Hiltner (ed.), Commission of Religion and Health, Federal Council of the Churches of Christ in America, 1945.

559. Hiltner, Seward, "Five Areas of Mutual Endeavor," *Psychiatry and Religion*, J. L. Liebman (ed.), Boston: Beacon Press, 1948.

565. ———, "Empathy in Counseling," *Pastoral Psychology*, I, No. 10 (1951), 25–30.

570. ———, *The Counselor in Counseling: Case Notes in Pastoral Counseling*, Nashville: Abingdon-Cokesbury Press, 1952.

571. ———, "Pastoral Psychology and Christian Ethics," *Pastoral Psychology*, IV, No. 33 (1953), 23–35.

572. ———, "Pastoral Psychology and Constructive Theology," *Pastoral Psychology*, IV, No. 35 (June, 1953), 17–26.

573. ———, "Freud for the Pastor," *Pastoral Psychology*, V. No. 50 (January, 1955), 41–57.

574. ———, "Bibliography and Reading Guide in Pastoral Psychology," *Pastoral Psychology*, V, No. 50 (1955), 8–21.

575. ———, "Freud, Psychoanalysis and Religion," *Healing: Human and Divine*, Simon Doniger (ed.), New York: Association Press, 1957.

589. Horton, Walker M., "A Psychological Approach to Theology—after Twenty-Five Years," *Healing: Human and Divine*, Simon Doniger (ed.), New York: Association Press, 1957.

596. Howe, Reuel L., "Counseling Theological Students," *Journal of Clinical Pastoral Work*, I, No. 1 (Autumn, 1947), 11–17.

598. ———, "A Pastoral Theology of Sex and Marriage," *Sex and Religion Today*, Simon Doniger (ed.), New York: Association Press, 1953.

600. Huckel, Oliver, *Mental Medicine: Some Practical Suggestions from a Spiritual Standpoint*, New York: Crowell and Company, 1909.

601. Hudson, Cyril Edward, *Recent Psychology and the Christian Religion*, New York: George H. Doran Co., 1923.

606. Hudson, R. Lofton, "The Psychiatrist and the Pastor," *Journal of Pastoral Care*, IX, No. 1 (1955), 8–21.

609. Hughes, Thomas H., "Freudism and Religion," *The Philosopher*, London, XII, No. 2 (April, 1934), 63–72.

611. Hulme, William Edward, "Counseling and Theology," *Christian Century*, LXVIII, No. 8 (February 21, 1951), 238–40.

612. ———, "How to Set Up a Counseling Program in Your Church," *Pastoral Psychology*, II, No. 20 (January 1952), 43–8.

616. ———, *Counseling and Theology*, Philadelphia: Muhlenberg Press, 1956.

618. Hurley, James, "The Priest and the Psychiatrist: Indispensible to Family Clinic," *Hospital Progress*, XXX (August, 1949), 245–6.

623. Irion, Paul E., "Toward an Ethical Understanding of Grief Situations," *Pastoral Psychology*, IV, No. 39 (1953), 19–26.

625. Jackson, Edgar N., "The Therapeutic Function in Preaching," *Pastoral Psychology*, I, No. 5 (1950), 36–9.

626. ———, *How to Preach to People's Needs*, New York: Abingdon Press, 1956.

639. Johnson, Paul E., "Clinical Training in Preparation for Classroom Teaching of Pastoral Subjects," *Clinical Pastoral Training*, Seward Hiltner (ed.), Commission on Religion and Health, Federal Council of the Churches of Christ in America, 1945.

643. ———, "The Problem of Guilt in the Adolescent," *Psychiatry and Religion*, J. L. Liebman (ed.), Boston: Beacon Press, 1948, 126–43.

647. ———, *Psychology of Pastoral Care*, Nashville: Abingdon-Cokesbury, 1953.

648. ———, "Jesus as Psychologist," *Religion and Human Behavior*, Simon Doniger (ed.), New York: Association Press, 1954, 47–57.

653. Jones, Ernest, *Essays in Applied Psychoanalysis (Essays in Folklore, Anthropolgy)*, Vol. II, London: Hogarth Press, Ltd., 1951.

662. Jung, Carl Gustav, *Psychology and Religion*, New Haven: Yale University Press, 1938.

666. ———, *Die Beziehungen der Psychotherapie zur Seelsorge* (The Relation of Psychotherapy to Pastoral Care), Zurich: Rascher, 1948.

687. Kemp, Charles F., *The Church: The Gifted and the Retarded Child*, St. Louis: Bethany Press, 1958.

690. ———, *Physicians of the Soul*, New York: Macmillan Company, 1947.

697. Kew, Clinton J., "Group Psychotherapy in a Church Setting," *Pastoral Psychology*, 1, No. 10 (1951), 31–7.

741. Kubie, Lawrence S., "Psychoanalysis of Healing by Faith," *Pastoral Psychology*, I, No. 2 (1950), 13–18.

742. Kuether, Frederick, Jr., "The Place of Clinical Training in the Theological Curriculum as Training Supervisors See It," *Clinical Training*, Seward Hiltner (ed.), Commission on Religion and Health, Federal Council of the Churches of Christ in America, 1945.

744. Kunkel, Fritz, *In Search of Maturity*, New York: Charles Scribner's Sons, 1943.

749. Lankler, Ralph Conover, "The Minister's Use of Psychiatry," thesis, Union Theological Seminary, 1931.

751. Latko, E. F., "Psychotherapy for Scruples," *Homiletic and Pastoral Review*, XLIX (May, 1949), 617–23.

755. Leonard, Augustin Gustave Pierre, "La Psychologie Religieuse de Jung" (The Religious Psychology of Jung), *Vie Spirituelle Supplement*, XVIII (1951).

765. Leslie, Robert C., "The Role of the Chaplain in Patient Relationships: Group Counseling," *Journal Pastoral Care*, VI, No. 1 (1952), 56–61.

766. ———, "Religion and Healing" (bibliography), *Bulletin of General Theological Library*, Boston, Mass., XLVI, No. 1 (October, 1953).

782. Liertz, Rhaban, "L'image du pere et son influence sur l'education religieuse" (The Image of the Father and His Influence on Religious Education), *Psyche*, VI (1951), 583–88.

813. Mailloux, Noel, "Psychology and Spiritual Direction," *Faith, Reason, and Modern Psychiatry*, F. J. Braceland (ed.), New York: P. Kenedy & Sons, 1955, 247–63.

830. Mathewson, Robert J. Watson, "An Estimation of the Psychoanalytical View of Man from the Standpoint of Christian Theology," thesis, Union Theological Seminary, 1940.

834a. Maves, Paul B., and Cedarleaf, Lennart, *Older People and the Church*. New York, Nashville: Abingdon-Cokesbury, 1949.

836. May, A. Mark, "The Factor of Conscience in Human Relations," *The Minister and Human Relations*, William Anderson (ed.), Nashville: The Methodist Church, 1943.

837. May, Rollo, *The Springs of Creative Living*, New York: Abingdon-Cokesbury, 1940.

853. McDonnell, Kilian William, "Psychiatrists in an Abbey," *America*, XCVII (August 31, 1957), 545–47.

854. McDonough, A., "Reliable Psychotherapy," *Sign*, XXVIII, No. 33 (January, 1949).

856. McGarry, William J., "Freud Has Passed on and Freudianism also Dies," *America*, VI, No. 1 (October 7, 1939), 606–7.

862. McKenzie, John Grant, *Souls in the Making*, New York: The Macmillan Company, 1929.

863. ——, *Psychology, Psychotherapy and Evangelicism*, London: Allen & Unwin, 1940.

869. McNeill, John Thomas, *The History of the Cure of Souls*, New York: Harper & Row, 1951.

875. Menninger, Karl A., *A Guide to Psychiatric Books, and Some Reading Lists*, 2nd revised edition, New York: Grune & Stratton, 1956.

904. Mollegen, A. T., "A Christian View of Psychoanalysis," *Journal of Pastoral Care*, VI, No. 4 (1952), 1–14.

908. Moore, Thomas Verner, "The Clergy and Mental Hygiene," *Ecclesiastical Review*, LXXXV (1931), 598–604.

909. ——, "Religious Values in Mental Hygiene," *Ecclesiastical Review*, LXXXIX (July, 1933), 13–27.

913. ——, *Personal Mental Hygiene*, New York: Grune & Stratton, 1944.

914. ——, *The Driving Forces of Human Nature and Their Adjustment*, New York: Grune & Stratton, 1950.

920. Moses (Morse), Josiah, *Pathological Aspects of Religions*, Worcester, Mass.: Clark University Press, 1906.

922. Moxon, Cavendish, *Freudian Essays on Religion and Science*, Boston: Gorham Press, 1926.

925. Muedeking, George H., *Emotional Problems and the Bible*, Philadelphia: Muhlenberg Press, 1956.

928. Mullen, Joseph J., "Psychological Factors in the Pastoral Treatment of Scruples," *Studies in Psychology and Psychiatry*, I, No. 3 (June, 1927).

931. Munsterberg, H., "Psychotherapy and the Church," *Psychotherapy*, Chap. 12, New York: Moffat, Yard and Company, 1900.

950. Neumann, Johannes, "Psychotherapy, Theology and the Church," *Journal of the Psychology of Religion*, Karl Beth (ed.), Gutersloh: Bertelsmann, 1929, 328–29.

954. Newman, Lewis I., "Self-Acceptance—A Jewish View," *Judaism and Psychiatry*, S. Noveck (ed.), United Synogogue of America, 1956.

973. Oates, Wayne E., "The Diagnostic Use of the Bible," *Pastoral Psychology*, I, No. 9 (1950), 43–6.

974. ——, *The Christian Pastor*, Philadelphia: Westminster Press, 1951.

978. ——, *Anxiety in Christian Experience*, Philadelphia: Westminster Press, 1955.

999. Oliver, J. R., "Psychiatry and Mental Health," *Catholic Mind*, LV (October, 1951), 413–21.

1005. Outler, Albert C., *A Christian Context for Counseling*, New Haven: The Hazen Pamphlets, 1948.
1022. Pfister, Oskar Robert. *Religionswissenschaft und psychoanalyse* (The Knowledge of Religion and Psychoanalysis), Geissen: Topelmann, 1927.
1023. ———, *Christianity and Fear*, London: G. Allen and Unwin, 1948.
1034. Pope Pius XII, "Ils qui interfuerunt Conventui primo internationali de Histopathologia Systematis nervorum, Romae habito," *Acta Apostolicae Sedis*, XLV (May 25, 1953), 278–86.
1051. Pratt, George K., "Psychiatrist and Clergyman," *Christianity and Mental Health*. A report of the Conference of the Committee on Religion and Health, held at Greenwich, Connecticut, August, 1938. Prepared by the Federal Council of the Churches of Christ in America.
1052. Preston, Robert A., "A Chaplain Looks at Psychiatry," *Bulletin Menninger Clinic*, XIV, No. 1 (1950), 22–6.
1054. Prinzhorn, Hans, *Psychotherapy, Its Nature, Its Assumptions, Its Limitations*, London: Johnathan Cape, 1932.
1059. Quayle, William A., *The Pastor Preacher*, New York: Methodist Book Concern, 1910.
1062. Rado, Sandor, "The Border Region between the Normal and the Abnormal," *Ministry and Medicine in Human Relations*, Iago Galdston (ed.), New York: International Universities Press, 1955, 33–48.
1068. Relk, Theodor, "The Therapy of the Neuroses and Religion," *International Journal of Psychoanalysis*, X (1929), 292–302.
1076. Riecker, Otto, *Das evangelische Wort* (Spiritual Communication), Gutersloh: Bertelsmann, 1953.
1085. Roberts, David E., *Psychotherapy and the Christian View of Man*, New York: Charles Scribner's Sons, 1950.
1087. Rochedieu, Edmond Robert, *Psychologie et Vie Religieuse* (Psychology and Religious Life), Geneva: Roulet, 1948.
1093. Rogers, William F., "Needs of the Bereaved," *Pastoral Psychology*, I, No. 5 (1950), 17–21.
1110. Sanders, Benjamin G., *Christianity after Freud*, London: B. Bles, 1949.
1111. Sandrow, Edward T., "Conscience and Guilt—A Jewish View," *Judaism and Psychiatry*, S. Noveck (ed.), United Synagogue of America, 1956.
1116. Saunders, K. J., *Adventures of the Christian Soul*, Cambridge: University Press, 1916.
1118. Schaer, Hans, *Erlösungsvorstellungen und ihre Psychologischen Aspekte*, Zurich: Rascher, 1950.

1121. Schaier, Immanuel B., "Religious Abnormalities," *The Psychology of Religion*, Karl Beth (ed.), Gutersloh: Bertelsmann, 1929.

1129. Schnitzer, Jeshaia, "Religious Counseling and the American Rabbinate," *Reconstruction Magazine*, XVI, November 3, 1950.

1138. Schulte, Chrysostumus, "Pastoral Treatment of Psychopaths," *Religion und Seelenleden*, Wilhelm Bergmann (ed.), Dusseldorf: L'Schwann, 1926.

1148. Shaw, Don C., "Some General Considerations on the Religious Care of the Mentally Ill," *Journal of Clinical Pastoral Work*, I, No. 2 (1947), 20–24.

1155. Sherrill, Lewis Joseph, *Guilt and Redemption*, Richmond, Virginia: John Knox Press, 1945.

1156. Shoemaker, Samuel Moore, *How You Can Help Other People*, New York: E. P. Dutton, 1946.

1157. Shrader, Wesley, *Of Men and Angels*, New York: Rinehart, 1957.

1174. Southard, Samuel, "Sectarianism and the Psychoses," *Religion in Life*, (Autumn, 1954).

1187. Steinbach, Alexander Allen, "Depression—A Jewish View," *Judaism and Psychiatry*, S. Noveck (ed.), United Synagogue of America, 1956.

1188. Steinthal, Erich Franz, "Physician and Minister," *Lutheran Quarterly*, II (1950), 287–97.

1190. Stern, Karl, "Religion and Psychiatry," *Commonweal*, XLIX (October 22, 1948), 30–33.

1193. ———, "Some Spiritual Aspects of Psychotherapy," *Faith, Reason and Modern Psychiatry*, F. J. Braceland (ed.), New York: P. Kenedy and Sons, 1955, 125–40.

1205. Strauss, Eric Benjamin, "Psychological Medicine and Catholic Thought," *Month*, XVI (October, 1956), 203–15.

1212. Stunkard, Albert, "Some Interpersonal Aspects of an Oriental Religion," *Psychiatry*, XIV (1951), 419–31.

1217. Terhune, William B., "Religion and Psychiatry," *Journal of Pastoral Care*, II, No. 3 (Fall, 1948), 15–21.

1226. Thomas, John R., "Evaluations of Clinical Pastoral Training and Part-Time Training in a General Hospital," *Journal of Pastoral Care*, XII, No. 1 (1958).

1231. Tillich, Paul, "The Relation of Religion and Health," *Review of Religion*, X (1946), 348–84.

1234. ———, "Anxiety, Religion and Medicine," *Pastoral Psychology*, III, No. 29 (1952), 11–17.

1251. Van der Veldt, James H., "Religion and Mental Health," *Mental Hygiene*, XXXV (1951), 177–89.

1252. ———, and Odenwald, Robert P., *Psychiatry and Catholicism*, New York: Blakiston, 1957.

1271. Waterhouse, Eric S., *Psychology and Religion*, New York: K. K. Smith, 1931.

1272. ———, *Psychology and Pastoral Work*, Nashville: Cokesbury Press, 1940.

1278. Weatherhead, Leslie Dixon, *Psychology in the Service of the Soul*, New York: The Macmillan Company, 1930.

1282. Weigert, Edith Hildegard, "Love and Fear: A Psychiatric Interpretation," *Journal of Pastoral Care*, V, No. 2 (1951), 12–22.

1286. Westberg, Granger Ellsworth, "Newer Approaches to the Care of the Sick," *Lutheran Quarterly*, I (1949), 255–62.

1290. White, Andrew Dickson, *A History of the Warfare of Science with Theology in Christendom* (2 Volumes), New York: D. Appleton and Company, 1896.

1291. White, Ernest, *Christian Life and the Unconscious*, New York: Harper & Row, 1956.

1295. White, Victor, "The Analyst and the Confessor," *Commonweal*, XLVIII (July 23, 1948), 346–49.

1297. ———, *God and the Unconscious*, Chicago: Henry Regnery Company, 1953.

1310. Wise, Carroll A., *Religion in Sickness and Health*, New York: Harper & Row, 1942.

1311. ———, "Clinical Training in Preparation for Institutional Chaplaincy and Clinical Training Supervision," *Clinical Pastoral Training*, Seward Hiltner (ed.), Federal Council of the Churches of Christ in America, 1949.

1313. ———, "The Pastor as Counselor," *Pastoral Psychology*, II, No. 11 (1951), 9–14.

1316. ———, *Psychiatry and the Bible*, New York: Harper & Row, 1956.

1326. Worchester, Elwood, *Religion and Medicine*, New York: Moffat, Yard and Company, 1908.

1327. ———, *Body, Mind and Spirit*, New York: Charles Scribner's Sons, 1932.

1337. Yoder, H. Walter, "Pastoral Counseling and the Church," *Pastoral Psychology*, 1958.

1343. Zilboorg, Gregory, and Henry, George W., *A History of Medical Psychology*, New York: W. W. Norton Company, 1941.

1347. ———, "Some Details and Assertions of Religious Faith," *Faith, Reason and Modern Psychiatry*, F. J. Braceland (ed.), New York: P. Kenedy and Sons, 1955, 99–121.

Bibliography

Aberle, David, "The Functional Prerequisites of Society," *Ethics*, LX (January, 1950), 100–111.

Bakan, David, *Sigmund Freud and the Jewish Mystical Tradition*, Princeton, N.J.: D. Van Nostrand Co., Inc., 1958.

Bales, Robert Freed, "The Equilibrium Problem in Small Groups," *Small Groups: Studies in Social Interaction*, A. Paul Hare, Edgar F. Borgatta, and Robert F. Bales (eds.), New York: Alfred A. Knopf, 1955, 498–515.

———, "The Therapeutic Role of Alcoholics Anonymous as Seen by a Sociologist," *Quarterly Journal of Studies in Alcohol*, V (1944), 278.

Barber, Bernard, "Resistance by Scientists to Scientific Discovery," *Scientific Manpower*, 1960, 36–47.

Barnard, Chester I., *The Functions of the Executive*, Cambridge, Mass.: Harvard University Press, 1938.

Berelson, Bernard, *Content Analysis in Communications Research*, New York: The Free Press of Glencoe, 1952.

Berger, Peter L., "Sectarianism and Religious Society," *American Journal of Sociology*, LXIV (July, 1958), 41–44.

Blumer, Herbert, "Collective Behavior," Alfred McClung Lee (ed.), *New Outline of the Principles of Sociology*, New York: Barnes & Noble, 1951, 167–224.

Bogue, Donald J., *The Population of the United States*, New York: The Free Press of Glencoe, 1959.

Buber, Martin, "Distance and Relation," *Psychiatry*, XX (1957).

Burchard, W. W., "Role Conflicts of Military Chaplains," *American Sociological Review*, XIX (1954), 528–35.

Bureau of Applied Social Research, Columbia University, "Annotated Bibliography and Directory of Workers in the Field of Religion and Psychiatry," New York, 1960. (Mimeographed.)

Campbell, Angus, Gurin, Gerald, and Miller, Warren E., *The Voter Decides*, New York: Harper & Row, 1954.

Cannon, W. B., *The Wisdom of the Body*, New York: W. W. Norton and Co., Inc., 1932.

Cantril, Hadley, *The Psychology of Social Movements*, New York: John Wiley & Sons, Inc., 1941.

Cassirer, Ernst, *The Philosophy of Symbolic Forms*, Vol. 1, New Haven: Yale University Press, 1955.

Cloward, Richard A., "Illegitimate Means, Anomie, and Deviant Behavior," *American Sociological Review*, XXIV (1959), 164-76.

Cohen, Albert, *Delinquent Boys*, New York: The Free Press of Glencoe, 1955.

Collingwood, R. G., *The Idea of History*, Oxford: Oxford University Press, Inc., 1956.

Cooley, Charles H., *Human Nature and the Social Order*, New York: Charles Scribner's Sons, 1922.

Crockett, Harvey J., Jr., "The Achievement Motive and Differential Occupational Mobility in the United States," *American Sociological Review*, XXVII (April, 1962), 191-204.

Devereux, Edward, "Parsons' Sociological Theory," *The Social Theories of Talcott Parsons*, Max Black (ed.), Englewood Cliffs, N.J.: Prentice-Hall, Inc., 1961.

Dubin, Robert, "Parsons' Actor: Continuities in Social Theory," *American Sociological Review*, XXV (1960), 467-82.

———, "Deviant Behavior and Social Structure, Continuities in Social Theory"; Cloward, Richard A., "Illegitimate Means, Anomie, and Deviant Behavior"; and Merton, Robert K., "Social Conformity, Deviation, and Opportunity Structures: A Comment on the Contributions of Dubin and Cloward," *American Sociological Review*, XXIV (1959), 147-88.

Durkheim, Emile, *The Division of Labor in Society*, Trans. George Simpson, New York: The Macmillan Co., 1933.

Eisenstadt, S. N., "Studies in Reference Group Behavior: Reference Norms and the Social Structure," *Human Relations*, VII (1954), 191-216.

Etzioni, Amitai, *A Comparative Analysis of Complex Organizations*, New York: The Free Press of Glencoe, 1961.

Festinger, Leon, Riecken, Henry W., and Schacter, Stanley, *When Prophecy Fails*, Minneapolis: Univ. of Minnesota Press, 1956.

Freud, Anna, *The Ego and the Mechanisms of Defense*, London: Hogarth Press, 1936.

Freud, Sigmund, *Moses and Monotheism*, New York: Vintage Books, Inc., 1958.

Fromm, Erich, *Escape from Freedom*, New York: Rinehart and Co., 1941.

Gerth, H. H., and Mills, C. Wright, *From Max Weber: Essays in Sociology*, New York: Oxford University Press, Inc., 1958.

Goode, William J., "Encroachment, Charlatanism, and the Emerging Profession: Psychology, Sociology, and Medicine," *American Sociological Review*, XXV (December, 1960), 902–14.

Graybeal, David, "Churches in a Changing Culture," *Review of Religious Research*, II, No. 3 (Winter, 1961), 121–28.

Gurin, Gerald, Veroff, Joseph, and Feld, Sheila, *Americans View Their Mental Health*, New York: Basic Books, Inc., 1960.

Hall, Oswald, "The Informal Organization of the Medical Profession," *Canadian Journal of Economic and Political Science*, XII (1946), 30–44.

Harnack, Adolf, *Outlines of the History of Dogma*, Boston: The Beacon Press, 1957.

Hollingshead, August B., *Elmtown's Youth*, New York: John Wiley & Sons, Inc., 1949.

Homans, George C., *The Human Group*, New York: Harcourt, Brace and World, 1950.

Hughes, Everett C., "The Making of a Physician," *Human Organization*, XIV (1956), 21–25.

Hyman, Herbert H., "Reflections on Reference Groups," *Public Opinion Quarterly*, XXIV (Fall, 1960), 389–96.

———, *Survey Design and Analysis*, New York: The Free Press of Glencoe, 1958.

———, "The Value Systems of Different Classes: A Social Psychological Analysis of Stratification," *Class, Status and Power*, Reinhard Bendix and Seymour Lipset (eds.), New York: The Free Press of Glencoe, 1953.

Jacquet, Constant H., Jr., *Missionary Research Library Occasional Bulletin*. 1954.

Johnson, F. Ernest, and Ackerman, J. Emery, *The Church as Employer, Money Raiser, and Investor*, New York: Harper & Row, 1959.

Johnson, F. Ernest, Ackerman, J. Emery, and Fichter, Joseph H., *Religion as an Occupation*, Notre Dame, Indiana: University of Notre Dame Press, 1961.

Jones, Ernest, *The Life and Work of Sigmund Freud*, 3 Volumes, New York: Basic Books, Inc., 1953, 1955, 1957.

Jung, Carl Gustav, *Modern Man in Search of a Soul,* New York: Harcourt, Brace and Co., 1933.

Kadushin, Charles, "Social Distance between Client and Professional," *American Journal of Sociology,* LXVII (March, 1962), 517-31.

———, "Paths to a Psychiatric Clinic," Unpublished dissertation, Columbia University, 1959.

Kaplan, Norman, "Reference Group Theory and Voting Behavior," Unpublished Ph.D. dissertation, Columbia University, 1955.

Katz, Elihu, and Lazarsfeld, Paul F., *Personal Influence,* New York: The Free Press of Glencoe, 1955.

Kelley, Harold H., "Two Functions of Reference Groups," *Readings in Social Psychology,* Guy E. Swanson, Theodore M. Newcomb, and Eugene L. Hartley (eds.), New York: Henry Holt and Company, 1952.

Killian, Lewis M., "Significance of Multiple-Group Membership in Disaster," *American Journal of Sociology,* LXVII (January, 1952), 309–14.

Klausner, Samuel Z., "Annotated Bibliography and Directory of Workers in the Field of Religion and Psychiatry," Bureau of Applied Social Research, Columbia University, 1958. (Unpublished mimeograph.)

———, "Images of Man: An Empirical Enquiry," *Journal of the Scientific Study of Religion,* Vol. 1, 1961.

———, "The Mellowing of the Religio-Psychiatric Movement," (H. Paul Douglass Lectures of the Religious Research Association, 1963), *Review of Religious Research* (in press).

———, "Methodology of Research in Religion and Psychiatry," *Journal of Religion and Health,* Vol. 1, July 1962.

———, "Methods of Data Collection in Studies of Religion," *Journal of the Society for the Scientific Study of Religion* (in press).

———, "Pastoral and Psychiatric Counseling: Some Philosophical Bases for Some Observed Differences," paper presented at the Clergy Conference on Mental Health sponsored by the Connecticut Mental Health Association and the Connecticut Department of Mental Health, May 1, 1963. (To be published by the Connecticut Department of Mental Health, Hartford, Connecticut.)

———, "Role Adaptation of Ministers and Psychiatrists in a Religio-Psychiatric Clinic," Bureau of Applied Social Research, Columbia University, New York, 1957. (Dittoed.)

———, "The Social Psychology of Courage," *Review of Religious Research,* III (Fall, 1961), 63–71.

———, "Some Differences in Modes of Research Between Psychologists and Sociologists," *Transactions of the Fifth International Congress of Sociology,* Geneva, International Sociological Association (in press).

————, "A Typology of Concept-Indicator Relations," Washington, D.C.: 1962. (Dittoed.)

La Piere, Richard, *The Freudian Ethic: An Analysis of the Subversion of the American Character*, New York: Duell, Sloan, and Pierce, 1959.

Lasswell, Harold D., et al., *Language of Politics, Studies in Quantitative Semantics*, New York: Stewart, 1949.

Lazarsfeld, Paul F., and McPhee, William, *Voting*, New York: The Free Press of Glencoe, 1954.

Lazarsfeld, Paul F., and Rosenberg, Morris (eds.), *The Language of Social Research*, New York: The Free Press of Glencoe, 1954.

Lecky, Prescott, *Self-Consistency: A Theory of Personality*, New York: Island Press, 1945.

Lennard, Henry, and Bernstein, Arnold, *The Anatomy of Psychotherapy*, New York: Columbia University Press, 1960.

Lenski, Gerhard, *The Religious Factor*, Garden City, N.Y.: Doubleday & Co., Inc., 1961.

————, "Status Crystallization: A Non-vertical Dimension of Social Status," *American Sociological Review*, XIX (1954), 405–13.

Lewin, Kurt, *A Dynamic Theory of Personality*, New York: McGraw-Hill Book Co., Inc., 1935.

————, et al., "Level of Aspiration," *Personality and the Behavior Disorders*, J. McV. Hunt (ed.), New York: Ronald Press (1944), 333–78.

Lieberson, Stanley, "Ethnic Groups and the Practice of Medicine," *American Sociological Review*, XXIII (1958), 542–49.

Linton, Ralph, *The Study of Man: An Introduction*, New York: Appleton-Century-Crofts, Inc., 1936.

Lynd, Robert S., *Middletown*, New York: Harcourt, Brace and Co., 1936.

McClelland, David C., *The Achieving Society*, New York: D. Van Nostrand Co., Inc., 1961.

Malinowski, Bronislaw, *Magic, Science and Religion*, New York: Doubleday & Co., 1955.

May, Rollo, Angel, Ernest, and Ellenberger, Henry F. (eds.), *Existence, A New Dimension in Psychiatry and Psychology*, New York: Basic Books, Inc., 1958.

Mayer, Albert J., and Sharp, Harry, "Religious Preferences and Worldly Success," *American Sociological Review*, XXVII (April, 1962), 218–27.

Mead, George, "The Genesis of the Self and Social Control," *International Journal of Ethics*, XXXV (1925), 251–77.

————, *Mind, Self and Society*, Chicago: University of Chicago Press, 1934.

Menninger, Karl, *The Theory of Psychoanalytic Technique*, New York: Basic Books, Inc., 1958.

———, *et al.*, *Reader in Bureaucracy*, New York: The Free Press of Glencoe, 1952.

Merton, Robert K., *Social Theory and Social Structure* (2nd ed. revised), New York: The Free Press of Glencoe, 1952.

———, "The Role Set: Problems in Sociological Theory," *The British Journal of Sociology*, VIII (1957), 106–20.

Merton, Robert K., Fiske, Marjorie, and Kendall, Patricia L., *The Focused Interview*, New York: The Free Press of Glencoe, 1952.

Merton, Robert K., Reader, George G., and Kendall, Patricia L., *The Student Physician*, Cambridge, Mass.: Harvard University Press, 1957.

Meyers, Jerome K., and Schaffer, Leslie, "Social Stratification and Psychiatric Practice: A Study of an Outpatient Clinic," *American Sociological Review*, XIX (1954), 307–10.

Moore, W. E., and Feldman, A. S., *Labor Commitment and Social Change in Developing Areas*, New York: Social Science Research Council, 1960.

Niebuhr, Richard H., *The Social Sources of Denominationalism*, New York: Henry Holt and Co., 1929.

North, Cecil C., *Social Differentiation*, Chapel Hill: University of North Carolina Press, 1926.

Ogburn, William F., *Social Change with Respect to Cultural and Original Nature*, New York: B. W. Huebsch, 1922.

Parsons, Talcott, "Illness and the Role of the Physician," *American Journal of Orthopsychiatry*, XXI (1951), 452-60.

———, "Phase Movement in a Theory of Action," *Working Papers in the Theory of Action*, Talcott Parsons, Robert F. Bales, and Edward A. Shils (eds.), New York: The Free Press of Glencoe, 1953.

———, *The Social System*, New York: The Free Press of Glencoe, 1951.

———, *The Structure of Social Action*, New York: The Free Press of Glencoe, 1937.

Parsons, Talcott, Bales, Robert F., and Zelditch, Morris, *Family: Socialization and the Interaction Process*, New York: The Free Press of Glencoe, 1955.

Parsons, Talcott, and Shils, Edward A., "Values, Motives, and the Theory of Action," *Towards a General Theory of Action*, Talcott Parsons and Edward A Shils (eds.), Cambridge, Mass.: Harvard University Press, 1951.

Parsons, Talcott, and Smelser, N. J., *Economy and Society*, Chicago: University of Chicago Press, 1956.

Patchen, Martin, "The Effect of Reference Group Standards on Job Satisfaction," *Human Relations*, XI (1958), 303–14.

Pfautz, Harold W., "Christian Science: A Case Study of the Social Psychological Aspects of Secularization," *Social Forces*, XXXIV (March, 1956), 246–51.

Piers, I., and Singer, M., *Shame and Guilt*, Springfield, Ill.: Charles C Thomas, 1953.

Pope, Liston, *Millhands and Preachers*, New Haven: Yale University Press, 1942.

Rieff, Philip, *Freud: The Mind of the Moralist*, New York: Viking Press, 1959.

Riesman, David, *The Lonely Crowd*, New Haven: Yale University Press, 1950.

Rivers, W. H. R., *Medicine, Magic, and Religion*, London: Kegan Paul, Trench and Treubner, 1924.

Rosen, Bernard C., "The Achievement Syndrome: A Psychocultural Dimension of Social Stratification," *American Sociological Review*, XVI (1951), 755–74.

Rosen, John, *Direct Analysis*, New York: Grune & Stratton, Inc., 1953.

Rosenberg, Bernard, and White, D. M., *Mass Culture*, New York: The Free Press of Glencoe, 1957.

Salisbury, W. Seward, "Faith, Ritualism, Charismatic Leadership, and Religious Behavior," *Social Forces*, XXXIV (1956), 241–45.

Sherif, Muzafer, *The Psychology of Social Norms*, New York: Harper & Row, 1936.

Shibutani, Tamotsu, "Reference Groups as Perspectives," *American Journal of Sociology*, LX (1955), 562–69.

Siegel, Alberta E., "Reference Groups, Membership Groups and Attitude Change," *Journal of Abnormal and Social Psychology*, LV (1951), 360–64.

Srole, Leo, *et al.*, *Mental Health in the Metropolis*, New York: McGraw-Hill Book Co., Inc., 1962.

Stanton, Alfred H., and Schwartz, Morris S., *The Mental Hospital*, New York: Basic Books, Inc., 1954.

Stouffer, Samuel, *et al.*, *The American Soldier: Studies in Social Psychology in World War II*, Vol. III: *Measurement and Prediction*, Princeton, N.J.: Princeton University Press, 1950.

Strodtbeck, Fred L., "Family Interaction, Values and Achievement," *Talent and Society*, D. C. McClelland (ed.), Princeton, N.J.: D. Van Nostrand Co., Inc., 1958.

Sutherland, Edward H. (ed.), *The Professional Thief*, Chicago: The University of Chicago Press, 1937.

Tolman, Edward C., *A Psychological Model*; Talcott Parsons and Edward A. Shils, "Values, Motives, and the Theory of Action," *Towards a*

General Theory of Action," Talcott Parsons and Edward A Shils (eds.), Cambridge, Mass.: Harvard University Press, 1951.

Tumin, Melvin, and Feldman, Arnold S., "The Miracle at Sabana Grande," *Public Opinion Quarterly,* (Summer, 1955), 125–39.

Turner, Ralph H., "Reference Groups of Future Oriented Men," *Social Forces,* XXXIV (1955), 130–36.

Veroff, Joseph, Feld, Sheila, and Gurin, Gerald, "Achievement Motivation and Religious Background," *American Sociological Review,* XXVII (April, 1962), 205–17.

Wach, Joachim, *The Sociology of Religion,* Chicago: University of Chicago Press, 1951.

Waples, D., Berelson, B., and Bradshaw, F., *What Reading Does to People,* Chicago: University of Chicago Press, 1940.

Warner, W. Lloyd, and Lunt, Paul S., *The Social Life of a Modern Community,* Vol. II; Yankee City Series, New Haven: Yale University Press, 1942.

Weber, Max, *Ancient Judaism,* Trans. H. H. Gerth and D. Martindale, New York: The Free Press of Glencoe, 1952.

———, *The Methodology of the Social Sciences,* New York: The Free Press of Glencoe, 1949.

———, *The Protestant Ethic and the Spirit of Capitalism,* New York: Charles Scribner's Sons, 1956.

———, *The Theory of Social and Economic Organization,* New York: The Free Press of Glencoe, 1947.

World Federation of Mental Health, *First World Mental Health Year: A Record,* London: A World Mental Health Year Publication, 1961.

Zelditch, Morris, Jr., "Role Differentiation in the Nuclear Family: A Comparative Study," *Family: Socialization and the Interaction Process,* New York: The Free Press of Glencoe, 1955, 307–51.

Zilboorg, Gregory, and Henry, George W., *A History of Medical Psychology,* New York: W. W. Norton & Co., Inc., 1941.